THE HOOPER TROPHY

Rivalry on the Western Border: The Story of LS "Buck" & Agnes Hooper and The Football Rivalry Between DeRidder & Leesville
Updated Edition

By Samuel Staples Lewis & Charles Anthony Owen

Published by Tim Temple Family of DeRidder

All proceeds to DeRidder High Schhol & Leesville High School

Edited by Clayton Iles

Copyright by Fiddle-Dee-Dee Entertainment Group, LLC 2020 & Charles A. Owen.

All Rights Reserved.

ISBNs

Paperbound 978-1-7356310-2-8

Hardcover 978-1-7356310-3-5

No part of this publication may be reproduced in any form without written permission of the publisher.

Table of Contents

Rivalry on the Western Border	2
Hooper Family Biography	3
First Hooper Trophy Game, by Louis Magee	26
I Ended Up a Dragon, by Dowd Douglas	27
Thoughts from David Doyle	28
Rivalry Like No Other, T.J. Moore	29
Perspectives of a Wampus Cat, by Sam Fertitta	30
Perspectives of a DeRidder Dragon, by David O'Neal	31
Reflections of a Dragon, by Jimmy Lestage	32
Coach Sedric Clemons	33
Series Standings	34
Game Tracker: All Time Results	35
All Time Scores	169
DeRidder All-State Players	172
Leesville All-State Players	173
Research: Sources and Methods	174
Benefactors and Sponsorship	175
Index	176

vs

Rivalry on the Western Border:
The Family Who Brought us the Hooper Trophy and the Football Rivalry Between DeRidder and Leesville

By Samuel Staples Lewis & Charles Anthony Owen

For as long as anyone in Western Louisiana can remember, there has been a rivalry between the cities of DeRidder and Leesville. The two towns developed in different ways and as a result of different economic and cultural reasons, but by the early 1900s, the center of the communities stood about 20 miles apart. Leesville was first settled in 1871 and incorporated in 1900. DeRidder was settled in 1897 and incorporated in 1903. The towns grew on parallel but differing tracks over the years, but a natural rivalry was birthed; starting in 1910, the two cities (at one time towns) have played an annual football game that has been the focus of much attention and excitement.

Records are available for games going back as far as 1910 and one report indicates a game was played in 1909, though no score has ever been discovered. The game became a highlight of the social scene in the two towns for many years up through the 1950s. There was a 6 year period in the 1920s when no games were played because the sport was suspended in Leesville.

In 1962, a family by the name of Hooper established a trophy that would be awarded to the winner of the annual fete. L.S. "Buck" Hooper, a graduate of Leesville High and Agnes Lewis Hooper, a graduate of DeRidder High were the couple behind the codifying of the rivalry; with affection for both cities they hoped to leave their mark on the fall event and the celebration of healthy competition. Since 1962, only three years have passed without the teams competing on the gridiron. A new Hooper Trophy is purchased any time one of the schools win the best of a 10-game series. At this writing, Hooper VII is being contested and the game between the schools is a mark on the calendar for many in Western Louisiana.

This book tells the story of the family behind the trophy. A review of the lives of Buck and Agnes and their motivations and family story is included. Results from the games through the years---with 99 contests in the books---are provided. Where possible, the story of the games are told through the eyes, typewriters and computers of local media. Most of the football portion of the book is picture-intensive, with box scores, articles and photos of players, teams and stadium crowds.

This effort is crafted as a tribute first to the communities involved. Since Buck and Agnes donated the Hooper Trophy out of love for their towns and schools, we dedicate the work to the towns and schools, but also to the Lewis and Hooper families, whose name lives on and will continue to live and be part of local lore. Proceeds from the sale of this book will be split between DeRidder High School and Leesville High School, to be used as seen fit by the educational leaders in those schools.

One author is a graduate of DeRidder High School, and one is a graduate of Leesville High School. There is no agenda, we do not takes sides, we simply wish to tell this tale.

Not really. One author will ALWAYS pull for the Dragons and the other will always pull for the Wampus Cats!

A Biography of the Hooper Family that Started the Hooper Trophy

Football fans in Leesville and DeRidder are keenly aware of the Hooper Trophy, but many are not familiar with the history of the Hooper Trophy and the Hooper family, respectively. While Chuck Owen writes about the trophy and the prep football rivalry, I'm writing about my relatives -- the Hooper family.

The Hooper Trophy exists, in large part, because Leesville High School alumnus, Louis Sylvester Hooper (age 27, nickname "Buck") married Catherine Agnes Lewis (age 16, addressed always as "Agnes"), a DeRidder High School graduate, on November 10, 1929. The Hooper-Lewis marriage eventually birthed the Hooper Trophy to honor the rivalry between the respective two alma maters. The following paragraphs report the history of Buck and Agnes Hooper's household and their respective family histories in Vernon and Beauregard Parishes (respectively in the older Rapides and Calcasieu Parishes). The final paragraph will close with personal thoughts from a nephew.

Hooper family at the beach *** circa 1936
L.S. (standing), Agnes (sitting), Catherine (front left), Buckie (front right)

Louis Sylvester Hooper, Sr. (1902-1984)
- Education: Leesville High School; Soule College.
- Military: United States Navy (World War I; 1918); American Legion.
- Career: business entrepreneur; United States IRS agent; tax consultant.

Buck Hooper was born April 28, 1902, in Pickering, Vernon Parish, Louisiana. Pickering, Rosepine, DeRidder, and other communities were created circa 1897 when the Kansas City Southern railroad line connected travel along the western half of Louisiana. Buck was the third of four children born to Louis Wilburn Hooper (1869-1943) and Isabella Frances Drummond (1879-1972). Buck's older brother was Walter R. Hooper (1897-1976). His older sister was Elizabeth ("Bessie") E. Hooper (1899-1982). Buck's younger sister was Lily May Hooper (1904-1994).

Buck's family moved to Leesville, where he received all his grade school education between 1906 and 1921. Buck's other formal education was at Soule College in New Orleans, where he studied with the school's founder, George Soule (1834-1926).

The Four Hooper Children

Bessie Lily Walter Louis
They started to school here in 1908 - on the hill.

Oh!. for the good old days - "spare the rod - spoil the child" - they gone forever.

In 1951 the late J. Ed Howe published HISTORY of SHREVEPORT and SHREVEPORT BUILDERS Vol. II

I helped him in a small way to get "the show on the road" and wrote a piece for the dust jacket.

He in turn put me in the book (see inside) and I later used it in un-successful political campaign as a 'FLYER' to better acquaint the voters with my background for candidacy. Lost - no regrets.

The sketch is produced again and used as FILLER for much correspondence with genealogists et al and especially members of Leesville, La. High School Alumni Association of which I was first president, and now LIFE MEMBER. Nostalgia - retrospect!!

Best wishes and may The Good Lord bless and keep you as HE has me these past 76 years.

Sincerely

L.W.(Buck) Hooper

195-98-94

APPLICATION FOR CERTIFICATE IN LIEU OF DISCHARGE

Personally appeared before me, a Notary Public, Clerk of Court and ex-officio
(Title of official administering oath)

in and for the Parish of Caddo, in the State of Louisiana

Louis Sylvester Hooper, a resident of Shreveport
(Name of applicant)

in the County of Caddo, and State of Louisiana

who, being duly sworn, declares that he enlisted in the Navy on or about the 7th day of January, 1918, at New Orleans, Louisiana, as Apprentice Seaman, for 4 years, and served on the following-named vessels, in the order stated, viz: Naval Training Station, St. Helena, Norfolk, Va. and Naval Operating Base, Hampton Roads, Va.

that some of the officers and men on the vessels upon which he served were as follows, viz:

Captain John H. Dayton, Chief Petty Officer Edwards, and Ramsey
(N.O.B. Hampton Roads, Va.)   (St. Helena)

that he was discharged on or about the 10th day of May, 1918 from the U.S.S. Naval Operating Base, at Hampton Roads, Va., in the State of Virginia, as Seaman 2nd Cl.; that his Discharge Certificate (or C.S.C.) was lost (or destroyed), "without the privity or procurement" of the applicant, on or about the 30th day of October, 1935, at De Ridder, Louisiana, in the State of _____, under the following circumstances:

Fire of unknown origin destroyed residence and all personal effects.

Applicant declares that he was born at Pickering, in the County of Vernon and State of Louisiana; date of birth April 28th 1902 (Navy records should show Jan. 5th 1899 or 1900 - my father, now deceased approved same) occupation INCOME TAX CONSULTANT; that his personal description at enlistment was as follows:

Color of eyes, grey; color of hair, brown or sandy; complexion, fair; height, 5 feet 8 or 9 inches; and had the following marks or scars, in india ink or otherwise, about the person: scar on right forearm - gray splotch of hair on top of head

This declaration is made for the purpose of securing a Certificate of Service, and the applicant desires that it be sent to the following address:

311 Elmwood   Shreveport   Louisiana
(Number) (Street)   (City)   (State)

WITNESSED BY—
H. Anderson
C. Senderman

L. S. Hooper
(Signature of applicant)

CERTIFICATE IN LIEU OF LOST OR DESTROYED
DISCHARGE CERTIFICATE

To all Whom it May Concern:
Know ye, That

Louis S. Hooper   A.S. No. 4,457,291 a Private of S.A.T.C., Southwestern Louisiana Industrial Institute, Lafayette, Louisiana, U.S. Army, who was inducted on October 14, 1918 at Lafayette, Louisiana to serve for the period of the emergency was Honorably Discharged from the service of the United States on December 15, 1918, by reason of demobilization.

Character: Excellent.

Given at the War Department, Washington, D. C., on September 9, 1942.

By authority of the Secretary of War:

Major General,
The Adjutant General.

This Certificate is given under the provisions of the Act of Congress approved July 1, 1902, "to authorize the Secretary of War to furnish certificates in lieu of lost or destroyed discharges" to honorably discharged officers or enlisted men or their widows, upon evidence that the original discharge certificate has been lost or destroyed, and upon the condition imposed by said Act that this certificate "shall not be accepted as a voucher for the payment of any claim against the United States for pay, bounty, or other allowances, or as evidence in any other case."

NOTE.—This certificate is issued from the office of The Adjutant General of the Army without erasure. Any addition, alteration, or erasure made thereon is unauthorized.

W. D., A. G. O. Form No. 0150-2
March 5, 1942

U.S. GOVERNMENT PRINTING OFFICE   16—27181-1

gsw Gp. 3

    Buck Hooper was a successful entrepreneur in DeRidder. He owned several small businesses, including "Beauregard Club" and "White Kitchen Cafe," at/near the corner of First Street and Stewart Street in downtown DeRidder. By 1932 in the Great Depression, Buck's businesses were starved of cash and went bankrupt. President Franklin D. Roosevelt's administration created the Works Progress Administration (WPA) to provide employment and build infrastructure throughout the United States of America. Buck's government job was to coordinate the construction of outhouses in Beauregard Parish. In 1937 Buck was hired to work at the federal Internal Revenue Service (IRS) office in Shreveport, Louisiana. This office served the eight parishes in the northwestern corner of the state. Buck used his experience with the IRS to become self-employed as a tax consultant. "Tax consultant" was the occupation identified by Agnes on Buck's death certificate.

L.S. "Buck" Hooper (left) and his father L.W. Hooper
Shreveport, Louisiana *** December 1941

Buck's first run for public office might have been for mayor of DeRidder in 1932. He received the least number of votes of all the candidates. In 1954 he ran unsuccessfully for the statewide office -- Louisiana Public Service Commissioner. As a registered Democrat, Buck was active in numerous elections for nearly 25 years. Some of the more prominent elections included those for Sam Rayburn (1882-1961), who served 25 terms in the United States House of Representatives. Buck's sister, Lily, married the distinguished Lether Edward Frazar. Lether experienced early success as the principal of Merryville High School, then president of the school currently known as the University of Louisiana at Lafayette, then president of McNeese State University, and then elected as the Lieutenant Governor of Louisiana. Buck's wife, Agnes, had several relatives run and be elected for numerous local and state government positions.

L. S. Hooper & Murrell Kilgore *** Monroe, Louisiana *** June 1954

DEMOCRATIC NATIONAL COMMITTEE
1001 Connecticut Avenue, N. W.
WASHINGTON, D. C.
April 6, 1955

Camille F. Gravel, Jr.
Member for Louisiana
611 Murray Street
Alexandria, Louisiana

Mr. L. S. Hooper
302 Ward Bldg.
Shreveport, Louisiana

Dear Mr. Hooper:

The Testimonial Dinner for SPEAKER SAM RAYBURN to be held in Washington, D. C. The evening of April 16th will be the most important meeting of its kind ever held in the Nation's Capital. Former President and Mrs. Truman, Mrs. Franklin Roosevelt, Mrs. Woodrow Wilson, Governer Stevenson, Governors Harriman, Leader, Clement, Griffin and Folsom are among the party stalwarts who will attend.

Since Congress is in session, the majority of the Democratic Senators and Members of the House of Representatives will be on hand to pay deserving tribute to MR. DEMOCRAT.

All Contributors of $100.00 to the Democratic National Committee will be invited guests at the dinner. How about sending me your check by return mail and plan to be with us. If you want me to, I'll be happy to attend to your hotel reservation.

In the event you can't be at the dinner, would you try to raise $100 for the National Committee so that Louisiana can make an adequate contribution to insure the financial success of this occasion. Checks should be made payable to the Democratic National Committee. Your aid and assistance at this time are needed and will be deeply appreciated.

Cordially,
/S / Camille Gravel

CFG:at
cc: Hon. Sam Rayburn
cc: Hon. Paul Butler

- -

April 11, 1955

Dear Camille:

Will see you at the Willard Hotel on Friday - dinner card and hotel reservation in hand. Took the liberty of sending copy of your letter to all Democratic Committeemen and Parish officials in the 4th Congressional District and now to those in attendance at the Red River Valley Association meeting. So you can see I'm trying to raise another hundred or so for the party.

Sincerely,
/S/ L. S. Hooper

SEATING ARRANGEMENTS ALPHABETICALLY

SAM **R**AYBURN TESTIMONIAL DINNER

Saturday, April 16

National Guard Armory

Washington, D. C.

Buck never fully retired. He worked less as the years passed and referred more work to his son, Buckie, in the 1970s. He continued to be involved in politics, genealogy, supporting local art and sports, Boy Scouts of America, and promoting the Hooper Trophy back in Vernon and Beauregard parishes. Buck died in the Veterans Hospital in Shreveport in January 1984. A Hooper section of burial plots rests in the lower eastside of Leesville Cemetery (near Kurthwood Road). Here rest Buck's parents, sister Bessie, Buck, Agnes, Buckie, and Catherine.

Memorial service

L.S. "Buck" Hooper (right) receives a book titled "Grierson's Raid" from Centenary College President Dr. Donald Webb Sunday during memorial services in Betty Virginia Park for the late actor John Wayne. Hooper, a devoted fan of "the Duke," directed a mock battle of the Grierson raid in the park July, 1959, as part of the premiere showing of the movie "The Horse Soldiers," filmed in 1958 in Natchitoches and starring Wayne. (Times Photo by Gerald McCarty)

To Agnes – with love

Creighton Owens
Pres. 1970-71

P.J. Sliman Jr.   L.S. Hooper
Treas   Pres. 1969-70

Rev. Everitt I. Carver
Board
1970-71

R.L. "Babe" Winfree
Sec. 1969-70

Leesville, LA. 16 Oct. 1970

Catherine Agnes Lewis (1912-2011)
- Education: DeRidder High School; several classes at Centenary College.
- Military Support: American Legion Auxiliary (Civil Defense).
- Career: proofreader for the Lousiana Legislature.

Catherine Agnes Lewis was born November 24, 1912, in DeRidder, Louisiana, to Elbert Nathaniel Lewis, Sr. (1888-1969) and Lola Melvina Carroll (1888-1991). She was born five weeks before the birth of Beauregard Parish -- of which DeRidder is the parish seat. Agnes had an older sister, Maurine Dee Lewis (1910-2005), a younger sister, Mary Virginia Lewis (1915-2007), and a significantly younger brother, E.N. Lewis, Jr. (1926-2018). Agnes, at age 16, married Buck Hooper in her parents' home at 221 Second Street, DeRidder, Louisiana -- located across the street from DeRidder High School (DHS).

early 1930s *** Maurine & Agnes Lewis *** Longbell Lumber Company *** DeRidder, Louisiana

While a senior in the eleventh grade in the 1928-1929 school year, Agnes represented DHS in Natchitoches at the competition known in recent decades as the Louisiana State Literary Rally. She advanced through the debate competition to reach the championship round, where Agnes won the state championship! The topic debated was whether or not there should be the addition of a twelfth grade in order to earn a high school diploma. DeRidder High School graduated its first student only twenty years earlier -- in 1909. Grade school education became compulsory in Louisiana in 1914. The twelfth grade was added to Louisiana public education in 1947.

Agnes Lewis *** circa 1928 (age 16)

Agnes, a mother of two young children, served as president of the Parent-Teacher Association (PTA) at Louisiana Avenue Elementary School in Shreveport in the late 1930s. She and the two children were active in numerous theatrical productions in Shreveport. All three performed in the April 1946 production of "I Remember Mama."

With her husband being a World War I veteran, her brother a World War II veteran, and numerous other relatives also military veterans, her family was proud of Agnes's service as district president of the American Legion Auxiliary for the 1945-1946 service year. Daughter Catherine Hooper served in the Junior American Legion Auxiliary. In 1955, Agnes attended the Federal Civil Defense Administration School at Olney, Maryland as a volunteer of the Auxiliary. While at the school, she was visited by her son, Pvt. L.S. Hooper, Jr. of the U.S. Army. Later in 1955, she visited Tinker Air Force Base to learn more about national defense.

Left to Right: Capt. Morton Weissman, commander of the Shreveport ground observer filter center; Mrs. Marion H. Porch, coordinator of women for Civil Defense; Mrs. L.S. Hooper, chairman of the auxiliary's state Civil Defense program; General Lewis J. Fortier, deputy state director of Civil Defense. Mrs. Hooper provided an educational presentation at the American Legion club house at Cross Lake, Shreveport, Louisiana, on May 3, 1955.

June 24, 1955 *** Tinker Air Force Base, Oklahoma City, Oklahoma *** Agnes L. Hooper (front center, dark dress and white gloves) respectively represented the American Legion auxiliary and the city of Shreveport at a meeting to discuss United States national defense.

OVERTON BROOKS, M. C.
4TH DIST., LOUISIANA

NATIONAL PRESIDENT AND DIRECTOR,
NATIONAL RIVERS AND HARBORS
CONGRESS

VICE CHAIRMAN,
COMMITTEE ON ARMED SERVICES

CHAIRMAN,
SUBCOMMITTEE NO. 1

MEMBER,
SUBCOMMITTEE FOR SPECIAL
INVESTIGATIONS

Congress of the United States
House of Representatives
Washington, D. C.

June 28, 1955

Mrs. L. S. Hooper
3872 Fairfield Avenue
Shreveport, Louisiana

My dear Mrs. Hooper:

    I note in the press dispatches reaching here that you were able to make the trip to Oklahoma City for the briefing of Brigadier General William P. Nuckols. I am very glad you were able to make this trip and I hope that this briefing gave you lots of valuable information which you may use in the defense of this country. I know that it was a great experience for everyone who was able to attend.

    You know that a large part of my work is with the military and with our national defense. I feel that I can cooperate with your group which attended the Tinker Air Force Base program to the fullest, with the idea of educating our people as to the needs of national defense and with the further idea of being of assistance to you and the others who attended. Perhaps I can send data, information or literature which may be of help from time to time and if so, I suggest that you not hesitate to call upon me for this assistance.

    Congress will adjourn some time after the first of August and I expect to be home at that time. I expect to get around and see all of my friends locally.

    With best wishes, I am

Regards to L. S.

Sincerely yours,

Overton Brooks, M. C.

OB:lab

After her children were grown and out of the house, Agnes was employed as a proofreader (a.k.a "bill drafter") with the Louisiana State legislature. One of her more challenging responsibilities was to take proposed legislation, written by persons without a legal education or background, and revise it in a timely manner so that it would meet legal and political standards. A funny story she told about her days working with the legislature involved a prank she and others played on a coworker, who attended potluck-style get-togethers but never contributed food or beverages. Some in the group, including Agnes, decided to pull a prank on him. They served canned cat food on crackers and a special plate just for him and called it pate (a spread made of finely chopped liver, fish, meat, etc., and served as an hors d'oeuvre). Yes, he ate it!

Agnes enjoyed relatively good health after being widowed in 1984. She and her cat continued living on Fairfield Avenue. Buckie had his own place only a block away and visited often. Agnes belonged to a bridge club, which involved going to different members' homes to play cards. The Shreveport Times newspaper published a feature story on how Agnes commonly used multiplied coupons to purchase groceries at 80-90% savings! In her 90s, she finally moved into an assisted living facility. Then she moved back to DeRidder, where her brother, Nathan, was able to oversee her affairs. Agnes outlived her two children, her husband, and her two sisters. She died at age 98 in DeRidder and is buried in Leesville.

L.S. "Buckie" Hooper, Jr. (1931-2001) and Catherine Hooper (1933-1952)

In rare genealogical fashion, both the firstborn son and daughter were respectively named after their parents. Louis Sylvester ("Buckie") Hooper, Jr. was born near the home where his parents were married two years earlier. Catherine Hooper was born two years later. As previously stated, the Hooper household moved from DeRidder/Ludington to Shreveport in 1937. Both Buckie and Catherine were active in Shreveport-area theater. Both attended Louisiana Avenue Elementary School, Alexander Elementary School, and then graduated from Byrd High School.

Agnes, Buckie, and Catherine Hooper visit DeRidder * mid-1940s
SecondStreet; Sheriff Cain's house; Beauregard Parish Jail and Courthouse

Catherine was enrolled at McNeese State College in Lake Charles, Louisiana when her life tragically ended at age 18 in a late-night car crash. Her uncle, Lether Frazar, was then president of McNeese and was called upon to identify Catherine's body. Catherine's death was a heavy blow throughout her extended family. Buck made a scrapbook of the whole event. Agnes' brother, Nathan Lewis, was in the Army during the Korean War, yet he hitchhiked from Newport News, Virginia, to Shreveport, Louisiana, to grieve with the family. Six years later (1958), Nathan named his firstborn daughter "Catherine" in honor of his deceased niece. Catherine Agnes Hooper was initially buried in Shreveport, but later she was reburied in Leesville.

Agnes & Catherine at Coney Island, N.Y. 1947

Buckie earned Eagle Scout in the Boy Scouts of America. According to oral history, Buckie and his high school friend, J. Bennett Johnston (later served as a U.S. senator, 1972-1997) engaged in some teenage shenanigans, but salacious details will not be divulged in this publication. Buckie initially attended Louisiana State University, where he was a cheerleader, yet he graduated with his baccalaureate degree at Centenary College of Louisiana (located in Shreveport, Louisiana). Buckie served in the United States Army in the 1950s. In the 1970s Buckie returned to Shreveport and learned the tax consultant trade with his father. Buckie continued the profession after his father's death in January 1984. Buckie died in the Veterans Administration Hospital in Shreveport, Louisiana, in 2001.

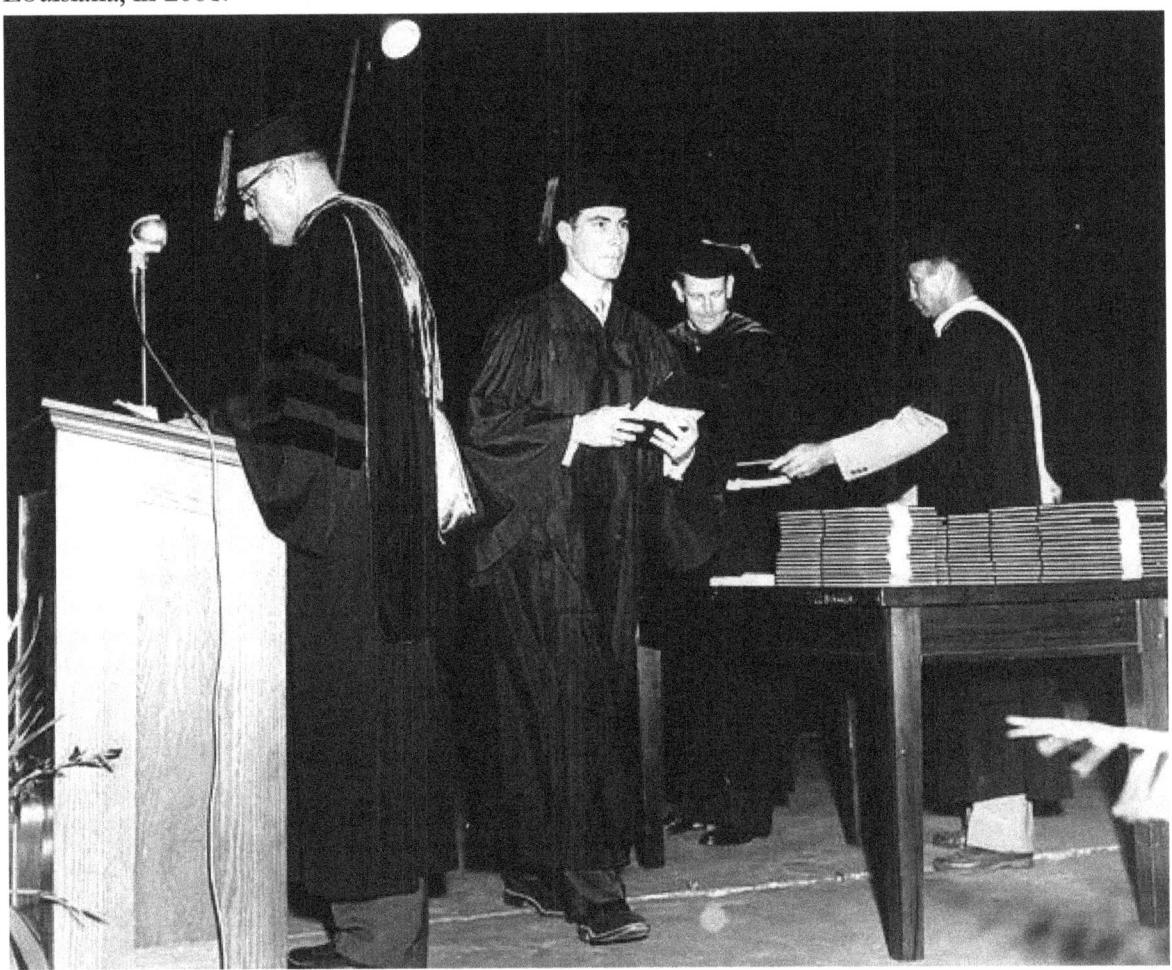

Catherine was never married and had no children. Buckie was married three times and had no children. Both Buckie and Catherine are buried in the Hooper section at Leesville Cemetery.

L.S. "Buckie" Hooper, Jr. *** Christmas 1964

Pvt Louis S. Hooper, Jr.
US 54149277
76th Trans Co (Med Trk)
APO 58
New York, NY

SPECIAL DELIVERY

Mr. L.S. Hooper
3872 Fairfield Ave
Shreveport, Louisiana
USA

Ancestry and Extended Family of L.S. "Buck" and Agnes Hooper

Agnes' grandparents are the following: Leah Emily (Williams) Lewis (1864-1945) and John H. Lewis (1856-1918), also Thomas J. Carroll (1848-1929) and Mary Ann (Eaves) Carroll (1850-1945). Dozens of Agnes' relatives have been educators, politicians, public servants, and business leaders in Vernon, Beauregard, and other nearby parishes. Her ancestors settled along local waterways like the Sabine River, Bayou Anacoco, and Bundick Creek in the 1830s-1850s era. All four of her great-grandmothers and two of her great-grandfathers are buried within a 30-mile radius of DeRidder. Great-grandfather, Elbert Lewis (1828-1864), died in Polk Hospital in Rome, Georgia, and is buried there alongside other fallen Civil War soldiers. Several distant grandfathers in her direct lineage served as Patriots in the American Revolutionary War.

Buck consistently highlighted his ancestry with a discussion about his great-great-grandfather, Thomas C. Hooper (1788-1851), who was born in Georgia, served in New Orleans in the War of 1812, and then settled as an early pioneer along the Red River in Rapides Parish. Thomas was buried in an isolated grave on a hilltop in the Fishville area. A large white marble monument was erected by his son to honor the father's legacy. Due to the grave's isolation, though, the grave was "lost" until 2009, when some local boys came across the toppled monument while walking in the woods. The Town Talk newspaper ran a cover story on December 6, 2010, about efforts to restore the grave of L.S. "Buck" Hooper's great-great-grandfather.

Author's Notes

The author is Samuel Staples Lewis. I am a nephew of L.S. "Buck" and Agnes L. Hooper. Information in this biography of the Hooper family comes mainly from respective discussions with my father (E.N. "Nathan" Lewis Jr.) and Aunt Agnes. Various historical documents were drawn from Buck Hooper's scrapbooks that I now steward.

A treasured memory I have of Uncle Buck is a story my father told me when he was nearly 90 years old. 29-year-old Buck took 5-year-old Nathan to the 1931 Beauregard Parish Fair and bought two tickets for a short plane ride at $1.25 each. When the plane flew over nearby Ludington, Buck asked Nathan, "Do you see those little white things moving down there? Those are Buckie's diapers flapping on the clothesline!" My father said this 1931 airplane ride with Buck proved to be one of the most thrilling experiences of his entire life.

Report from the First Hooper Trophy Game

By Louis Magee, LHS Class of 1963

The first Hooper Trophy game between Leesville High School Wampus Cats and the DeRidder Dragons was held in November 1962. Leesville and DeRidder had been long-time rivals and the game always provided extra enthusiasm and hoopla from each community. The idea of presenting a trophy for the winner of the game was presented by Mr. and Mrs. Hooper and the era of the Hooper Trophy began.

In November 1962 the Wampus Cats traveled to DeRidder for the first game involving the Hooper Trophy. It was a cold November night with intermittent rain and a wet football field. The Wampus Cats entered this last game of the year with only one loss for the year; however, in these games won-lost records could be thrown aside as each team played with extra incentive, enthusiasm and commitment.
This game was no exception.

In 1961 the DeRidder Dragons had come to Leesville and had won by a score of 45 to 7. This was an exception to the normal games. DeRidder running back Tommy Allen had scored 4 touchdowns on only 5 carries with each touchdown being from 40 yards or more. He later went on to be highly successful running back at LSU.

In this game both teams entered the game with an exceptional rushing game. Tommy Allen was back as the running back for the Dragons. Coaches Paris, Munyan and Bullock had prepared the Wampus Cats well for this game. The game was a slugfest as both teams were determined to shut down the opposing team's rushing game. Leesville held DeRidder to only 123 total rushing yards and DeRidder held Leesville to 126 yards. Neither team was able to cross the goal line with their rushing game.

The only scores in the game came on a counter pass play from DeRidder's quarterback to his tight end who broke loose behind the Leesville Defensive secondary and scored on a wide open pass play. One score was just before the half and the same play was ran in the second half with the same result. Leesville's defense shut down both extra point attempts by the Dragons. Those two scores proved to be the difference in the game as the Dragons beat the Wampus Cats 12 to 0.

It was a great football game resulting in the DeRidder Dragons winning the first official Hooper Trophy. The Wampus Cats had a great year and finished the season with only two losses.

Louis Magee, LHS Quarterback
First Team All-District 1962

I Ended Up a Dragon

By Dowd Douglas, DHS Class of 1985

I guess you could say the route I took to play in the annual Hooper Trophy game was more unusual than most. I had grown up 15 miles north of Leesville in the small town of Hornbeck where they didn't even play football. My dad, being a former college football player, would take me once a year to watch the Wampus Cats. It was then that I decided I wanted to play football and one day be a Wampus Cat!

As my elementary school years came and went, I realized in the 7th grade that this probably wasn't going to happen. I was going to be a basketball and baseball player in Hornbeck. Then it happened. At 13 years old, my parents decided we were moving to DeRidder where I would become a Deridder Dragon.

I began playing football as the quarterback at DeRidder Junior High where I quickly learned about and began to experience the great rivalry between the dragons and the Leesville Wampus cats. Though I played against them, we never even came close to beating them while I played in junior high. Then came high school.

I look back fondly on my high school Hooper Trophy Days where I continued as quarterback. Each year brought the anticipated rivalry game between the DeRidder Dragons and the Leesville Wampus cats. I'm proud to say that we won the Hooper Trophy my sophomore year and my senior year, but sadly never got to experience defeating them at their home Wampus Cat Stadium.

Years later as an adult in the coaching profession, I found myself back at DeRidder High coaching against Leesville in Wampus Cat stadium. It was then that I came to fully realize what an awesome atmosphere it was there. No track going around the field, so the crowd would always be right there on top of you. You couldn't help but get caught up in the incredible football fever created by the students and fans, and yes the rivalry continued. As a coach, we did defeat them at the Wampus Cat stadium bringing the Hooper Trophy home, but it just wasn't the same experience as being a player at 17. Those were the days that almost didn't happen!

Dowd D. Douglas

DeRidder High School Class of 1985

Thoughts from Mr. David Doyle
DHS Class of 1965, Son of Legendary Dragon Coach Cecil Doyle

I played 4 time in these three years and DeRidder was victorious in 3 of the 4 games.

In 1963, we played two times. First time was a regular scheduled game, and the second time was a Bi-District Playoff Game.

Leesville was the 3-AA District Champions and DeRidder was the 4-AA District Champions. At this time, a team had to win the District Championship to be in the playoffs (a lot harder to get in playoffs than it is now).

Leesville won the first game (regular season) and DeRidder won a hard fought second game. One thing I remember most about playing Leesville is my friend, R.J. Fertitta was one tough football player.

My dad, Coach Cecil Doyle, would always put in our minds that if we lost to Leesville (our closest geographic opponent), we would have to live with the thought of being second best to Leesville. That was a very motivating statement.

We would always have a packed house no matter where we played the game. This added to our intensity to play our very best against a worthy opponent which made us play our best. Lots of fun and great memories.

Leesville vs DeRidder: Rivalry Like No Other

T.J. Moore
Wampus Cat Class of 83

When I moved to Ft Polk from Berlin, Germany in the summer of 1977 as a 12 year old I quickly became aware of the importance of football in Leesville especially the rivalry with DeRidder. Even though I played football for the terrific youth team at Ft Polk, I attended Leesville Junior High and became friends with many of the players on the awesome junior high team. The guys constantly talked about the DeRidder game. So the rivalry wasn't just a high school rivalry. It existed at every level of competition in every sport involving DeRidder. We ran faster, jumped higher and played harder whenever we played DeRidder.

I remember the tremendous excitement I felt as my freshman year got underway. That meant football. That meant we (the Ft Polk kids) would join forces with the Leesville kids to form a monster freshman team. This was a problem for every team on our schedule especially DeRidder because of our rivalry. I remember the excitement level being super high before the DeRidder game. All we talked about all week was just how badly we wanted to beat DeRidder. I loved every minute of it. And yes we gave DeRidder a sound beating. We went on to beat DeRidder 2 more times, our sophomore and junior seasons.

Coming off a terrific Junior season capped by our 3rd win against DeRidder, we were fired up looking to make it 4 in a row to go out undefeated against DeRidder our senior season. Well, we hit a major bump in the road when Oscar Joiner, our star running back, went down with an ACL injury in our season opener. Losing Oscar for the remainder of the season was devastating. He was such a weapon. Without our star running back, we suffered our 1st defeat against a really good DeRidder team. Finishing 3-1 against DeRidder is one heck of an achievement and a terrific way to close out my high school career. I'll alway cherish my many fond memories of the Leesville vs DeRidder rivalry and cheer on the lucky players who get to experience it in the future.

Perspectives of a Wampus Cat

By Sam J. Fertitta, LHS Class of 1976

In the eyes of a Leesville Wampus Cat, there is no bigger event during the school year that surpasses a contest with DeRidder. If we play DeRider in anything, I care about what happens. But, if we play the Dragons on the football field, in varsity football, nothing comes close. It just doesn't. This is the game of the year. This is Alabama vs Auburn. This is our Bayou Classic. This is our Egg Bowl. Nothing is any bigger. Well, if we got back to the Dome, I'd say it's on par. But that's about it.

I say these things through the eyes of a family who has been on the football field since the first year of the Wampus Cats. My father (Sam Fertitta) and his brothers (Anthony and Fatty) were on teams beginning in 1929 and stringing along through 1935. Thirty years later, my cousin, RJ Fertitta would fiercely lead the Cats to their first playoff game and district championship. RJ's brother, Ronald, and I also played for the Cats in the 1970s. My sisters were cheerleaders and loved the black and gold! My daughters cheered on the sideline at Wampus Cat stadium.

My uncle Anthony was on the team in 1931 when Leesville defeated DeRidder for the first time. RJ was on the team in 1962 in the first year of the Hooper Trophy rivalry; he was also on the team that played DeRidder in the playoffs the first time. His brother Ronald scored a touchdown in the 1971 game against DeRidder. I played in the 1975 contest and DeRidder squeaked out a 50-0 win over us, but it might not have been that close.

For some mystical reason, being at Wampus Cat stadium means a lot to me. It meant a lot to everyone in my family, including my mother who wasn't from the area. She married my dad and moved here in 1948. There is something extraordinarily special about football in our town.

As a broadcaster for now over 25 years, I have vivid memories of the Leesville/DeRidder games, but they all seem to run into one, long contest. The rivalry goes from one year to the next, with memories of the previous year fresh on my mind until the next year starts. I can't recall many final scores, but I can sense the excitement. If I close my eyes, I can see filled stands from the vantage point of both sides of both fields. I can smell the grass in both stadiums. I can hear both bands. I can see both teams charging out from their end zones. The excitement and pageantry of it all never leaves me.

As young athletes, coaches used the rivalry to motivate us. Our families told us the stories of games gone by, and got us excited about the fall event. In reality, I didn't know anything about the rivalry or the Hoopers until I was well out of high school. What I really knew was that the people in Beauregard Parish were the ones we wanted to beat. I'm very grateful the Hoopers established this trophy, because it means a lot to us all!

In the years since high school, I found out our communities had a lot in common, the main one being we were here in Louisiana together, trying to build life and take care of the blessings of God. I've grown to admire the City of DeRidder and certainly respect the blue and the white. I pull for DeRidder every week, except when they plays us. I wish my father, my uncles and all my cousins had lived to see what an important thing the rivalry had become and to see a book, dedicated in the event's honor.

Perspectives of a DeRidder Dragon: Hooper Trophy
By David O'Neal, DHS Class of 1983

The infamous Hooper trophy existed long before my time. In fact, I quickly learned in seventh grade that the Leesville Wampus Cats was a monster that had to be defeated at all cost. We did not know why, but we circled this date as the day we as very young men had to defend our Dragon honor against the school "up the road".

As with most influences as young men, our thought processes was a learned behavior. We looked up to our older peers, family members, coaches, teachers and community leaders to align our beliefs, good or bad. We learned at an early age that Leesville was to be our enemy! Athletic rivalries are good. I do not know of a sport at any level that does not have one? It inspires and motivates us to give our best and provides ownership of our accomplishments and unfortunately our defeats. It provides fan and community support and the "talk of the town" every fall. We were not allowed in High Scholl to travel to Leesville unless accompanied by an adult. Of course, we challenged this rule many times to test the waters of our manhood. Not a good idea!

I vividly recall playing Leesville Junior High in seventh grade. As the Wampus Cats got off the bus, I remember thinking these guys look and are built like the Pittsburgh Steelers!! They were huge! Actually they played like them as well. The Wampus Cats were blessed to have Oscar Joiner as their tailback. He wore number 32 (Franco Harris of the Steelers) and we saw the back of his jersey the whole game. In fact, we saw the back of 32 for five years. He was a man among boys! My class never beat Leesville until our senior year of ball 1982.

The Hooper Trophy sat proudly in the trophy case at Leesville High School (1980-1982) for my first three years of high school ball. As freshman we were not a part of the Hooper war as we were young Dragons waiting to play with the big boys! We had never laid hands on the trophy until 1982 when The Cats came to DeRidder to routinely hand us another defeat.   If I recall, Oscar was battling a knee injury and we saw this as our opportunity to make our town proud. We won this game decisively 37-12 in front of our home crowd. It was the war we had been waiting on. In fact, both benches cleared right before the game clock was at zero and the officials called the game. Unfortunately, sportsmanship did not prevail! There was not a more proud moment in my high school career than this victory. Finally, the giant fell!

As I continued my playing days at Louisiana Tech, I always called home to get the Leesville game score and highlights involved. I remember a couple of my high school teammates attending college with a couple of the Leesville players and they became good friends their freshman year. I could not fathom the boys in blue associating with the with black and gold. What are they thinking? Not long after, I met these guys and found out they were just like us! We all became friends.

My career provided us the opportunity to move back to DeRidder in 1999. I could not wait for the Hooper Trophy game. My business sent me "up the road" and I quickly met and established lifelong relationships with the fine folks of Leesville, LA. I am always supporting the Cats as long as they are not playing the Dragons. The Wampus Cats program has put out some of the best athletes in the state and I am proud to tell folks along my travels the rich history of The Hooper Trophy and what this contest and the game of football has taught me!

Reflections of a Dragon

Jimmy Lestage, DHS Class of 1993

The Hooper Trophy. The Dragons versus the Wampus Cats! The rivalry. THE GAME. If you don't know about it, then you are definitely not from DeRidder or Leesville.

This annual Fall Friday night showdown is a year in the making. Either team could be having a great season, or one that they feel could be better. But on THAT Friday and the days in the week before, all of that is out the window. The Dragons and the Wampus Cats will put on a gridiron show that will make both look like warriors. Every player on both sides of the field wants to win this game. They want the Hooper. They want the bragging rights. They want to make their town and their alums proud.

Although it is a different group of young men out there battling every year, they all have the same understanding. This game is bigger than them. It is about civic pride as much as it is about improving their season record. Their teachers, parents, fellow students, and community members all talk about the prior year's game leading up to each new one. If you have the trophy, you can't lose it. If you don't have it, you have to get it back!

At some point, those players, and those spirited cheerleaders and students in the bands or student sections, move on to adult life. I can assure you that their passion for The Hooper Trophy moves on with them. I know that I have spirited discussions with Wampus Cat friends and colleagues every year about the two teams, the season they are having, the star players they may have, the offense, the defense, and always The Hooper.

Coach Sedric Clemons

Linebackers
Leesville High School
1992-1996

"Cats eat, dragon meat! Cat's eat, dragon meat!" The rhythm of 50 Wampus Cats fill the air as Coach Rodger Causey slowly walks through the stretch lines while looking each player in the eyes. His focus is intense before he blows the whistle and yells as only he could do, "ITS DRAGON WEEK BOYS"! September 1991.

I was an eighth grade Leesville Junior High Wampus Cat. I was indoctrinated into the Leesville vs. Deridder rivalry by a victory that week at Deridder's (the team down the road) home stadium. The indoctrination continued throughout my high school career. I was there in the fall of 1993 when Leesville Wampsus Cats were down at half-time to Deridder High School. The Cat's emerge from the locker room with the the birth of the fight song that has been adopted by all generations of Wampus-Cat faithful courtesy of Chalmicah Wilson, "I'm so Glad I AM A WAMPUS CAT". The most satisfying victory came in 1995 my senior year over the team down the road at Cecil Doyle Memorial Stadium in a Quarter-Final playoff game. Leesville had not seen a quarter-final game since the mid-80's. Wampus Cats arrive at the stadium around 5p.m. The stands were already full of Wampus-Cat fans..standing room only.

The atmosphere was electric from the first minute of the 1st quarter to the final buzzer of the 4th as we battled. Everything was on the line. Leesville's first semi-final appearance in school history, crushing our heated rivals playoff dreams, and bragging rights for years to come over the team down the road for our families and friends. Nothing was sweeter than a 29-0 victory as we left no doubt who was the better team. The Hooper was ours, the fans got the bragging rights, we solidified our claim as the best team in Wampus Cat football history, and we got to do it burning down our rivals home stadium with a shut-out victory.

To my shame my first coaching job was in 2000 for the "team" down the road. The Dragon fans love the rivalry is just as intensely as the Wampus Cat faithful. During the pep-rally that week in 2000 I vividly recall every dragon in the Gym going crazy as the band played, "I'm So Glad....I'm NOT a Wampus CAT". I joined the Leesville High School coaching staff in 2001. I continue to have the awesome responsibility of indoctrinating our Cats and ensuring the rivalry is kept alive and well: the Hooper Trophy, my town vs your town, my boys vs your boys, the fight song, the history, and record. Lock the gate, turn on the lights, ring the bell it's time to fight. Put the ball down and lets play!!

The Series: Current Standings

As of the first printing of this book, the DeRidder Dragons lead the all-time series with 55 wins in 102 contests. Leesville has picked up 44 wins and there have been four ties in games between the two schools.

The series began in 1910, and DeRidder dominated the early decades of the fete. From 1910 until the Hooper Trophy Series came into effect in 1962, the Dragons prevailed in 29 of 39 games, with the Cats tallying seven wins and three games ending in ties. The series has been much more of an even tenor since the Trophy came into existence, with Leesville having a slight edge.

Between 1962 and 2019, Leesville won 33 games and DeRidder prevailed in 25. A lone game in 1972 was the only tie in the series. Leesville was awarded a win in that contest, based on most first downs achieved in the game.

The teams have met three times in the post season. DeRidder won the first contest in 1963, and Leesville captured the next two---1995 and 2011. Playoff games do not count in the tally for the Hooper Trophy.

Some interesting points in the series: There is no valid documentation of DeRidder losing to Leesville prior to 1931. The series began in 1910 and DeRidder won all but one contest with a lone game ending in a tie. The longest winning streak in the series in 10 games; Leesville won all games between 1998 – 2008 (no game was played in 2005 due to Hurricane Rita). DeRidder did not lose a game to Leesville for the entire decade of the 1970s; the Dragons won nine games and tied the Cats once. The most lop-sided score in a game was 1945, when DeRidder won 61-7. The most points scored in a game was 2008, when the Cats put 68 points on the board.

The series is set up in a 10-game cycle, with the first team to win six games in the series becoming the permanent home for series trophy. A new trophy is purchased after a series is concluded. The results of the Hooper contests, as they stand today:

- Leesville won Hooper I which spanned from 1962 – 72
- DeRidder captured Hooper II, which included the years 1973 - 79
- Leesville won Hooper III, which spanned the years 1980 – 87
- DeRidder won Hooper IV, which ran from 1988 – 1997
- Leesville won Hooper V, which included 1998 – 2003
- Leesville won Hooper VI, spanning the years 2004 - 2014
- Leesville won Hooper VII 6-2, which ran from 2015-2023

Game Tracker: Results of the Contests

This seciton of the book provides a narrative and results of the games played between Leesville and DeRidder.   To the greatest degree possible, the story is told through the eyes, typewriters and computers of local media.   News reports form the day are provided when possible. A running tally of the now seven Hooper Trophy Series is provided.

The early years of the series saw dominance by DeRidder.   For some time, reporting on this series indicated the first contest between the two schools was in 1910.   All of the "lists" that have been disseminated indicate the first game was in 1910, but in researching this book, a lone report indicated the first game was in 1909.   No data was found on the outcome of that game.   Research is still underway.

In a number of instances, no news reporting is available on contests, espeically prior to the 1940s.   Much of the data from the early years of the rivalry was provided via the research of Brian Trahan, former editor of the Leesville Leader and Daniel Green, former Sports Writer for the Leader and Beauregard Daily News.   The goal to provide the score, a media report, one or more photographs and a box score from each game.

1910: DeRidder 35   Leesville 0

No report or photographs discovered.

1911: No game was played, but a photograph from the 1910 team from LHS and 1911 DHS team were discovered.   It is assumed that some of the players on the 1911 team also played in 1910.

DERIDDER'S FIRST TEAM — BOTTOM ROW: Wiley Abner, unknown, Rush Crocker, Homer Doane, Marvin Sharpless, Jimmy Jones, Allen Abney. MIDDLE ROW: unknown, Chester LaGrone, Ira Baden, unknown. TOP ROW: Ed Shaw (coach), Winfred "Poss" Green, Marion Abney, V. E. "Chick" Green, Bill Lewis, Ward Anderson (principal and coach). "Poss," "Chick," and Bill later played together on the LSU varsity.

1913:   DeRidder 24 Leesville 0. No articles or photographs discovered

1914:   Leesville victory, as per 1934 newspaper article; score is unknown (see 1934 results)

1915:   DeRidder 6 Leesville 0. No articles or photographs discovered

1920:   DeRidder 6 Leesville 6. No articles box scores were found, but a picture of the 1920 was published prior to the 1960 DHS Homecoming, courtesy Beauregard News.

Here are the District Football Champs of 1920 ... the DeRidder Dragons, from left, first row, George White, John Warren, Dank Shirley, Pete LaCaze, Sid Crocker, Marvin Baden and Bill Sanders; 2nd row, Robert Lewis, Harry Warren, George Crocker, Howard Patterson, Ralph Sweet, Percy Winberry, and at center back, Coach Bob Brown who is now superintendant of school of Lafayette Parish.
(Photo reproduction, Barrie-Shaw, Courtesy Pete LaCaze.)

1921: DeRidder 49 Leesville 0. No articles or game photos were found. Below is an excerpt from the 1922 DHS Yearbook

Sid Crocker, (Captain)
Quarterback

Robert Lewis
Left Halfback

Lloyd Gibson
Fullback

1922: DeRidder 53 Leesville 0. The DeRidder team of 1922 was very accomplished and they trounced the Leesville squad. The series went on hiatus from 1922 – 1929, as football was disbanded for a 6 year period in Leesville between 1923 and 1928.

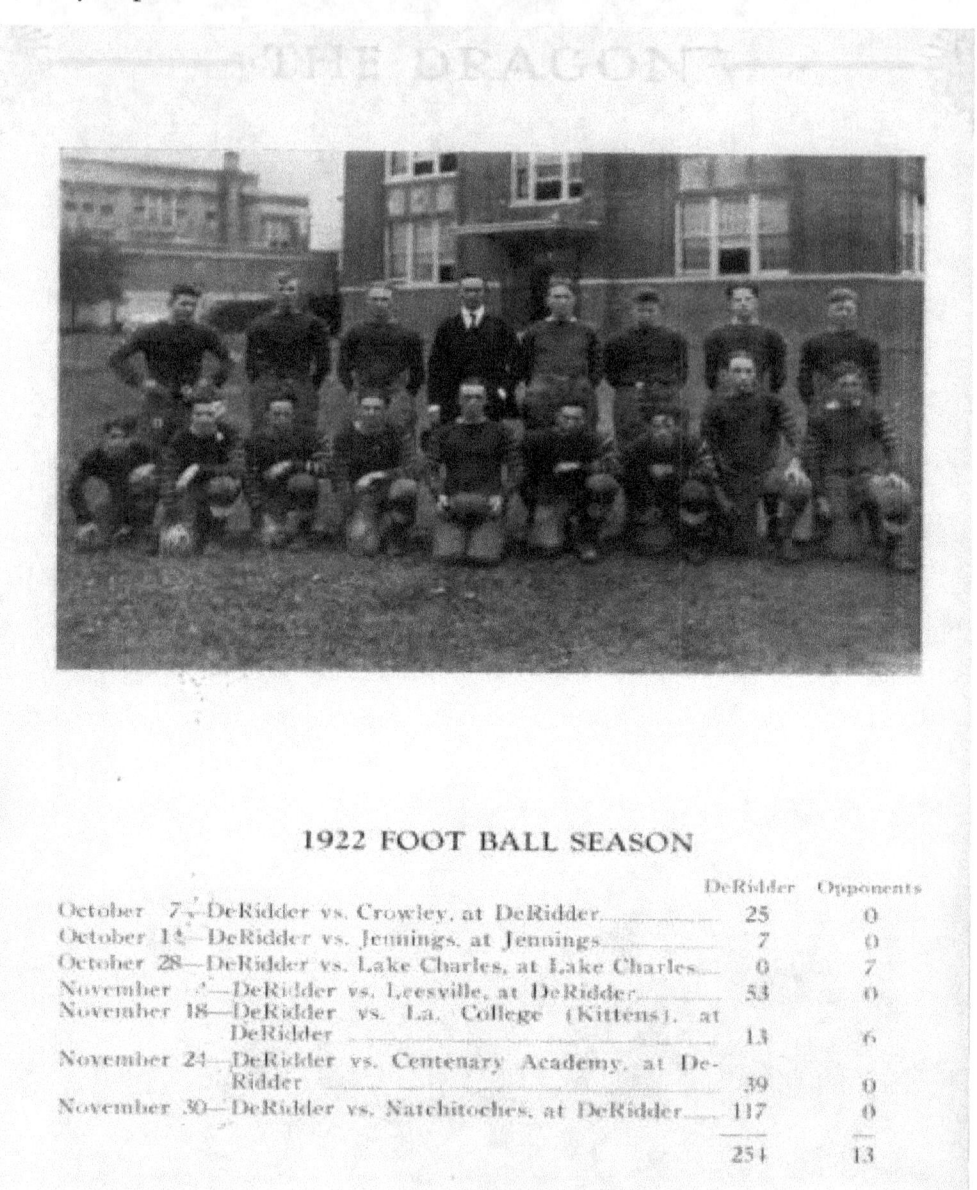

1922 FOOT BALL SEASON

	DeRidder	Opponents
October 7—DeRidder vs. Crowley, at DeRidder	25	0
October 14—DeRidder vs. Jennings, at Jennings	7	0
October 28—DeRidder vs. Lake Charles, at Lake Charles	0	7
November 7—DeRidder vs. Leesville, at DeRidder	53	0
November 18—DeRidder vs. La. College (Kittens), at DeRidder	13	6
November 24—DeRidder vs. Centenary Academy, at DeRidder	39	0
November 30—DeRidder vs. Natchitoches, at DeRidder	117	0
	254	13

GREAT 1922 TEAM beat Natchitoches 117-0, lost only to Lake Charles High School (7-0) and were district champs in '21 with virtually the same team. Members were: Robert Lewis, Sheldon Blue, Ray Simmons, Ernest Crocker, Pete Terry, Alvie Huffman, George White, Lloyd Wiggins, Ellis Nichols, Porter Bilbo, Hubert Stracner, Milford Green, Jack Gardiner, Lois White.

1929:   DeRidder 13   Leesville 0.   Football returned to Leesville in 1929 and the Dragons took up where they left off, dominating the rivalry.   Below is an article from the Leesville paper that reported the results.   A picture of the LHS team is also provided

Leesville Football Team Played Well

In the great footballball game Saturday between the Leesville Wampus Cats and the DeRidder Red Devils, the devils finally won but it was after the hardest contest they had ever been in. The strenuousness of the fray may be judged by the fact that several of the players were badly hurt. It was the most exciting game ever played in Leesville, and though they did not win the Wampus Cats showed the devils that they were "foemen worthy of their steel."

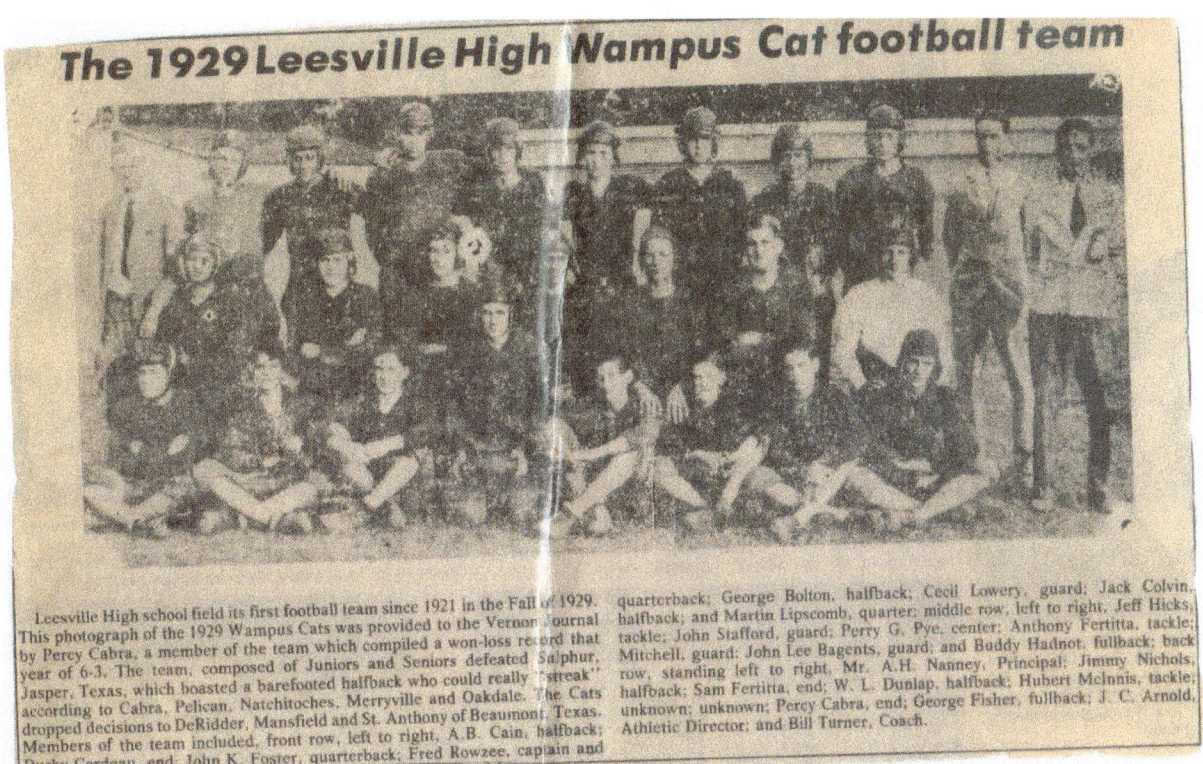

The 1929 Leesville High Wampus Cat football team

Leesville High school field its first football team since 1921 in the Fall of 1929. This photograph of the 1929 Wampus Cats was provided to the Vernon Journal by Percy Cabra, a member of the team which compiled a won-loss record that year of 6-3. The team, composed of Juniors and Seniors defeated Sulphur, Jasper, Texas, which boasted a barefooted halfback who could really "streak" according to Cabra, Pelican, Natchitoches, Merryville and Oakdale. The Cats dropped decisions to DeRidder, Mansfield and St. Anthony of Beaumont, Texas. Members of the team included, front row, left to right, A.B. Cain, halfback; Ducky Cordeau, end; John K. Foster, quarterback; Fred Rowzee, captain and quarterback; George Bolton, halfback; Cecil Lowery, guard; Jack Colvin, halfback; and Martin Lipscomb, quarter; middle row, left to right, Jeff Hicks, tackle; John Stafford, guard; Perry G. Pye, center; Anthony Fertitta, tackle; Mitchell, guard; John Lee Bagents, guard; and Buddy Hadnot, fullback; back row, standing left to right, Mr. A.H. Nanney, Principal; Jimmy Nichols, halfback; Sam Fertitta, end; W.L. Dunlap, halfback; Hubert McInnis, tackle; unknown; unknown; Percy Cabra, end; George Fisher, fullback; J. C. Arnold, Athletic Director; and Bill Turner, Coach.

1930: DeRidder 13 Leesville 0.   The Dragons continued their dominance in the series in 1930. Two articles from the local papers tell the story of the game.   Of note is the reference to the Leesville "Bob Cats."   The school's mascot was changed from Wampus Cats to Bob Cats from 1930 – 1932.   Also of interest is the idea that the 1930 game was the 15th between the school; this work has records of nine games by 1930 and research is continuing to compile the historical site picture.

LEESVILLE.

Leesville, Oct. 23 (Special).—The practice field of the Leesville Bobcats is a scene of bustling activity as they go through their final rehearsals for the clash with the DeRidder Dragons Friday.

This will be the fifteenth year the two teams have met, during which time Leesville has never won a single game, although each year the game has been close and stubbornly contested. Last year the score was 12 to 0, DeRidder scoring two touchdowns in the last period.

Coach W. H. Beeson is working this year with the finest material ever assembled to represent Leesville, and local fans are of the belief that "the worm will turn" against their DeRidder adversaries. This prediction is based on the increased strength of the line and the running and passing ability of Captain Anthony Fertitta and Fred Rowzee, two of the flashiest backs in Class A football.

Due to the pronounced rivalry of the neighboring towns and the bright prospects of a win for Leesville the game is attracting unusual attention throughout this section.

DERIDDER WINS OVER LEESVILLE

The big football game here last Friday between Leesville and DeRidder was a glorious scrimmage, which many of the business men of Leesville turned out to see. Leesville was defeated but went down fighting most gallantly.

The line up was as follows:

DeRidder—Clinton, left end; Donald, left tackle; Sigler left guard; Welborn, center; Donald, right guard; Branch, right tackle; Morrison, right end; Swearingen, full back; Olds, right half; Pernici, left half; Perry, quarterback.

Leesville—Winfree, left end; Gamblin, left tackle; Owens, left guard; Stevens, center; Bush, right guard; Cordeau, right tackle; Cabra, right end; Fertitta, full back; Brock, right half; Hadnot, left half; Rowzee, quarterback.

Refree, F. L. Miller of the state university. Umpire, F. Pfos; Head line man, Ray Weeks, Time keeper, Julian Atkins.

1931: Leesville 7   DeRidder 0.   The team from Leesville notched their first recorded win in the series in the 1931 contest. The news article indicated the game took place on Armistice Day (now called Veterans' Day); for several years to come, the game would be played on this date.

1932:   Leesville 19   DeRidder 19.   The series saw its first of four ties in the 1932 event. No articles or photographs related to the game have been discovered.

1933: DeRidder 13   Leesville 0.   No articles or photographs were discovered.   A ticket to the Armistice Day game was retained by the Lewis family of DeRidder.

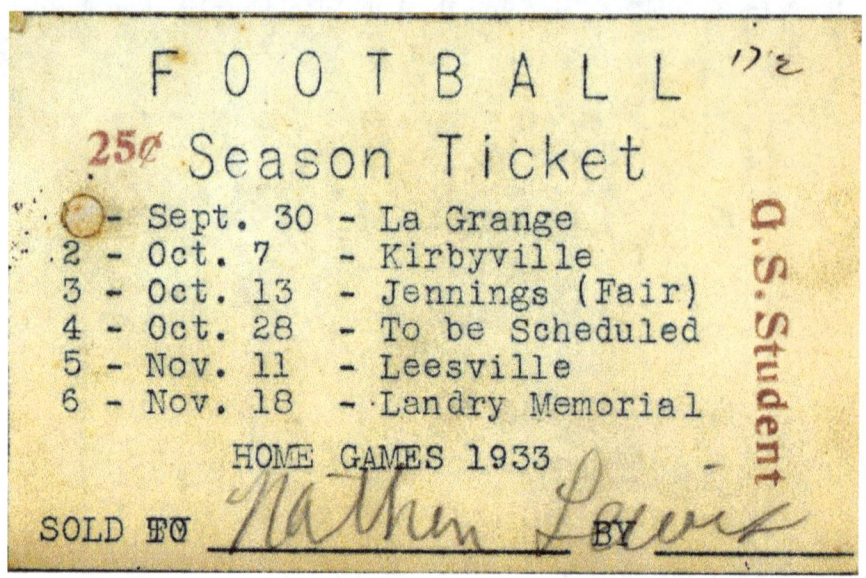

1934: Leesville 25   DeRidder 13.   The Wampus won the 1934 contest. The article from the Shreveport paper indicates that Leesville notched their first win since 1914, a disputed point. The Cats won the 1931 contest, but the reference to 1914 provided a new clue as to a game that took place but whose results were not discoverable.

DEFEATS DE RIDDER.

Leesville, La., Nov. 13 (Special).— For the first time in years, some say as far back as 1914, Leesville high school team, coached by Wood Osborne, Monday defeated DeRidder eleven. The score was 25 to 13. All of the scoring was done in the first half. Fertita scored for Leesville on passes in the first and second quarters and Roy Jones scored once on a blocked punt and Anderson tallied through the line. Herrington recovered a loose ball behind the goal line for one of DeRidder's touchdowns after Fidler had fumbled and Beard scored on a pass. Leesville made 17 first downs and DeRidder four.

1935: DeRidder 35 Leesville 0. No articles or photographs were discovered. However, news articles about both teams doing other things in this year merit note. DeRidder played Fair Park High School in Shreveport in the first night game in Shreveport history, mostly likely the first in DeRidder's history. The team from Leesville traveled to Mexico City for the first of what would be a number of trips to play an American team in the Mexican Capitol City.

Prep Grid History Made Here

Prep school football history was made in Shreveport Friday night when the Fair Park Indians of this city and the Dragons of DeRidder met on the gridiron at Fair Park Friday night. It was the first after dark pigskin battle waged by prep school elevens in this city. The pictures show the two teams as they struggled under the lights before about 3,000 fans.—(Photo by Gasquet, Times photographer.)

Leesville Team To Figure In International Grid Battle

Above is pictured members of the Leesville high school football squad which will battle the American Foundation school at Mexico City in October. First row (sitting) left to right—R. Smart, Hamersly, Koen, Robinson, M. Smart, Sepeda, Grade, Lyons; second row—Watson, McClure Wells, Booker, Burnett, Word, Lyles, Vidler, McBroom; third row—Martin, Russell, Mattison, Fertitta, D. Smart, Bill Adams, Harrison, Keller, Craft, James; fourth row—Elois Robertson, Bert Adams, R. Robinson, Guidry, Stanley, Hillman and Coach Osborne.

1936:   Leesville 7   DeRidder 0.   No post game article or photographs were discoered.   However, an article appearing in the Shreveport media makes reference to the initial contest in 1909, the results of which are still unknown

> **LEESVILLE.**
>
> Leesville, Nov. 5 (Special).—The Leesville high school Wampus Cats play the DeRidder Dragons here Armistice Day. This game is one of the oldest in tradition of any schools in the sate. The first game having been played in 1909.
>
> The Wampus Cats have not lost a high school game this year and have played such teams as Winnfield, Boyce, Oakdale, Merryville, and Hemphill, Texas. The only setback they have had was at the hands of Normal Imps.

1937:   Leesville 7   DeRidder 7.   The schools tied in the 37 contest.

DRAGONS HOLD CATS FOR 7-7 DEADLOCK FRI.

Just an upset, still a mighty thrilling and exciting game, was the annual clash between the Leesville Wampus Cats and the DeRidder Dragons on the sandy DeRidder grid last Friday night which ended in a 7-7 deadlock.

The Wampus Cats, over-anxious and over-excited failed to display their usual form in the tussle with their arch enemies DeRidder, on the other hand, played inspired ball, far outdoing any previous performance, and holding a Leesville that only the over-weight Jena eleven has been able to slow down.

The first three quarters found the two teams still deadlocked, each determinedly guarding its goal posts. It was the Wampus Cats, who so far had to click, that broke the tie with a touchdown and conversion. The Dragons then wasted no time in making up the loss.

The fast Leesville back field slipped up on its usual brilliant yard-making. It was Clyde McClure who finally scored.

With only six minutes to play, the Dragons started their touchdown march. Hicks and Bennett hit the line and Carter and Hernandez gained on passes for the score, actually made by Carter. Carter's pass to Bennett for the extra point tied the final score.

The game, full of thrills ended with the ball in the center of the field after several upset plays, neither team threatening to score.

Starring Draggon linesmen were Harmon, guard, Lewis, tackle, Cryer and Donald, whose catch of a forward pass while lying prone during the Dragon's goalward punch was a high point. In the backfield, Carter's passing and punting and Captain Hicks' line plays were outstanding. Bennett and Hernandez were also good.

In the Cat's backfield, Cotton Mc-Clure did the most successful scratching. Mattison and Smart also starred, and Sepeda did good work. Martin, Harrison and Robinson starred in the line.

———oOo———

1938: Leesville 49   DeRidder 0.   The Wampus Cats got their first lopsided win in the series in the 38 contest. An excerpt from the Leesville yearbook provides interesting but biased details

Leesville 49, DeRidder 0

On Armistice Day came the highlight of the football season, the traditional game with DeRidder played this year on Gilbert Field. It was in this game that the "Dragons" lost their scales. It all started when Sepeda, on a well-directed spinner, on the third play of the game brought the ball to DeRidder's one-foot line. When the game ended, the "Cats" had dragged the "Dragons" all over the field for a good clean "skunking."

BACK ROW: Klyde McClure, Norris Bush, Peter Anderson, Ira Cratt, Homer Robinson, Douglas Sartin, Ernest Franklin, Aubrey Bunch.

MIDDLE ROW: George Walker, manager, Kemp Tucker, Allen Wood, Howard Martin, Louis Moses, Darrell Smart, Howard Ford, Wood Osborne, Coach.

FRONT ROW: Pete Sliman, Clayton Lyons, John Sepeda, I. B. Dowden, Danny Ferguson, Malcolm Smart.

1939: DeRidder 33 Leesville 0.   The Dragons returned the 1938 favor with a throttling of their own in 1939

DE RIDDER IN 33-0 WIN

DeRidder, La., Nov. 11 (Special).— The DeRidder Dragons trounced the Leesville Wampus Cats, their old rival by a 33-0 victory. Through the entire game the Dragons was master of the situation, the rain being no hindrance to the hard-fighting team. The Wampus Cats could make no headway through the strong Dragons rock-like line, which has not been scored through in the past six games.

1940: DeRidder 39 Leesville 0. The Dragons again had the upper hand against the Cats. An excerpt from the Leesville yearbook tries to cushion the blow on the lop-sided game.

Leesville 0
De Ridder 39

The Leesville High Wampus Cats lost their traditional game to the De Ridder Dragons on Gilbert Field by a score of 39-0. It was the first time in several years that the Dragons beat the Cats on Leesville soil. The game was, however, much closer than the score indicates. The Cats came very close to scoring in the scoreless first quarter. Bill Carlock due to a knee injury that he received in the first period was lost for the remainder of the season. Martin, who captained the De Ridder game, was shifted to the backfield to fill the vacancy.

1940 Leesville team

1941:   DeRidder 14   Leesville 6

No articles discovered, but a team photo of the Wampus Cats was discovered during research.

1942:   No results, articles or photographs discovered.   As per article in Leesville Leader, the game was to take place on November 6, 1942

1943: Two games were played in the tumultous year of 1943. With World War II in its mid stages, the towns and communities were no doubt bustling with activity from Camp Polk but were also depleted of men and young men who had joined the war effort.

Game 1: DeRidder 13   Leesville 7

Game 2: Leesville 7   DeRidder 6

DeRidder Dragons Defeat Wampus Cats

Last Friday night the Wampus Cats were defeated by the Dragons of DeRidder by the score of 13—7. This was the toughest and hardest game of the season for both teams.

By the injuries on both teams you could tell the old rivialry between the two teams still exists.

The Dragons two touchdowns and extra point came early in the first half.

The Wampus Cats lone tally came late in the last quarter, it was made by Leesville's quarterback Pinchback, he also ran the ball over for an extra point.

Even though the Wampus Cats went down in defeat they showed good spirit and determination to win by coming from behind and making the lone toughdown in the last ten minutes of play.

On the forward defensive wall the brilliance of play by Brown and Hughes sparked the Leesville defense, also quarterback Pinchback was in on many tackles.

On the offensive Pinchback and Dunn were consistant ground gainers.

The teams will play a return game in Leesville Nov. 19 and Wampus Cats hope to reverse the score with decisive victory.

Wampus Cats Defeat DeRidder Dragons Here Friday Night

The Wampus Cats broke a record in closing their 1943 gridiron season, Friday night, on Gilbert Field, by defeating the DeRidder Dragons by ascore of 7-6. This marks the first win for Leesville over DeRidder in five years. It was the cats fourth victory o fthe year, against four defeats and one tie.

The Dragons drew blood by pushing over a tally early in the second quarter. However, the combination of Culpepper and Hunt soon put the Wampus Cats back in the game. Culpepper threw a beautiful pass to Hunt, who made a nice catch, and carried the pigskin to the goal line. On the next play Pinchback carried the ball over for a touchdown, Leesville converted and the score stood 7-6.

This ended the scoring for the evening; the two teams battling each other to a standstill the rest of the game.

The forward wall of the Wampus Cats stood like the proverbial "Rock of Gibralter" and checked the Dragon's plays throughout the major part of the game.

The backfield composed of Dunn, fb; Culpepper, rh; T.W. Lee, lh; and Pinchback, qb, played an outstanding game.

Most of the ball carrying was handled by Dunn. Pinchback carried for Leesville, in the early part of the game, but was removed for a rule infrac-

1944: No game played. Leesville did not compete in football in the 1944 season. DeRidder, did however, and the team lost only one game, the entire season. An excerpt, probably from a DHS annual is below

FLASHY HALFBACKS (left), Wayburn Henderson (21) and Frank Delia were members of the '44 team that lost only to Sulphur, state champions that year. Bill Lewis, voluntary coach during the World War II period, helps Wayburn understand game.

1945: Two games were played in 1945 as the rivalry picked up where it left off, with DeRidder continuing to hold the dominant, upper hand.

DeRidder 61 Leesville 7

DeRidder 27 Leesville 7

1945 DeRidder Dragons

DHS's Frank Delia

1946:   DeRidder 53 Leesville 0

No articles or game details were found outside of yearbook reporting

1946 LHS Team

DHS's Jimmy Simmons

1947: DeRidder 25   Leesville 0.

No newspaper articles were discovered.   An excerpt from the LHS annual and a team photo are below.

1948: DeRidder 20   Leesville 6

No newpaper articles or pictures were discovered.

1949: DeRidder 20   Leesville 19

No newspaper articles were discovered.   A lone photograph, from a game between DeRidder and Crowley highlights two Dragon players from some point in the season.

1950: DeRidder 32   Leesville 0

Newspaper article from the Dragons trouncing the Wampus Cats is below.

Cats Defeated By Dragons; Play Bunkie Friday

Displaying considerable power on both offense and defense, the DeRidder Dragons rolled over the Leesville Wampus Cats 32-0 in a game played last Friday night at DeRidder.

Statistically there was no comparison between the two teams, with DeRidder marking up 15 first-downs to 2 for the Cats. The Dragons tried seven passes, completed one for 13 yards and had one intercepted, while Leesville attempted eleven passes, made one click for 11 yards and had three intercepted. DeRidder fumbled twice with Leesville recovering one of them and Leesville's only fumble was recovered by the Dragons. The Cats Cats were not penalized during the game, but DeRidder lost a total of 55 yards by this route. The big difference was in yardage gained, where the Dragons ran up a total of 315 yards against only seven yards for the Cats.

DeRider's first score came in the initial period after a blocked punt and recovery by Rusty Temple on the Leesville 31. On the next play James Shirley skirted right end and went all the way for the touchdown. Walden converted.

The Dragons scored twice in the second quarter with Shirley and Mac Bryan doing the honors. Walden added the extra point after Bryan's score, but his kick was wide on the other occasion.

In the third period, a 68-yard drive, featuring a 27-yard run by Shirley was climaxed by Bryan scoring around end. Walden's kick was blocked.

The final touchdown was added in the fourth period, when Boudreaux went twenty yards through the middle of the Cats line for the score. Again the kick was blocked.

The Cats did not play the football of which they are capable, while on the other hand, DeRidder seemed definitely up for this game. Suffering from injuries before the game started, the Cats practically lost the services of Moses and White in the first three plays. In addition, Paris, Bolgiano and Hicks were forced out at various times during the contest.

DeRidder's entire team played well, and Coach E. D. Kelly's substitutions, while frequent, were just as effective as his starting line-up. The Dragons have a better-than-average assortment of backs, with Shirley, Bryan, Boudreaux and Walden all showing to good advantage. For the Cats Brumley, Grant, Clark and Pollard battled it out all the way. Paris, Bolgiano and Penrod, hampered by injuries, were not at their best, but also gave a good account of themselves.

DeRidder
LE—Hamilton, 165 lbs.
LT—Turner, 175 lbs.
LG—Temple, 140 lbs.
C—Ford, 155 lbs.
RG—Perkins, 145 lbs.
RT—O'Neal, 185 lbs.
RE—Jones, 160 lbs.
QB—King, 135 lbs.
HB—Bourdreaux, 155 lbs.
HB—Bryan, 155 lbs.
FB—Shirley, 155 lbs.

DHS Starters 1950

Leesville's Ted Paris

1951:   DeRidder 28   Leesville 7

The Dragons continued their winning ways in 1951. Newspaper article is below from the Leesville Leader. Both teams would have players make the Associated Press "All State Team" in 1951; the Dragon's Bob Hamilton (E) and the Cat's Ted Paris (T) were named to the squad. Hamilton would serve many years as a pastor, passing away in 2018. Paris, a member of LHS Sports Hall of Fame, returned to Leesville as a coach and served a full career as an educator in the Vernon Parish school. No box scores nor articles detailing the game were found in research. Of note is the mention of a plot to steal the "live" Wampus Cat and the ensuing high school prank and discussions.   Further researched is required to find out about the mysterious animal.

Didja Kno
By Ludie Zell

The DeRidder Dragons downed the Leesville Wampus Cats by a score of 28-7, Friday night. Of course we were disappointed as we would have liked to have won. But win or lose we are still all out for the Wampus Cats. They are still IT with us.

One thing the boys from DeRidder didn't succeed in doing, and that was to steal our real live Wampus Cat. Thursday night a group of DeRidder boys paid Leesville a visit with the intention of taking our Wampus Cat back to DeRidder with them. The trick turned on them however, when one of our good citizens upon hearing the misbehavior of the boys and thinking it a bunch of drunks called the law. Imagine the boys embarrassment when they had to tell the officers the truth in preference to going to jail.

The 'Wampus Cat' was a gift to the school by Mr. Dale Werner and all the kids seemed to get a kick out of seeing him. However, he is still in my possession but anyone wanting to donate some meat for his dinner is entirely welcome to do so. How that cat can eat.

LHS's Ted Paris

DHS's Bob Hamilton

1952: Deridder 39   Leesville 0.

The Dragons embarrassed the Wampus Cats in 1952, dominating the contest from start to finish. An excerpt from the Opelousas Daily World chronicles the game. 1952 would be a very successful year for the team from DeRidder, with the Dragons going undefeated in the regular season, winning all games and advancing to the State Semi-finals, where they lost to eventual State Champion Spring Hill.

DeRidder Sweeps On. Handcuffs Leesville

DeRIDDER. — Rampaging De-Ridder High's Lions swept onward toward a district Class A title by outclassing and handcuffing Leesville 39-0 here Friday night.

DeRidders' line charged so hard that Leesville's net ground yardage was exactly one yard. Four DeRidder backs took turns scoring, with Tom McCaig — who tallied twice — snagging a Leesville pass and running it back 85 yards to score.

DeRIDDER.		
41	Marion	7
52	Vinton	0
32	Natchitoches	7
12	La Grange	9
26	West Lake	0
28	Eunice	0
39	Leesville	0
37	Mansfield	6
33	DeQuincy	12
19	Oakdale	6
12	Morgan City	7
331		54

DHS Coach E.D. Kelly

1953:   Leesville 18   DeRidder 7

Leesville took the 1953 in a game that captivated the fans in Vernon Parish.   Report of the game from the 1954 Wampus Cat Annual is below.

LEO BASS
Fullback

On Armistice Day came the highlight of the football season, the traditional game with DeRidder played this year on Gilbert Field. It was in this game that the Dragons lost their scales. It all started when Sepeda on a well-directed spinner, on the third play of the game brought the ball to DeRidder's one foot line. When the game ended, the Cats had dragged the Dragons all over the field for a good clean skunking.

Here is an account of this years game:

Dick Berry, after throwing a 21 yeard pass to Fisher, went over for a T.D. from the one yard line. Coburn's kick was blocked and the score stood Leesville 6, DeRidder 0.

At the first of the second quarter, a heartbreaker was witnessed. Sonny Byrd raced 90 yards for a T.D. only to have it nullified by a clipping penalty.

DeRidder scored in the third quarter with a pass from Frank Roe to Leo Bass. The Dragons' kick was good leaving the score 7-6.

Leesville made their last two scores in the last quarter when helped by 25 yards in penalties went to the 3 yard line. Dawin Smart went over for the tally. Coburns kick was no good. The score was then 12-7.

The last score came when the Dragons lost the ball on the Cats 21 yard line. Leesville assisted by 35 yards of penalties went to the 13 yard line. Dawin Smart carried the ball over from there. Berry's pass to Fisher for the extra point was no good.. When the game ended Leesville was well on the way to another touchdown.

If the sportsmanship in the future is like this year, we should have little trouble in downing the Dragons for many years to come.

DICKIE BERRY
Quarterback

DAWIN SMART
Fullback

Wampus Cat Stadium – First Year

1954: DeRidder 12   Leesville 6

DeRidder took the 1954 contest by a single score. News report from the Alexandria Town Talk is below.

DeRidder Tags Leesville With First Defeat, 12-6

(Special to The Town Talk)

DERIDDER, La. — The DeRidder Dragons handed Leesville's Wampus Cats their first loss of the season here Friday night by edging out a 12-6 victory.

DeRidder, in Class 4-AA and Leesville is in 4-A.

The nondistrict tilt found DeRidder scoring in the first quarter when Leo Bass went over from six yards out after Dan Cooley had recovered a Leesville fumble on the Wampus Cat 14-yard marker.

Bass scored again in the second from one yard out after a long pass play had set up the advantage.

DeRidder stopped Leesville twice inside the 20 in the first half.

In the second quarter James Coburn scored for Leesville on a one-yard buck. Coburn, gaining 71 of Leesville's 170 yards, was the individual scorer for the night.

Leesville made 14 first downs compared with seven for DeRidder and gained 209 total yards to DeRidder's 102. Three pass interceptions and four fumbles helped sink Leesville.

STATISTICS

DERIDDER		LEESVILLE
7	First Downs	12
94	Yards Rushing	121
38	Yards Passing	33
4 of 12	Passes Completed	3 of 13
3	Passes Intercepted By	0
5 for 35	Punts, Ave. Ydge.	2 for 20.5
0	Fumbles, Ball Lost	3
50	Yds. Penalized	25

Score By Quarters

DeRidder .... 6 6 0 0—12
Leesville .... 0 0 6 0— 6

LHS's Lewis Reid Brown   DHS's Billy O'Neal   DHS's Larry Simmons

1955   DeRidder 32   Leesville 6

The Dragons took an easy win in 1955, in what would be a banner year for the team from Beauregard Parish. DHS advanced to the State Semi-Finals, losing to Neville of Monroe. Tackle Melvin Branch and End Gary Crowe made All State for the Dragons on the year; Branch went on to a storied career, playing at LSU for Legend Paul Dietzel as a member of the famous "Chinese Bandits" and as a star in the American Football League.

DeRidder Takes 32-6 Easy Win

(Special to The Town Talk)

LEESVILLE, La.—The DeRidder Dragons defeated Leesville's Wampus Cats by a 32-6 score here Friday night in a hard-fought 32-6 game.

DeRidder made 13 points in the first period, 19 in the second. Leesville scored in the final period.

Gary Vaughn scored two touchdowns for DeRidder. Larry Simmons also picked up a pair of touchdowns for the victors and Melvin Branch, a tackle, recovered a blocked punt in the end zone for the other score by the winners.

Ed Allen scored on a 50-yard pass play for Leesville. He took the ball from Leesville's quarterback Charles Smart.

Leesville led in first downs by seven to five. DeRidder paced in rushing 104 to 63 yards. Leesville led in passing, 57 to 41 yards.

EDWARD ALLEN
Halfback

DHS's Melvin Branch

1955 CHAMPS—BOTTOM ROW: Lewis, Vaughn, Cooley, Schmidt, Cagle, Simmons, Goodeaux, Sexton, Anderson, Cooper. MIDDLE ROW: Coach Kelly, Davis, Hodge, Williams, Mulkey, Downs, Eubanks, Russell, Day, Lyon, Wellborn, Nelson, O'Neal, Coach Jantz, Coach Doyle. TOP ROW: Harbison, Marsalise, Brister, Hinson, White, Blake, Vaughn, Mangano, Stewart, Durand, Hanchey, Crowe, Branch.

1956:   DeRidder 34   Leesville 7

DeRidder handled Leesville easily in the 1956 contest.   Excerpts from the Leesville Leader and the DHS yearbook are below.

Cats Close Out 1956 Grid Season With Loss To Dragons

Friday night the Wampus Cats of Leesville High school closed out their 1956 football season with a 34-7 loss at the hands of the DeRidder Dragons. The game, between two of the bitterest rivals in the state, was played at DeRidder.

The Dragons jumped off to a quick lead in the opening minutes of the first quarter when they took the kickoff and marched to paydirt with Larry Simmons taking the mail over on a 21-yard run.

From them until the closing seconds of the half the game was a rock-'em-sock-'em defensive battle between the Dragons, a member of District 4-AA and the Cats, an injury-racked representative of District 4-A. The defense of the Cats was exceptional in the second quarter, especially when you consider that five Leesville players (including their leading TD maker, Wayne Morris) were hobbled with injuries. The Dragons managed to score again with only a few seconds left on a 12-yard pass from Quarterback Murphy Ashworth to Harvey Cryer.

Leesville, who was hurt by three fumbles and two pass interceptions, surrendered three TDs in the third quarter, as the weight, depth (of which Leesville has practically none) and experience began to show. Those scores came on a 43-yard run by Simmons, an 18-yard dash by Ashworth and the final a 28-yard ramble by Adrian Vaughn. Little Don Cagle made four of five place-kicks for the extra points to round out the tallies.

In the final stanza, Leesville's little Cats rocked the Dragons back to register their touchdown. The payoff came with Quarterback Sam Piranio racing the last 10 yards of a 35-yard Wampus Cat drive. J. C. Welch, who ran brilliantly all night, on the end-around play, made the extra point via that specialty.

Defense had the better of the game from them on and the score at the end read Leesville 7, DeRidder 34.

First downs favored the Dragons 9 to 12 and in rushing yardage they came out on top 365 to 163. For the first time this year,
continued on page eight

STATISTICS
	Leesville	DeRidder
First down	9	12
Rushing yardage	163	365
Passing yardage	24	31
Passes	2-11	2-5
Passes intercepted by	1	2
Punts	4-40	3-22
Fumbles lost	3	2
Yards penalized	5	80

DRAGON CAPTAINS WAIT ON SIDELINE before going to the center of the field for the toss of the coin. They are Robert Welborn (60) and Garey Vaughn (23).

DHS's Simmons lead blocks for Ashworth   DHS's George Leray   LHS's Kenneth Magee

1957: Leesville 33   DeRidder 6

The Wampus Cat returned the favor from the previous year's drubbing. Local media reporting is attached.

Leesville 33 DeRidder 6

LEESVILLE, La. — Leesville's Wampus Cats smashed hapless DeRidder 33-6 Friday night on the strength of four first-half touchdowns.

Robert Pynes scored twice for the winners, once on a pass from Sam Piriano and again on a nine-yard sprint. Wayne Morris ran 29 yards, John Hall went three, and Piriano sneaked over from the one for the other Cat scores.

Piriano ran two extra points and Hall bucked for another.

Tommy Blakes cracked over from the seven for the Dragons' only score.

LHS's John Hall   DHS's Don Cagle (33) and teammates

LHS's Robert Pynes

1958:   DeRidder 14   Leesville 0

The Dragons shut out the Wampus Cats in the 1958 contest.   Media reporting from the Leesville Leader is provided

Rain, Mud, and Dragons Halt Wampus Cats

The Leesville Wampus Cats dropped their second game of the season Monday night when the DeRidder High Dragons "outkicked" them 14-0 in a game played under the most adverse conditions. The entire game was played in a driving rain and the whole field was covered with water. The game was originally scheduled for last Friday night and then again Saturday night, but was postponed until Monday because of the weather. As it turned out it wouldn't have mattered when the game was played.

The game, which did little to decide which team was really the best went scoreless through the first half and it seemed that it might end that way. But DeRidder wisely chose to punt on first down and wait for LHS to commit and error. The Cats did just that in the third period when the ball was fumbled on the Cats 38 yard line on a fourth down punt try. DeRidder recovered and Benny Brown some how got loose on the first try and ran the 38 yards to the goal line. The PAT was good.

Then in the final stanza with DeRidder still resorting to punting on first down, the locals fumbled again and the Dragons took over on the Cats 11. Quartreback Lewis Roberts bootlegged the final eight yards for the tally and the ball game.

Outside of the two scores it was mostly just a matter of a few offensive plays and then punting as neither team could do much with the girdiron in such terrible shape.

Despite the fact that they lost Leesville did manage to gain the most ground — or mud — however you want to look at it. LHS sloshed for 143 yards on the ground and DeRidder managed but 90. Those totals aren't much to brag about but were surprising in view of the way things were. DeRidder threw the only pass of the night but it was intercepted. There were 13 fumbles in the game with Leesville losing four and DeRidder three. In the punting department the Dragons came out on top with a 35 yard average on seven kicks and LHS could manage only a 21 yard average on four and therein lay the matter of victory and defeat. Only five yards were assessed in penalties in the hurriedly played game with that being stepped off against DeRidder.

DHS's Bennie Brown, tackled by Dick Bedell of Eunice

LHS's Billy Lewis

DHS's Larry Faulks, Ernest Colquette and George Bass

1959:   DeRidder 7   Leesville 6

The contest in 1959 came down to an extra point, and the Dragons prevailed. Excerpts from the Leesville Leader and Alexandria Town Talk are provided.

Cats Edged By Dragons, 7-6, in Thriller Here

Last Friday night the Leesville High Wampus Cats wound up their regular season play by dropping a close, hard fought ball game to the heavily favored DeRidder Dragons. The final score was by the narrowest of margins, 7-6, in a game that was just as close and exciting as the score would indicate.

DeRidder had to come from behind to nip the underdog squad of Coach Ted Paris.

DeRidder, a 14 to 20 point favorite before the game, found themselves behind in the first quarter as the Wampus Cats jumped aboard a big break to get their touchdown. The Dragons fumbled a Leesville punt with the Cats recovering and the locals quickly punched over the tally. John Terry, one of the hardest running backs in the state, slammed over from the three yard line to score. The then seemingly unimportant try for the extra point failed.

DeRidder came back in the second quarter to gain the lead they never relinquished. Bobby Slaydon's four yard run was good for the TD and Jimmy Clark ran over what proved to be the deciding point.

The second half proved to be just as exciting as the first although neither team could score. The game ended with Leesville in possesion of the ball driving deep into DeRidder territory only to be stopped by the clock.

The win gave DeRidder an 8-2 season record and Leesville's now stands at 5-4-1.

DeRidder had a slight edge in statistics although the Cats led in first downs 10 to 9. The Dragons gained 170 rushing and added 28 more on one pass completion out of five tries. LHS rushed for 147 yards and Quarterback Warren Norris completed four of ten aerials for 19 yards.

This Friday night the Cats get a chance to improve on their season record by taking on the Oakdale Warriors in the first annual Lions Club Bowl for Crippled Children. Proceeds of the game go toward the Crippled Childrens' summer camp being built near Leesville.

Oakdale and Leesville will be tangling for the second time this year. The two teams battled to a 7-7 tie in the season opener here. Oakdale, which hasn't shown too much offensively, has shown they can be pretty tough to score on and should be a better team than they were at the beginning of the season. The same holds true for the Wampus Cats and quite a battle should be in store for the fans.

DE RIDDER - LEESVILLE

Leesville scored first, but missed the try for extra point. DeRidder made its touchdown in the second period, ran over the extra point and then the two teams settled down to a defensive battle in the second half.

Bobby Slaydon plunged one yard for DeRidder's score and Jerry Clark ran over the extra point.

Fullback John Terry scored Leesville's touchdown on a three-yard run. It was Terry who tried the run for extra point.

Leesville led in first downs, 12-9, but DeRidder had the edge in rushing, 207 to 165.

It was the second straight loss for the Wampus Cats, after winning five in a row. They wound up with a 5-4-1 record. DeRidder won eight and lost only two.

DHS's Bobby Slaydon   LHS's John Terry

DHS's Bobby Iles   LHS's Ronnie Byrd

DHS's George Bass

1960: DeRidder 14 Leesville 13

Once again, the Dragons edged the Cats by one point.

DERIDDER 14, LEESVILLE 13

DERIDDER, La. — DeRidder made the most of its extra point scoring ability to nip Leesville 14-13 in the season closer for both teams.

However, Leesville came out on the long end of the statistics despite losing a heartbreaker.

The Wampus Cats of Coach Ted Parish, who compiled a 4-6 record this season, rushed for 145 yards and added 125 with some accurate passing to out gain the Dragons by 35 yards. DeRidder rushed for 230 yards and failed to complete a single pass.

It was passing that brought Leesville its two scores. The first coming when quarterback Ronnie Byrd passed three yards to halfback Sid Morris and the second was a 65-yard pass play involving the same combo.

Leesville drew first blood in the second quarter, but Ken Anderson put DeRidder out front 7-6 when he ran the extra point following halfback Bill Green's four-yard touchdown run in the third period.

DeRidder, owner of a 7-3 record, scored again in the fourth quarter when Green smashed over from the two. Green ran the extra point that put the game out of reach for Leesville.

The second Byrd-to-Morris TD pass play came with but one minute left in the game — too late for the Cats to pull out the victory, but Byrd passed to Morris for the extra point.

Sidney Morris

1961:   DeRidder 47   Leesville 7

In the year prior to the commencement of the Hooper Trophy, the Dragons mangled the Wampus Cats yet again.   A lengthy report from the Leesville paper provides details. The Dragons had a strong season in 1961, finishing 8-1 and placing two players on the All State team, Shirley Smith (T) and Tommy Allen (E).

```
Score by Quarters:
DeRidder      0 27 13 7 — 47
Leesville     7  0  0 0 —  7
```

Dragons Speed By LHS Wampus Cats in Season's Finale

The Leesville Wampus Cats rang down the curtain on the 1961 football season, and it fell with a thud! The Cats played their worst games of the season and were walloped by their arch rivals, the DeRidder Dragons, 47-7. The game left LHS with a 4-6 mark to show for the year.

A Dragon win wasn't surprising considering DeRidder's 8-1 record, but the ease with which they won was certainly unexpected.

Leesville began out like they had really come to play. The Cats kicked off and DeRidder promptly drew a 15 yard penalty for clipping. Leesville held and the Dragons punted. LHS then began to move steadily down the field. They consumed most of the opening period with their methodical march, finally climaxed by Robert Mock's eight yard smash over the goal. George Smith kicked the extra point.

DeRidder began to bellow smoke and in the second quarter the roof fell in. After Ronnie Black had got off two good gainers for the Dragons, Touchdown Tommy Allen went to work (if you could call it that) and zoomed to four of the quickest touchdowns ever regestered against the Cats. Allen, a sophomore, handled the ball only five times in scoring those four second period TDs. He scored on runs of 20, 22, 60 and 69 yards. All the youngster had to do was turn on the speed and set sail. There weren't any Cats around to stop him.

Down by the big margin the locals came back and it seemed they had a touchdown only to be denied when Louis Magee's perfect toss was dropped just over the goal line without a Dragon near.

In the second half, things weren't quite so explosive. Ronnie Black marked up a touchdown in the third quarter for the Dragons and Billy Whiddon blocked a Leesville punt and just had but to field the ball and step (continued on page five)

(continued from page one)
over the goal for another tally.

In the final quarter End Johnny Lewis picked off a Leesville aerial and romped over untouched for yet another marker.

One of the bright spots for the Cats was the inspiring play of the second stringers who entered the game in the fourth period. The young Cats with Roy Trahan, a sophomore, Mike Carver, a junior, Jimmy Haymon, a freshman, Richard Schwartz, a sophomore, doing the running with Ray Montgomery at the controls, found their line opening good holes against a mixtures of Dragon first liners and subs. The Wampus Cats reeled off four quick first downs before being stopped at the Dragon five.

In saying that Leesville played bad is putting it mildly. The Dragons, who seem to have a hex on the Cats and bring out the worst in them, rushed for 255 yards against 95 for the Cats. Surprisingly the Cats had 13 first downs to 11 for the Dragons. DeRidder went for TDs while Leesville got first downs. Leesville had 43 yards passing.

The Dragons were helped along by three Cat fumbles and four intercepted passes. The Cats gave little protection on passing and the punter was rushed badly every time. Their blocking was off and their tackling wasn't any better.

The 47-7 margin was the largest since Leesville's 33-6 victory in 1957.

DHS's Tommy Allen, Jerry Bailey and Louis Peavey

DHS's Shirley Smith

In the weeks and months leading up to the innaugual Hooper Trophy game, there was much talk in the local media about the Trophy that would be presented. Mr. and Mrs. Hooper made several trips down to publicize the event and generate excitement. The establishment of the rotating trophy solidified the importance of the annual game and rivalry.

Hooper Trophy to Be Presented at LHS Assembly

Wholesome competition between Leesville and DeRidder, already at a high pitch, will be heightened by entrance of the L. S. Hooper Trophy at the Nov 16 game.

Mr. Hooper played "a game or two" for Leesville High back in 1917, according to his recent correspondence with Joe Parker, principal. Mrs. Hooper is a graduate of DeRidder High School.

Both schools have accepted the trophy for competition. Struggle for the trophy will begin at the November game; the winner will keep it for one year. This pattern will persist until the game of 1971 at which time it will be retired to one of the schools.

The impressive momento is already in the hands of the engraver and will be displayed for the first time by Mr. and Mrs. Hooper. The display and a talk by Mr. Hooper will occur at the assembly at L. H. S. Friday morning, November 2, at 10:30 A. M. The public is invited.

The Hooper Trophy stands almost 2 feet high. It is crested by a male "Victory" statue. At the base are located four statuettes of football players. These include a lineman, a runner, a passer and a kicker. Appropriate plates carry replicas of the Wampus Cats and the Dragon school mascots. The silver plated trophy is on a wood base. A plate will be used to list the winner for each year.

After spending the week of November 2 in DeRidder, the Hooper Trophy will be on display in a downtown Leesville store window. It will be initially awarded at the November 16 game in DeRidder.

Leesville Leader, 1 Nov

Hooper Trophy On Display Here

The L. S. "Buck" Hooper is on display at Brother's-Word sporting good Store on Third Street. The memento was presented for Winners of the competition between the Leesville Wampus Cats and the DeRidder Dragons. Ten games will be placed before permanent ownership is determined but the winner of the Oct. 16, 1962 game will determine which school receives the prized possession for 1962-63.

Fans of the football team are invited to drop by the display for a close inspection of the strikingly handsome prize.

The Leesville Wampus Cats, riding a successful seaon record of 7-1-1 and a perfect home game win record, will be expending their best efforts to bring home the Hooper Trophy. Award will be made be Mr. Hooper at the close of the game Friday night, According to Mr. Jack Gormley and Mr. Joe Parker, principals of the competing schools.

Leesville Leader, 15 Nov

Leesville To Play at DeRidder

LEESVILLE — A traditional football rivalry in Vernon and Beauregard parishes will be renewed tomorrow night when Leesville's Wampus Cats, (7-1-1) for the season, go to DeRidder for a game with the Dragons. The winner will get the floating L. S. (Buck) Hooper trophy.

The traditional rivalry means more than a district title to fans from both Leesville and DeRidder. Principals Jack Gormley of DeRidder and Joe Parker of Leesville said the Hooper trophy will be awarded to the winners at the end of the game.

The trophy is now on display at Brother's Word Sporting Goods in Leesville, where tickets to the game are also available.

Shreveport Journal, 15 Nov

Buck & Agnes Hooper

1962:   DeRidder 13   Leesville 0

DHS Took the Inaugural Win in the Hooper Trophy Series.   Series DHS 1   LHS 0

Hooper Trophy Is Won By DeRidder

DERIDDER (Spl.) — The DeRidder Dragons completed the first leg in their quest for permanent possession of the newly inaugurated Hooper trophy here Friday night.

The trophy, to be given to the team which gets the most victories in a 10-game series, will stay with DeRidder for the next year after the Dragons' 12-0 triumph over Leesville.

If last night's game is any indication, the series, which has always been a good one, should continue to be so.

A closer contest would be difficult to find, disregarding the score. The Wampus Cats and Dragons each picked up 10 first downs. Leesville had 126 yards rushing to DeRidder's 123. The Dragons had a slight edge in passing with 56 yards to the Cats' 29.

And it was passing which proved the margin for victory.

DeRidder's initial score came as a climax to a 61-yard drive with a 31-yard pass from Mac Crider to Stewart Martin in the second period.

In the third quarter, Martin again scored on a heave from Crider, this one of 25 yards to complete a 54-yard drive.

Leading the DeRidder offense before the overflow crowd was Paul Nicholas who ran 14 times for 66 yards.

```
Leesville ................... 0 0 0 0— 0
DeRidder ................... 0 6 6 0—12
   DERIDER SCORING:   TD—Stewart
Martin 2 (31, 25 passes from Mac Crider).
             STATISTICS
                        Leesville  DeRidder
First downs ................ 10        10
Rushing yardage ......... 126       123
Passing yardage ..........  29        56
Passes .................... 3-8       2-2
Passes intercepted by...    0         1
Punts .................... 4-33.1   4-39.0
Fumbles lost ..............  1         1
Yards penalized ..........  75        10
```

DHS's Seniors: Kneeling L-R: Gary Colquette, Jerry Russell, Hank Bryan, Ed McDonald, Mac Crider. Standing Butch Pedersen, John Burdish

1962 Wampus Cats

1963: Leesville 28   DeRidder 6   Hooper I Series: DHS 1   LHS 1

In the second game of the Hooper Series, the Wampus Cats notched a win.   Talk in the communities around game time was that DHS Coach Cecil Doyle would be sitting some of his starters to get ready for the playoffs in the ensuing week. Both teams entered the season finale with clinched playoff berths.

Tuneup for Playoff Game

DeRidder Held Out Regulars in 28-6 Loss to Leesville

LEESVILLE, La. — A playoff victory is more important than a regular season victory. At least, that's the thinking of DeRidder coach Cecil Doyle.

The Dragons, who were ranked No. 3 in the state and had only a 7-7 tie with Natchitoches to blemish their unbeaten record, dropped a 28-6 decision to Leesville Thursday night in a non-district game.

These same two teams will meet again next Friday night, at a site to be determined today, in the opening round of the state playoffs.

Doyle elected to have his first stringers sit back and watch the action Thursday night, thus eliminating any chance of their being injured.

Coach Ted Paris of Leesville played his first unit for about two-and-a-half quarters before letting his second unit take over. Other than the regular aches and pains incurred in a football game, the Wampus Cats came away in good physical shape.

The game, played before some 5,000 fans, is an annual grid rivalry between these two neighboring communities.

Leesville scored a single touchdown in the first period, added two more in the second quarter, and after DeRidder scored its lone tally early in the fourth period, finished up with its fourth TD of the night late in the game.

Don Jackson got the first Wampus Cat score when he raced 20 yards.

Halfback Paul Nicholas added the extra point, and the Cats had a 7-0 lead in the initial period.

Nicholas scampered 15 yards early in the second quarter and fullback Mike Shockley ran the PAT to make it 14-0. Later in the period, Richard Schwartz, a regular end who was shifted to halfback for this game, ran it over from the three yard stripe, for the third Leesville TD.

Quarterback Billy Salim tossed a pass to Schwartz for the extra point, and Leesville left the field at halftime with a comfortable 21-0 lead.

After a scoreless third period, DeRidder got on the scoreboard when Wayne Green streaked 70 yards for a touchdown. The extra point try failed.

Leesville's final touchdown came when Danny Catchings climaxed a drive by taking it in from the one yard line. Quarterback Keith Carver passed to Catchings for the extra point to round out the scoring.

Score by Quarters:
DeRidder   0 0 0 6—6
Leesville 7 14 0 7—28

SCORE BY QUARTERS
DeRidder   0 0 0 6— 6
Leesville 7 14 0 7—28
 L—Don Jackson, 20 yard run (Paul Nicholas (run).
 L—Paul Nicholas, 15 yard run (Mike Shockley (run).
 L—Richard Schwartz, 2 yard run (Richard Schwartz pass from Billy Salim)
 L—Danny Catchings, 1 yard run (Danny Catchings, pass from Keith Carver)

LHS Seniors

RJ Fertitta and Buck Hooper

The controvery of the 1963 game made news as far north as Shreveport. The Shreveport Times published their own editorial on the Dragon's not playing first team playes and their story produced a response from both high schools and others in the communities. The stories below were printed in the Shreveport Times on 17, 19 and 20 November.

17 November

BILL McINTYRE
'L' for Lack Of an Effort?

Rules of the 'Game'

On Page 4 of the 'Constitution and Directory' of the Louisiana High School Coaches Assn., 1962-63 edition, is a list of ten 'commandments' set forth under the high-sounding title of "Our Code."

We take the liberty here of quoting from this "Code" as supposedly followed by the brethren of the LHSCA . . .

"It is the duty of all concerned with high school athletics:

"1. To emphasize the proper ideals of sportsmanship, ethical conduct, and fair play.

"2. To eliminate all possibilities which tend to destroy the best values of the game.

"3. To stress the values derived from playing the game fairly.

"4. To show cordial courtesy to visiting teams and officials.

"5. To establish a happy relationship between visitors and hosts.

"6. To respect the integrity and judgment of sports officials.

"7. To achieve a thorough understanding and acceptance of the rules of the game and the standards of eligibility.

"8. To encourage leadership, use of initiative, and good judgment by the players on the team.

"9. To recognize that the purpose of athletics is to promote the physical, mental, moral, social and emotional well-being of the individual players.

"10. To remember that an athletic contest is only a game—not a matter of life or death for player, coach, school, official, fan, community, state, or nation."

We suggest that you refer constantly to the above reprint as we delve further into an event that took place at Leesville last Thursday evening.

'Say It Ain't So!'

. . . Because, if it is, the goal of amateur athletics among high school teen-agers in Louisiana has become distorted in translation from theory to practice.

It appears, from reliable reports, that last week's schoolboy football game between DeRidder and Leesville, played at Leesville, fell far short of being a legitimate contest . . . In that the visiting Dragons struggled from start to finish with nothing but second-and third-stringers against a Wampus Cat squad that figured to be tough enough minus any artificial assistance.

Without detracting from Leesville's fine performance, an effort that produced a 28-6 victory, it is blatant fact that DeRidder surrendered without a fight in what was billed as a big year-end 'traditional' between natural Double-A rivals from the parishes of Vernon and Beauregard.

DeRidder had gone into the game with an unblemished 8-0-1 record, and was ranked third among Louisiana Class AA ballclubs. Leesville had come off an eight-game winning streak that had produced an 8-2-0 record. The Dragons had won the 4-AA championship, the Cats had captured the 3-AA crown.

This was the 'big one' for both sides. It had been that way for years.

But for the spectators in the stands it must've been an evening of frustration. DeRidder's starting lineup, including halfback Tommy Allen, a lad being boomed for all-state recognition, was kept chained to the bench and never played so much as a down.

Coach Cecil Doyle undoubtedly had his reasons for refusing to employ his first-stringers. The Dragons, for instance, were reportedly bruised and battered from physical punishment absorbed in recent victories over Jennings and Oakdale. Then, too, the Dragons and Wampus Cats are booked for an encore on Friday next in the opening round of the state playoffs.

Thus Doyle may have been looking ahead to their second meeting, this time with the playoff chips stacked up on the table. To some this might be a stroke of shrewd strategy—refusing to tip one's hand ahead of time—but we would assume that the Leesville high command, namely Coach Ted Paris, already had a fair impression of what the Dragons could and could not do with a football.

Going into the game with the pre-conceived intention of losing certainly didn't enhance DeRidder's reputation, nor did it sweep up Leesville in a false sense of superiority. Instead, it strikes us as a rebuttal of the axiom that "it's not who wins or loses, but how you play the game."

We remember when an undefeated season was something to be proud of.

One does not "play the game" with the intention of losing. In professional sports this would be branded, and with justification, as an outright "fix."

We respectfully submit that the Executive Committee of the Louisiana High School Athletic Assn., which sits at Alexandria this afternoon, take stock of such shenanigans within its jurisdiction.

It would appear on the surface that Cecil Doyle has bent, if not broken, at least eight of the ten "commandments" in the Code!

19 November: A response from a DHS player and the high school principal

A Defense for Doyle

In response to Sunday's column, dealing with last week's pre-determined outcome of the scheduled "contest" between DeRidder and Leesville, there came in Monday's mail several letters in rebuttal. Among them:
"Dear Sir:

"I am Johnny Lewis, senior guard for the 1963 DeRidder Dragons.

"I know it is your job to criticize or praise when you feel it is necessary. In the case you described in the Sunday, Nov. 17, 1963, issue of The Shreveport Times I think you should have praised Coach (Cecil) Doyle for his farsightedness and judgment in the DeRidder-Leesville game.

"Here are the facts: Tommy Allen has some bruised ribs, Billy Loftin has a pulled "hamstring," John Welborn, Kenneth Palmer and Buckie Nugent have sprained ankles, Bobby Hernandez got knocked out in the Oakdale game, Ricky Marshall has a hurt shoulder, Jimmy Lewis has a "trick knee," and I myself have a pulled groin muscle. Do you think these boys warrant a rest? Do you think they should play? All these injuries are temporary and most of these players will be able to go in our next game with Leesville.

"Some more facts: Jennings has replaced Leesville as a traditional rival. We, the players, have had to "get up" for the last 3 ballgames, which were all hard fought. We, the players, want DeRidder to have a state team so bad that it hurts our insides. 16 seniors will be leaving the varsity squad with graduation. (Do you think the experience that the 2nd team received in the Leesville game was valuable?)

"Coach Doyle, in all the players' opinions, is the best coach in the state of Louisiana! Who, in the state, has been able to stop the mighty single-wing of Jennings? Who would not put hurt players on the field for a chance of re-injury, just to win? As you say yourself, "It's not who wins, but how you play the game." But more than all these things as a coach, we the players, feel in our hearts, that Coach Doyle contains the best asset of all; He is a man!

"I, as well as all the members of the 1963 mighty Dragons, am sorry we lost. Our second team did a magnificent job and the coaches as well as the players are proud of them. But more than anything we thank them for giving the Dragon first-team a physical and mental rest to prepare us for state.

Thank you for listening. Your article was well-written but I don't care too much for the body.
Sincerely yours,
Johnny Lewis"

* * *

A Voice of Authority

Along with the daily mail came a Western Union wire above the signature of Jack Gormley, principal of DeRidder High School . . .

"Mr. McIntyre, I am one who reads your column with a great deal of interest, respect for your opinion, and often in complete agreement with your viewpoint; however, it was with a sense of keen disappointment that I noted the extreme inaccuracies in your comments in the editorial in the Sunday issue of The Shreveport Times, titled, "Rules of the 'Game'."

"As principal of DeRidder High School, I wish to present these facts to clarify a situation that, because of incomplete or inaccurate information, has led to unjust criticism of our coach Cecil Doyle.

"Knowledge of events before the game might shed some light on the situation. We had made sincere efforts to come to some agreement that would eliminate the game as a game that would have no bearing on the championship. It is regrettable that the demands of finances for a school's athletic program can be the main reason for playing an extra game.

"Our team was literally crippled up in a series of injuries that occurred during the latter part of the season. The one and only reason for not throwing in the injured players to satisfy the "win at any cost" crowd, or to pacify the complaining gamblers, was in the interest of not jeopardizing the well-being of the individual players.

"I have worked in close association with a number of highly respected coaches in our state and have found that the typical modern coach is a man of good character and personal integrity, who is sincere in working to achieve the goals set forth in what you have termed "the high sounding title of 'Our Code'."

"Of the many coaches I know, none exceed Cecil Doyle in real concern for his players, and in his efforts to promote those finer qualities of the game. We at DeRidder High School are behind coach Doyle 100 per cent."

* * *

We reprint Mr. Gormley's telegram primarily for the purpose of presenting both sides of the existing situation. . . . Although we reserve the right to take exception to the statement that Sunday's piece included "extreme inaccuracies."

20 November: Response by LHS high school, junior high and elementary principals

The Case Is Closed...

This corner has no intention of prolonging the pros and cons regarding last week's DeRidder-Leesville football conflict, other than to present a couple of closing comments from school officials in Leesville.

Since Jack Gormley, principal of DeRidder High School, was allowed to sum up his opinions on the Dragon-Wampus Cat meeting of last week in yesterday's column, it is only fitting and proper that Joe Parker, principal of Leesville High School, be allowed equal space...

"Dear Bill:

"You were most courteous and kind to print the full text of letters received from the player and the officials of DeRidder High School.

"Much has been said through the press since the morning following DeRidder's victory over the great Oakdale team and Leesville's defeat of the stalwart Red Devils of Natchitoches. Please note that this telegram marks the first public utterance from Leesville High. We have not nor will we attempt dictation of strategy to a fellow coach. Criticism, if any is warranted, must stem from fans and sports writers.

"Yes, we asked DeRidder to fulfill her agreement to play the annual Leesville-DeRidder football classic on November 14, 1963. We are delighted at the possibility of hosting that great Dragon team not just once but twice in a single year. We have friends that have followed our team for many years. We have almost 500 fans who reserve seats on a full season basis. These were eagerly awaiting the climaxing game of the regular schedule. Not only did we want to play that eleventh seasonal game on November 14, but we are proud that our decision to allow a forfeiture was a solid "No."

"You see, Bill, we enjoy football here in Leesville. It is evidenced by our fine facilities. It is evidenced by the many boys of high academic standing who play the game. It is evidenced by the fact that we bring in every junior and senior in the parish as guest to the first game of each year. We extend the same courtesy to uniformed scout troops. It is evidenced by the fact that we accept the military at student prices.

"No, Bill, Leesville High is not and will never, under my direction, be a school that plays the wonderful game of amateur football for money. Nor will any decision of mine or that of my coaches who are Christian gentlemen be influenced by complaining gamblers or any other pressure group. Incidentally, the gambling group, if it exists, is not known to me.

"Bill, we will never accept the awarding of the great L. S. "Buck" Hooper trophy on any basis other than that of the regular season game—the way "Buck" intended it.

"We, too, have had injuries. We, too, declined to used injured players. Some are among our most dependable, but our boys played November 14th like the happy sportsmen which they are. Entertaining well that capacity crowd of 5,000 loyal football fans.

"Leesville High stands ready to compete with energy and enthusiasm November 22. Leesville High stands ready to continue annually the competition with DeRidder—a competition enjoyed by so many for so long. Leesville High will do everything possible to serve those who come to enjoy the game Friday.

"Sincerely,
Joe Parker"

...And a Final Word

"Dear Mr. McIntyre:

"We appreciate your comments in Sunday's Shreveport Times relative to the Leesville-DeRidder football game. In our opinion your evaluation is an excellent means of keeping the public informed as to the coaching tactics that are unethical when preparations are made and admissions paid to see a regular scheduled football game, especially one that has been traditional between Leesville and DeRidder for many years.

"Would all the first team boys have been held out of the game if the state playoffs had not been involved in a future game? And why was an aching and bruised team permitted to suit out and take warm ups on the playing field? Will the disregard for the final annual Buck Hooper trophy be shown by DeRidder authorities in the future?

"Your editorial should do much in interpreting this type of a football game to the people and in securing their support to denounce practices of this kind in our fine high schools. Patrons and supporters of the athletic teams deserve the facts and unbiased opinion of the press which you have very ably expressed regarding this contest.

"There is an old saying that the wheel that squeaks the loudest needs the grease and from the bickering that is coming from DeRidder school authorities you have greased the guilty.

"Sincerely yours,
"C. A. Hughes, principal Leesville Junior High School, Lyons Palmer, principal West Leesville Elementary School"

With the above we sign "Thirty."

1963 Playoff Game: DeRidder 34   Leesville 19

In the first of what is now three clashes in the post season, the Dragons beat the Wampus Cats handily.   In what was probably the largest crowd ever to see a game at Wampus Cat Stadium, Coach Cecil Doyle's Dragons dominated the first round playoff contest.   Incidentally, this game was Leesville's first ever venture into the State playoffs and came on the heels of LHS's first District Championship. The game was played on the Saturday after US President John F. Kennedy was assasinated in Dallas; the original contest was slated for Friday, but moved for obvious reasons. The event did not count in the Hooper Trophy series as it was a playoff and not a regular season game. Of note from the game: DeRidder's Tommy Allen (RB) and John Moses (G) were first teamm All-State selections on the year, and Leesville's RJ Fertitta (G) was on the second team. DeRidder would lose in the second round of the playoffs in the 1963 season to Minden.

Allen Sparks Dragons Past Leesville 34-19

By FRANK ADAMS

LEESVILLE — The DeRidder Dragons stormed to a 28-0 lead then battled a Leesville passing blitz to fashion a 34-19 victory and advance in the state AA playoffs here Saturday night.

DeRidder will meet Minden Friday at 8 p.m. at Northwestern's football field in Natchitoches.

The Dragons, sparked by the running of Tommy Allen, pushed over two touchdowns in the first quarter and held a 14-0 halftime lead. A wild, 26-point third quarter left DeRidder in front by 28-12.

Allen carried the ball 17 times and gained 142 yards.

Allen, living up to his all-state billing, sparked the Dragons to a touchdown the first time they got the ball after a poor snap from center proved costly to Leesville.

The Wampus Cats were in a kicking situation at the Dragon 43, but the snap to punter Dewayne Palmer was low and wide and he had to chase it all the way to the Leesville 41 where Bob Teston dropped him.

Jimmy Lewis shook Stuart Martin loose the first time and flipped for a touchdown but the play was nullified by an offside call. Then Allen took over, reeling off sprints of 10, 11 and five yards to move to the Leesville 20.

Lewis tried the air unsuccessfully, then called on Allen again. Allen picked up five in two tries, then turned decoy. With the Wampus Cats chasing Allen to the right, Bobby Hernandez steamed through a gapping hole on the left side and sailed untouched into the end zone. Martin's kick made it 7-0 with 5:50 elapsed.

A few minutes later an Allen fumble was snared by Gary Treme but the pendulum swung right back on the next play when Billy Salim's pass skittered off Paul Nicholas' fingertips and was intercepted by Ricky Marshall at the Dragon 30.

Allen gained three, then Lewis, failing to find a receiver open, ducked through left guard, found daylight and raced 56 yards to the Leesville 11 before Richard Schwartz knocked him out of bounds. A personal foul call on the play moved the ball to the five. Hernandez banged to the three, then rammed left tackle. He fumbled, but Ben Mason scrambled to recover it in the end zone for a touchdown and Martin again converted.

DeRidder took the second half kickoff and marched 65 yards in 12 plays. Allen provided 21 yards on the ground and hauled in a pass for 10 more. Hernandez set things up by snaring a pass for six yards, then dashing nine yards to the two. Ricky Marshall failed to gain but Lewis sneaked in on the next play and Martin converted the extra point.

Leesville took to the air effectively at this point and the complexion changed completely. Billy Salim hit Roy Trahan for nine yards, Paul Nicholas gained eight, and then Salim shook Richard Schwartz loose and hit him with a jump pass at the 50. Schwartz slanted to the left and raced all the way to the DeRidder four before Marshall ran him out of bounds.

Nicholas barged for three at right guard, then hit right guard for the touchdown. Salim's attempt to run the extra point was short.

It didn't stay that way long. On the first play after the kickoff, Allen raced around right end for 10 yards to the Dragon 35. Then he skirted the right side, hit the open at the Leesville 45 and showed his fabulous speed on a 65-yard touchdown gallop. Martin's kick made it 28-6.

Things weren't calm yet. DeRidder started at its own 46 on an on-side's kickoff try. Marshall got eight but a penalty cost the Dragons five. Allen reeled off 17, Marshall got five more but a penalty nulified that gain. Then, with only 50 seconds of the fourth quarter gone Larry Rhame took a handoff from Allen, swung around the left side and raced 36 yards for a touchdown. Martin missed his first conversion of the night.

Leesville's final marker came in the fading minutes as reserves sprinkled both teams. Keith Carver pitched to Don Jackson for eight, to Martinez for eitht more and Jackson gained three moving to the DeRidder 40. Then the Wampus Cats pulled the end around, Schwartz to Martinez trick again and this time Martinez was all alone at the 10 and hauled it in for the touchdown. Danny Catchings ran the extra point.

```
DeRidder ............... 14  8 14  6—34
Leesville .............. 0  0 12  7—19
```
D—Bobby Hernandez, 15 run. Stuart Martin kick.
D—Ben Mason, recovered fumble in end zone. Stuart Martin kick.
D—Jimmy Lewis, 2 run. Stuart Martin kick.
D—Tom Allen, 65 run. Stuart Martin kick.
L—Paul Nicholas, 1 run. Run failed.
L—John Martinez, 74 pass from Richard Schwartz. Pass failed.
D—Larry Rhame, 36 run. Kick failed.
L—John Martinez, 10 pass from Richard Schwartz. Danny Catchings run.

STATISTICS

	DeRidder	Leesville
First downs	12	12
Rushing yardage	325	85
Passing yardage	16	292
Passes	2-5	14-27
Passes intercepted by	1	0
Punts	3-43.0	2-42.8
Fumbles lost	1	0
Yards penalized	45	66

LHS's Paul Nicholas

DHS's Tommy Allen

DHS's Tommy Allen, LHS's RJ Fertitta (63) and Don Jackson (22)

1964: DeRidder 40   Leesville 13   Hooper I Series: DeRidder 2   Leesville 1

The Dragons continued their dominance in 1964. Excerpt from the Shreveport Times

DeRidder Dragons Romp Past Leesville in Traditional, 40-13

DeRIDDER — The DeRidder Dragons scored early and late here Friday night to rout Leesville 40-13 in a non-conference game which is a traditional rivalry.

Eugene Kulaga and Bobby Hernandez scored quick markers for the Dragons in the first period and quarterback Bill Hyde threw for two scores in the second as the winners built a 27-0 halftime edge.

Steve Spann took an eight-yard pass from Hyde to make it 33-0 before Keith Carver put Leesville on the scoreboard on a seven-yard run.

Hernandez took a 16-yard pass from Jimmy Lewis for the final Dragon score and Billy Salim tossed 25 yards to Jimmy Skinner for Leesville and end scoring.

Cecil Doyle's Dragons ended the season with a 7-3 record. Leesville finished up 4-4-2 for the campaign.

Leesville .... 0 0 6 7—13
DeRidder .... 13 14 6 7—40
D—Eugene Kulaga 2 run. Kick failed.
D—Bobby Hernandez 56 intercepted pass. Bobby Hernandez kick.
D—Clarence Swilley 10 pass from Bill Hyde. Bobby Hernandez kick.
D—Steve Spann 53 pass from Bill Hyde. Bobby Hernandez kick.
D—Steve Spann 8 pass from Bill Hyde. Kick failed.
L—Keith Carver 7 run. Pass failed.
D—Bobby Hernandez 16 pass from Jimmy Lewis. Kick failed.
L—Jimmy Skinner 25 pass from Billy Salin. Keith Carver run.

STATISTICS
	Leesville	DeRidder
First downs	12	20
Rushing yardage	93	261
Passing yardage	106	105
Passes	7-18	7-8
Passes intercepted by	0	2
Punts	3-39.3	1-43.0
Fumbles lost	0	0
Yards penalized	15	65

Leesville .... 0 0 6 7—13
DeRidder .... 13 14 6 7—40
D—Eugene Kulaga 2 run. Kick failed.
D—Bobby Hernandez 56 intercepted pass. Bobby Hernandez kick.
D—Clarence Swilley 10 pass from Bill Hyde. Bobby Hernandez kick.
D—Steve Spann 53 pass from Bill Hyde. Bobby Hernandez kick.
D—Steve Spann 8 pass from Bill Hyde. Kick failed.
L—Keith Carver 7 run. Pass failed.
D—Bobby Hernandez 16 pass from Jimmy Lewis. Kick failed.
L—Jimmy Skinner 25 pass from Billy Salin. Keith Carver run.

1965: DeRidder 13 Leesville 0   Hooper I Series: DHS 3 LHS 1

The Dragons collected their third win out of four in the burgeoning Hooper series

Dragons Topple Stubborn Cats

By LYNN MARTIN

A pair of fourth quarter scores spoiled a fine defensive effort by the Leesville Wampus Cats as the DeRidder Dragons edged the Cats 13-0 in the annual grudge match between the two neighboring Double AA schools. By virtue of the win the Dragons won the Hooper Trophy for the third time in four years.

The game was played at Wampus Cat Stadium.

DeRidder, a heavy favorite, was hard-pressed by a stout LHS defense and the Cats held them scoreless until there were eight minutes lift in the game. Then quarterback Jimmy Lewis hit Clarence Swilley with a 16-yard scoring pass to climax a 39-yard DeRidder drive Center Steve Cagle kicked the extra point.

With 3 15 left in the game, the Dragons scored again. Steve Spann turned in a 50-yard scoring romp to ice the game.

Three times before the first DeRidder score, the Cats had repelled the Dragons. In the second quarter the Dragons drove to the LHS fourteen, but the aroused locals threw back the visitors with their stubborn defensive line play.

In the third quarter the Beauregard team moved to the Leesville fourteen again, but the Wampus Cats had the answer this time too and a 12-yard loss inflicted on Lewis halted that Dragon threat.

The Cats also stopped another DeRidder drive with a fumble recovery at the Leesville 26.

Leesville's most serious threat came after stopping the first DeRidder effort at the fourteen. From there, LHS moved to the Dragon 19, sparked by a 38 yard run by fullback Keith Carver. The Cats lost the ball then and the half came at that time, too.

During the first half the Cats shoved out a 4-3 first down edge and also held a 83 to 52 rushing yard margin. But even with their offensive edge, it was the defense that sparkled for the Cats and this seemed to keep the Dragons unsure of themselves.

For the night the DHS team managed to rack up 12 first downs and 185 yards rushing. They also picked up 65 yards in the air.

Leesville's offense tailed off in the final two stanzas and the Cats finished with six first downs, 94 yards on the ground and 40 in the air.

The game closed out the season for the hometown squad. They finished with a 4-6 record on the year.

	DeRidder	Leesville
First downs	12	6
Net yards rush	186	94
Net yards pass	65	40
Passes (A-C)	8-13	3-10
Had Intercepted	1	0
Punt-Avg	2-40.2	7-30.5
Fumble-Lost	1	0
Penalties-Yds	70	52

Score by quarters:
DeRidder   0 0 0 13—13
Leesville   0 0 0 0— 0

Scoring summary:
DeR—Clarence Swilley, 16 pass from Jimmy Lewis (Steve Cagle kick)
DeR—Steve Spann, 50 run (kick failed)

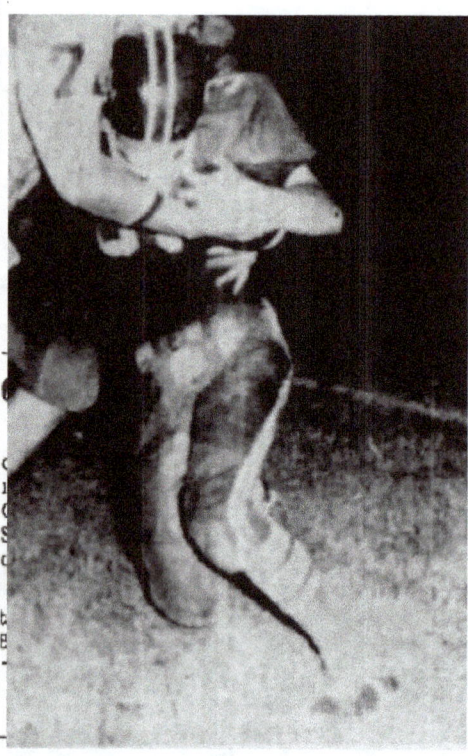

DHS's Paul Shirley

NOV 19 1965

LEESVILLE WAMPUS CATS

No.	Name	Class	Pos.	Wt.	No.	Name	Class	Pos.	Wt.
10	Roland Breaux	Soph.	QB	150	64	Bill Prassell	Sr.	G	135
11	Brown Word	Jr.	QB	140	65	Dennis Karamales	Soph.	G	150
12	Donnie Gill	Soph.	QB	110	66	Mike Cohen	Jr.	G	155
20	Jack Gross	Sr.	HB	150	67	Rick Morrison	Jr.	G	155
21	Charles Ross	Soph.	HB	140	70	Ulrich McClain	Jr.	T	170
23	Ronnie Morrow	Jr.	HB	140	71	Bobby Craft	Soph.	T	170
24	Carl Williams	Sr.	HB	155	72	Wayne Cavanaugh	Jr.	T	170
25	Joe Gendron	Jr.	HB	175	73	Craig Jeane	Soph.	T	140
26	Pat Garner	Soph.	HB	145	74	Walt Winton	Jr.	T	165
27	John Smith	Soph.	FB	150	75	Tom Heisman	Soph.	T	215
31	Keith Carver	Sr.	FB	180	76	Richard Carr	Soph.	T	225
32	Randy Martin	Jr.	FB	150	77	Larry McRae	Sr.	T	175
33	Rodger Causey	Jr.	FB	165	81	Billy Laurent	Sr.	E	
50	Dickie Bailes	Jr.	C	185	82	Mark Wilhelmy	Sr.	E	165
52	Allen Nickerson	Sr.	C	205	83	Don Dryden	Soph.	E	140
53	Thad Bailes	Soph.	C	175	84	Larry Caldwell	Jr.	E	165
53	Allen Fertitta	Jr.	G	150	84	Butch Mohl	Sr.	E	165
61	Richard Karamatic	Jr.	G	140	85	Jack Hadnot	Soph.	E	150
62	Rodger Welch	Soph.	G	145	86	Jimmy Funderburk	Soph.	E	125
63	Darwain Davis	Soph.	G	180	87	Don Davis	Sr.	E	165

NOV 19 1965

DeRidder Dragons 13

No.	NAME	Pos.	Wt.
10	Jimmy Lewis	QB	155
11	Johnny Hyde	QB	130
12	Donald Milner	QB	160
20	Johnny Granger	HB	130
22	Mike Maroney	HB	135
23	Wayne Green	HB	190
24	Steve Spann	LHB	160
30	Eugene Kulaga	FB	165
31	Johnny Frusha	FB	150
33	Steve Pinkley	FB	185
36	Paul Shirley	RHB	170
40	Ronnie Hayes	LE	155
41	Tommy Roberts	E	150
42	Marvin Lee	G	130
43	Rickey Alston	HB	132
44	Clarence Swilley	HB	150
50	Steve Cagle	C	165
51	Donnie Cline	C	160
53	Tommy Cooley	C	145
55	Tommy Granger	C	135
60	Richard Rathburn	G	148
61	Milbert Doyle	T	185
62	Ronald Banks	E	145
63	Willis Lange	G	147
64	Charles Travis	LG	155
66	John Hoss	G	150
68	Darrell Harper	RG	170
70	Bill Storms	C	160
71	Ronald Chelette	RT	175
72	Frank Mills	T	205
73	Lawrence Miller	E	135
74	Daniel Wyatt	T	172
75	Buddy Kenner	T	185
76	Donald Wiegand	B	160
77	Jerry Craig	T	225
80	Nick Capano	E	180
81	Raymond Teston	E	170
82	Bobby Green	E	150
83	Jeff Kern	LT	183
84	Mike Hyde	E	180
85	Robert Teston	RE	190
86	Gerald Banks	E	182

1966: Leesville 21   DeRidder 6   Hooper I Series: DHS 3   LHS 2

The Cats pulled of the first of what would be four, consecutive wins in the series.   A great photo appeared in the Leesville Leader, with both teams handling the trophy

Leesville Latest Contender After Roaring by DeRidder

Wampus Cats Paste Rivals 21-6;

Wampus Cats Paste Rivals 21-6; Natchitoches Bows 6-3 to Jena

Leesville is the latest team to file a claim in the scrambled District 3-AA football race, and the Wampus Cats used arch-rival DeRidder as a stepping stone.

Coach Bill Hickman's Cats, who showed only one victory and a tie for their first four weeks of the season, used a fumble recovery and an interception to stun their bitterest rival 21-6 Friday night.

DeRidder, which moved from District 4-AA this season, had been co-favored with Natchitoches, which is winless in five games.

Natchitoches was a 6-3 victim of all-winning Jena, the state's sixth-ranked team in Double-A, and a long-time member of 3-AA before helping form the new conference (2-A) this season.

Tioga was 3-AA's only other winner Friday night. The Indians ran their string of unscored-on quarters to 19 in beating arch-rival Buckeye 6-0 in a non-league game.

fense, 95 rushing and 29 passing. DeRidder led 13-7 in first downs.

Just as last week, when they beat Caldwell in the district opener, the Jena Giants got their only touchdown in the fourth period.

Gene Wilbanks rammed over from the one to climax a 55-yard drive.

Until this time, Natchitoches' defense had stopped the Giants cold, and the Red Devils were leading 3-0 on Petey Johnson's 26-yard field goal in the second quarter.

Tioga At Leesville

Tioga and Leesville clash at Leesville in the feature game next week, with the winner earning the favorite's role in the district. In other 3-AA games, Menard meets Pineville and Natchitoches plays DeRidder.

DeRidder, which entered the game with a 1-1-1 record against outside opposition, had it all over Leesville in statistics. But games are decided by points, and this was all Leesville, which never trailed.

Dennis Karamales put the Wampus Cats ahead to stay with a 10-yard touchdown run in the first period. Larry Caldwell kicked the first of his three extra points.

Johnny Hyde threw a 30-yard pass to Ray Teston for a DeRidder score later in the first quarter, but the kick for extra point was wide and the Dragons were never able to catch up.

In the second period, Rodger Causey scored the first of his two touchdowns for Leesville by intercepting a pass and running it back 73 yards.

Causey led Leesville's ground attack with 47 yards in 18 carries.

DeRidder rolled up 329 yards in total offense, but made 193 of these yards with a fruitless passing game, completing 11 of 26. Two were intercepted. Leesville had only 124 yards in of-

DISTRICT 3-AA

Team	Season	District
Tioga	3-1-1	1-0-1
Leesville	2-2-1	1-0-0
Menard	2-1-2	0-0-1
DeRidder	1-3-1	0-1-0
Natchitoches	0-5-0	0-1-0
Pineville	0-3-0	0-0-0

Friday's Scores
Tioga 6, Buckeye 0
Leesville 21, DeRidder 6
Winnfield 13, Menard 6
Jena 6, Natchitoches 3
Ferriday 21, Pineville 0

Next Week's Schedule
Tioga at Leesville*
Pineville at Menard*
Natchitoches at DeRidder

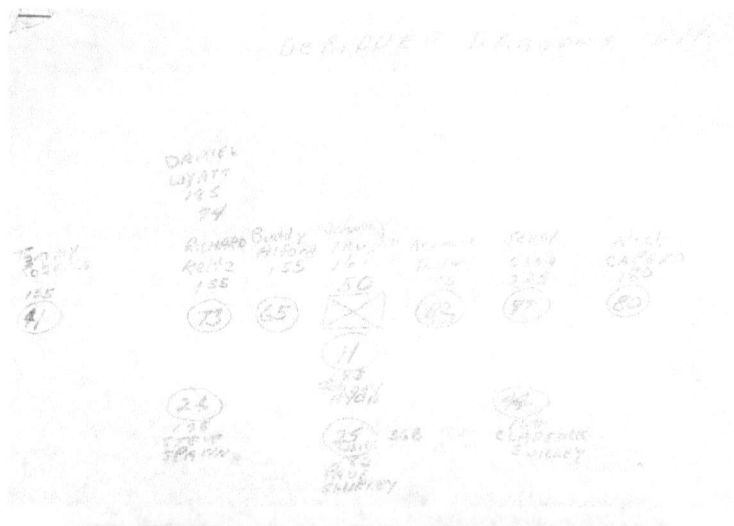

Fans at Wampus Cat Stadium

1967: Leesville 21   DeRidder 0   Hooper I Series: DHS 3   LHS 3

Leesville Blanks DeRidder in Bow
Wampus Cats 21-0 Winners in First 3-AA Battle

(Special to The Town Talk)

DERIDDER, La. — Leesville kicked off its District 3-AA slate on a successful note, defeating rival DeRidder 21-0 Friday night here.

The win gave Coach Charlie Edwards' Wampus Cats a 4-0-1 record for the season, while the loss was the fifth in a row for the Dragons, who are the defending champions in 3-AA.

Leesville's defense played a prominent part in the tough battle, one that really wasn't decided until the fourth period, a quarter that saw the Cats push over two clinching TDs.

Leesville had taken a 7-0 lead late in the second period when it marched 48 yards in 10 plays, with quarterback Donnie Gill going in from the one with 3:58 showing on the clock.

Mike Dudley split the uprights for the first of three successful conversions, and the Cats went into the dressing room holding on to their 7-0 lead.

After a scoreless third quarter, Leesville put together a 13-play, 81-yard drive that was climaxed when fullback Darwin Davis bulled his way into the end zone from one-yard out.

An interception by Victor Ortiz got the Wampus Cats in motion for their final TD, which came when James Arms fell on Davis' fumble in the DeRidder end zone with only two seconds left in the game.

DeRidder managed only threat during the game, and that came after Leesville scored its first touchdown.

The Dragons took the kickoff and marched to a first down at the Wampus Cats' 27, but that was as far as they could get as the Leesville defense stiffened and took over on downs.

Leesville hits the road for the second week in a row next Friday night, traveling to meet the tough Tioga Indians. DeRidder is also on the road for a game against undefeated Natchitoches.

The Wampus Cats controlled the statistics almost as one-sided as they did the score. In first downs, the Cats held a 12-6 advantage, and piled up a 190-43 margin on the ground.

DeRidder, connecting on 6-of-17 passes, accumulated 59 yards while Leesville managed 46, completing only 2-of-11. In total offense, Leesville commanded a 236-102 bulge.

Score by Quarters:
Leesville   0 7 0 14 — 21
DeRidder   0 0 0 0 — 0
Scoring:
Leesville — Touchdowns: Gill, 1-run; Davis, 1-run; Arms, recovery of fumble in end zone. Extra points — Dudley 3, kick

SCORE BY QUARTERS
Leesville   0 7 0 11 21
DeRidder   0 0 0 0—0
Score Summary:
L — Donnie Gill, 1 run, (Mike Dudley kick)
L — Darwin Davis, 2 run, (Dudley kick)
L — fumble in end zone, (Dudley kick)

Hooper Trophy Presentation

SENIOR PLAYERS, 1967

DHS Seniors 1967

1968: Leesville 26   DeRidder 20   Hooper I Series DHS 3   LHS 4

The Cats pulled ahead in the series for the first time.

Ortiz' Three TD Passes Spark Leesville Over DeRidder 26-20

(Special to The Town Talk)

LEESVILLE, La.—Quarterback Vic Ortiz, with three scoring passes, ran his touchdown production to 11 in leading Leesville to a 26-20 victory over arch-rival DeRidder Friday night.

In posting their third consecutive victory, following a 7-6 loss to Oakdale in the season opener, the Wampus Cats took a 4-3 lead over DeRidder in their Hooper Trophy series. The school that wins the most games over a 10-year period, ending in 1971, gains permanent possession of the cup.

Three straight Leesville touchdowns, after DeRidder had taken a 7-6 lead in the first period, put the game on ice.

Ortiz, in four games, has thrown seven touchdown passes, for distances of 60, 45, 40, 35, 18, nine and six yards, and added four touchdowns on runs from scrimmage.

Ortiz started the scoring Friday night with a nine-yard strike to Paul Sliman, with 4:45 left in the first quarter. Before the period ended, quarterback Mike Harris reeled off a 98-yard touchdown run from scrimmage and Wade Miller kicked the extra point for a 7-6 Dragon lead.

Then Leesville scored three straight times, twice in the second period and once in the third. Ortiz threw to end Daniel Ayala for the first two, for 45 and 18 yards, for a 19-7 halftime lead. In the third quarter, halfback Jack Ashfield ran 55 yards for another Wampus Cat TD, making the score 26-7.

Harris tried his best to pull it out for DeRidder after that, but the clock was against him. He threw a 77-yard touchdown pass to Miller in the third period, and ran four yards for another score in the fourth quarter.

Because of the long touchdown plays, there were only eight first downs in the game, five for Leesville and but three for DeRidder.

The Wampus Cats piled up 326 yards, including 236 on the ground and 90 on Ortiz' five completions in eight attempts.

Harris hit on six of seven aerials for 107 yards as DeRidder had a total offense of 252 yards.

Leesville lost four fumbles and DeRidder lost three.

Another factor was the punting of Ortiz, who averaged 40.5 yards on four kicks.

Score by quarters:
DeRidder   7 0 7 6—20
Leesville   6 13 7 0—26

Scoring:
DeRidder — Touchdowns: Harris 98-run, 4-run; Miller, 77-pass from Harris. Extra points: Miller 3.

Leesville—Touchdowns: Ashfield 55-run, Ayala 2, 45-pass from Ortiz, 18-pass from Ortiz; Sliman 9-pass from Ortiz. Extra points: Laurent 2.

Wade Miller

Fans at Wampus Cat Stadium

1969: Leesville 25 DeRidder 0   Hooper I Series: DHS 3 LHS 5

Goldsby Provides Leesville's Spark

(Special to The Town Talk)

DERIDDER, La. — Leesville's Wampus Cats, unbeaten but once tied this year, went into the second half in a scoreless tie with winless arch foe DeRidder here Friday night.

Then senior end Doug Goldsby decided he had had enough and took things in his own hands to start the second half. Goldsby took the kickoff at his own 30 and didn't stop until he was 70 yards away in the Dragon end zone.

This brilliant touchdown sparked the Wampus Cats and they went on to down DeRidder 25-0 in a non-district tilt.

The Wampus Cats held a substantial bulge in statistics. Leesville led 11 to two in first downs and 196 to minus 13 in rushing yardage. DeRidder led only in passing yardage, 59 to 28.

Goldsby's TD run broke what had been a series of frustrating events for the Wampus Cats. Fumbles and a pass interception stalled Leesville drives in the thirst half.

Following Goldsby's TD and John Driscoll's successful PAT kick, the Wampus Cats came back in less than four minutes to score another six-pointer. Jack Asrfield, who paced the Wampus Cat ground attack, hit the end zone from one yard out.

Early in the fourth quarter, Leesville quarterback Steve Hays went into the DeRidder end zone from 14 yards out and minutes later Goldsby picked up his second TD. This one came on a 20-yard pass from alternating Wampus Cat quarterback Billy Wood.

Score by quarters:
Leesville   0 0 13 12—25
DeRidder   0 0 0 0— 0
Scoring:
L-TD: Goldsby 70-kickoff return (Driscoll kick)
L-TD: Ashfield 1-run (kick failed)
L-TD: Hays 14-run (kick failed)
L-TD: Goldsby 20-pass from Wood (kick failed)

In 1964 the St. Louis Cardinals went into the month of September 7½ games out of first place. Yet they roared to the National League pennant and a World Series victory over the New York Yankees.

1969 DeRidder Dragons

Steve Hays (26) flies the last two yards of a 15-yard touchdown run in last Friday's Hooper Trophy Leesville-DeRidder Game. DeRidder's Mark Dees (30) and Buddy Whiddon (10) look on after having both missed tackling Hays.
Clarion-Ledger Photo

1970:   No Game Between LHS and DHS

1971:   DeRidder 21   Leesville 6   Hooper I Series: DHS 4   LHS 5

After a one year hiatus, the series picked back up and DeRidder got the 9th win in the Hooper series. DeRidder would lose NO games to Leesville in the 70s.

Young Leesville Bows To Rival in Opener

(Special to The Town Talk)

LEESVILLE, La. — It wasn't a district game, but the keen rivalry between Leesville and DeRidder made it just as important Friday night when the two teams met.

And DeRidder came away with the win, leading all the way in posting a 21-6 victory over the young Wampus Cats of coach Douglas Creamer.

The Dragons posted a 7-0 lead in the first quarter when Malcolm Chisson plunged into the end zone from one yard out and Johnny Hubbard kicked the extra point.

The Cats closed the gap to 7-6 in the initial period on a five yard run by Ronald Fertitta, but missed on a pass for the two-point conversion.

After a scoreless second period, DeRidder put the game away with 14 points in the third quarter. Lloyd Wildblood got the first TD on a 15-yard run and Hubbard ran for the PAT to make it 15-6. Hubbard got the clincher later in the period on a five-yard run, but missed the kick for the point after.

The one-mile Freehold, N.J., pacing record of 1.58.2 was set by Honest Story, driven by Ed Cobb, in 1970

STATISTICS

	D	L
First Downs	18	9
Yards Rushing	204	90
Yards Passing	34	59
Total Offense	238	149
Passes	6	9
Passes Completed	3	2
Interceptions by	2	1
Fumbles Lost	2	3
Punts	2	0
Average	31.5	0
Penalties	30	55

Score by Quarter:
DeRidder   7 0 14 0—21
Leesville   6 0   0 0— 6

Scoring:
D—Chisson (1-yd. run), Hubbard kick.
Y—Fertitta (5-yd. run), pass failed.
D—Wildblood (15-yd. run), Hubbard run.
D—Hubbard (5 lyd. run), kick failed.

RONALD FERTITTA

THE HOOPER TROPHY, long the symbol of football superiority in the traditional competition between DeRidder and Leesville, is proudly displayed by Frankie Harris, and Bobbie Hennigan, co-captains in Friday night's game with Leesville, and Head Football Coach Al Sandahl.

1972:   DeRidder 14   Leesville 0   Series: DHS 5   LHS 6

In an odd twist, DeRidder beat Leesville, but the Dragons were forced to forfeit the game, and thus forfeit the Hooper Trophy.   The Dragons self-reported playing an ineligible athlete and the game was forfeited. On the field, the Dragons won, but Hooper I was awarded to Leesville.

DeRidder Is 14-0 Victor

DeRIDDER — Malcolm Chaisson rambled 63 yards for a touchdown on the second play of the game to spark DeRidder to a 14-0 season - opening victory over Leesville Friday night.

Chaisson also tallied te Dragons' final marker in the fourth period, breaking three tacklers on his way to a 21-yard scoring dash. Frank Johnson ran for the two pointer after the first TD.

The game was the first to be played in DeRidder's new stadium.

Only six passes were thrown in the contest, Leesville hitting one of three and DeRidder failing to hit on three attempts.

THE YARDSTICK

	LEESVILLE	DeRIDDER
First downs	6	8
Net Yards rush	109	145
Net Yards pass	8	0
Passes (a-c)	3-1	3-0
Had Intercepted	0	0
Punt-Average	4-42.5	5-36.2
Fumbles-Lost	3-2	2-1
Penalties-yds.	9-85	5-45

Leesville	0	0	0	0—0
DeRidder	8	0	0	6—14

Scoring Summary:
D—Malcom Chiasson, 63 run (Frank Johnson run)
D—Chiasson, 21 run (run failed)

DeRidder plays ineligible man, game forfeited to Wampus Cats

Dr. H. Lynn Russell, principal of Leesville High, has announced that he had been informed by Principal James Haley of DeRidder that it had been learned that DeRidder had unknowingly played an ineligible student in the recent Wampus Cat-Dragon tilt, and that it would be necessary for DeRidder to forfeit the game to Leesville.

"Mr. Haley and his coaches discovered the error themselves," said Russell, "and they immediately contacted the Louisiana Athletic Association. If they had not done so, it would probably have gone without notice. We commend Mr. Haley and the DeRidder coaching staff for acting quickly and in the best tradition of sportsmanship to correct the error."

Arrangements are being made to transfer the Hooper trophy to Leesville from DeRidder, where it was placed in the showcase after DeRidder defeated the Wampus Cats on September 8.

Both Russell and Head Coach Doug Creamer expressed their regrets over the situation, stating that the Dragons had played an excellent game and had won the trophy fairly. "These things do happen," said Coach Creamer. "We certainly understand and wish the Dragons good season for the rest of the year."

THURSDAY, SEPTEMBER 21, 1972

LHS's James Dean and DHS's Jeremy Chaisson

The 1973 game saw the introduction of the second Hooper Trophy. The presentation was covered in media around the state. The below excerpt is from the Shreveport Times in September in 1973.

Another Hooper Trophy For Leesville-DeRidder

Times Sports Service

There's a new reward this year for the winner of the Leesville-DeRidder football game — the Hooper II Trophy.

It's the successor to Hooper I, retired after last year's game, and the arch-rivals will battle for it Friday night in their season opener at Leesville.

Like Hooper I, permanent possession of Hooper II will be determined on a 10-year basis.

The original series began in 1962 and the trophy is now in Leesville's possession. Actually, the series appeared to be tied 5-5 after DeRidder's 14-0 win last year. But the Dragons were found to have an ineligible player, had to forfeit and Leesville took home the trophy on a 6-4 margin.

The trophies are donated by a Shreveport couple, Mr. and Mrs. L. S. Hooper, who left a big part of their hearts in Southwest Louisiana. And they don't see eye-to-eye on the series.

Mr. Hooper, known as "Buck," is a 1919 graduate of Leesville High. Mrs. Hooper, the former Agnew Lewis, graduated in 1929 from DeRidder High.

The football rivalry, one of the state's oldest, began in 1910 and available records show DeRidder with a 31-13-1 lead. The Dragons won the opener 35-0.

Leesville enters its third season under Head Coach Doug Creamer. The Wampus Cats were 7-3 last year and Creamer says his club "could do a pretty decent job this year, once we get it together."

They'll have to get together without 5-11, 240-pound linebacker Johnny Mapu, who will be out much of the season with a broken leg.

Back to head the offense are junior quarterback Dennis Driscoll and halfback Donel Johnson. Tackle James Self (206) is the leader up front. The defensive is led by linebacker Albert Sherrill (202) and tackle Danny Turick (195).

The Wampus Cats have switched to a new league (4-AAA). But DeRidder has moved up to Class AAAA (District 4) with a new head coach, Charles Montgomery.

An eight-year coaching veteran at Prescott, Ark. — with a five-year head coaching mark of 37-19-1, Montgomery succeeds Al Sandahl.

"We're big and slow up front," says Montgomery, "and we'll play power football.

His offensive line includes all-district tackle Bobby Durham (230), guards Robert Hines and Sam Lampo (both 175) and tight end Robert Burby (190) and the defensive front includes nose guard Darrel Cade (225), tackle Earl Bos (225) and Durham with returning regular Mitch Manuel (180) at a linebacker.

L. S. HOOPER
. . . with new trophy

1973: Leesville 6   DeRidder 6   Series: DHS 0 LHS 0 1 tie

In what would be the last tie of the series, the Dragons and Cats finished in a deadlock. Leesville led until the last play of the game, when DHS scored on a long pass. The Wampus Cats blocked the PAT to salvage a tie.

DeRidder 'Stole' Victory from Cats

LEESVILLE, La — The law of average caught up with DeRidder here Friday night, and it gave the Dragons a license to steal a victory from their biggest rival, Leesville.

DeRidder didn't win, but the Dragons scored a touchdown on the last play of the game for a 6-6 tie.

The horn went off while Raymond Chaisson was racing for the end zone with a pass thrown by Gary Fuller from the Leesville 34-yard line.

It was the only time during the game that DeRidder came close to scoring.

In fact, the Dragons had lost six fumbles and had a pass intercepted, the latter setting up Leesville's touchdown, nine minutes before the end of the game.

Something good had to happen for DeRidder, and it came just in the nick of time.

The good fortune didn't last long enough, though. It remained for Michael Brown to save Leesville from defeat. He blocked DeRidder's try for extra point.

Although the Dragons twice stopped Leesville at the DeRidder two-yard line and made no serious threats of their own, the statistics were practically even. DeRidder actually out-gained Leesville in total offense, 141 to 139, but the Wampus Cats had two more first downs, 9-7.

In addition to turning the ball over seven times, DeRidder was penalized five times for 60 yards.

Lionel Casarez, who recovered a DeRidder fumble on the opening kickoff, intercepted a pass to start Leesville on its 35-yard touchdown drive, with Raymond Mapu running the last six yards for the score. Mapu led the Leesville attack with 34 yards rushing.

Danny Turrick's try for extra point was wide.

The missed PAT didn't seem important at the time. And when Leesville punted with 35 seconds left in the game, some of the fans left. Then, on fourth down, Fuller connected with Chaisson, and suddenly Leesville wasn't a winner, after all.

Giants Win LaSalle Title, Post 20-0 Win

JENA, La — The Jena Giants were victors Friday night in the battle of LaSalle Parish, whipping the LaSalle High Tigers 20-0.

Quarterback Larry McCartney had a hand in two of the Giants' scores, booming over

HOOPER II TROPHY PRESENTED--The beautiful new trophy being held by Dr. H. Lynn Russell, left, principal of the Leesville High School, and James Haley, right, principal of the DeRidder High School, is the new Hooper II trophy which has been donated for competition between the two schools by L.S. "Buck" Hooper, center, and Mrs. Hooper of Shreveport. Hooper, a 1919 graduate of LHS and Mrs. Hooper a graduate of DeRidder High in 1929, donated the original Hooper Trophy which was retired last year. The trophy is awarded permanently to the team which wins the best of a 10-game series. Leesville, although playing to a 6-6 tie with DeRidder Friday night, was awarded possession of the trophy on first downs.

1974:   DeRidder 28   Leesville 6   Series II   DHS 1   LHS 0

DeRidder took an easy victory in the Fall of 1974, getting their first win of the second series. Reporting from Shreveport Times. This game featured future LSU and Miami Dolphins star from DeRidder, John Adams.

Dennis Driscoll Some Consolation

DE RIDDER, La.—Julius Robichaux, Leesville High's new head football coach, learned a lot in his Wampus Cats' season opener here Friday night, but almost all of it was bad.

Robichaux discovered, in a 28-6 loss to arch-rival DeRidder, that his team has a long way to go.

However, Robichaux found some consolation in his debut. Quarterback Dennis Driscoll is a pretty hand around which to build.

Despite the one-sided game, Driscoll's talents stood out. The 170-pound senior ran for 111 yards and in the third period ripped off a 38-yard touchdown run.

DeRidder, though, had already put the game away when Driscoll burst into the end zone, taking a 13-0 first half lead and scoring again before Leesville could get on the board.

John Adams made two of the DeRidder touchdowns, on runs of one and five yards. Tim Harris dashed 10 yards for another score, and John Cooper ran back an intercepted pass 20 yards for the other touchdown.

First Quarter
DeRidder: Mike Adams 5 yard run (John Adams kick)
Second Quarter
DeRidder: John Cooper 28 yard interception return (John Adams kick)
Third Quarter
DeRidder: Tim Harris 10 yard run (John Adams Kick)
Fourth Quarter
Leesville: Dennis Driscoll 39 yard run (kick failed)
DeRidder: Mike Adams 1 yard run (John Adams kick)

John Adams

1975: DeRidder 50 Leesville 0 	Series: DHS 2 LHS 0

The Dragons trounced the Wampus Cats in a downpour at Wampus Cat stadium. The 1975 contest would be the most lop-sided in series history since 1945.

All DeRidder

LEESVILLE — It was all DeRidder and Randy Bosway in the opening game of the season, the annual grudge between Leesville and DeRidder for the Hooper trophy.

Bosway scored once and passed for three other touchdowns in a 50-0 DeRidder romp.

Randy scored on a 22-yard pass to open the onslaught and then passed to Gary Adams for 23 yards and another score. Another Bosway touchdown pass made it 20-0 by the end of the opening quarter.

Adams boomed through a 28-yard field goal for the lone score of the second quarter but then the DeRidder defense got in on the act, blocking a kick for a touchdown.

Bosway's last touchdown strike was a 71-yarder.

Mac McClendon capped scoring for DeRidder with a 63-yard run.

Mike Bosway

DHSs John Adams, John Cooper, Mike Bosway

1975 DHS Team

1976: DeRidder 42 Leesville 6   Series DHS 3 LHS 0

The Dragons, once again, had no trouble with the Wampus Cats. This game featured future McNeese star running back Theron McClendon.

Leesville Bows To DeRidder

The unranked DeRidder Dragons rolled up 373 yards on the ground and added 118 through the air to smother the Wampus Cats of Leesville High School 42-6 here Friday night.

Thereon McClendon scored three of the Dragon TD's. One on a 52-yard run for the games longest TD run and he passed for another 6-pointer hitting Williams Stevens on a 57-yard scoring play to get the scoring underway in the first quarter.

James Galloway broke loose on a 16-yard run in the first quarter and Larry Jackson rocketed 35 yards just before the half for the Dragons.

Leesville's TD came in the final quarter when Terry Hanes bowled over from two yards out. The PAT kick failed. This was the 16th loss in a row for the Wampus Cats.

DHS's Theron McClendon   LHS's Terry Haynes

1977:   DeRidder 6   Leesville 0   Series: DHS 4   LHS 0

The Cats took the Dragons to overtime and DeRidder won in dramatic fashion.   The defensive struggle was played in front of a capacity crowd at Wampus Cat Stadium

DeRidder..........................7
Leesville..........................0

LEESVILLE — Chris Spence scored from four yards out to lead DeRidder to a 6-0 overtime win over Leesville here in a tough defensive battle Friday night.

DeRidder's Dragons consequently won the "Hooper Trophy", the symbol of victory in the annual clash between the two schools.

Leesville was led by two-way player Terry Haynes, who had two interceptions and a fumble recovery, and also caught a 40-yard pass from Bobby Stephens.

The Wampus Cats also held DeRidder midway through the second quarter on four straight downs inside the one-foot line. That effort was led by linebacker Joe Mastrachio and end Richard Bastedo.

DeRidder is now 2-0, Leesville is 1-1.

Score by Quarters
DeRidder   0 0 0 6—6
Leesville   0 0 0 0—0
Scoring:
D— Chris Spence (4-run).
Yardstick:
First Downs: D 9, L 9; Yards Rushing: D 265, L 102; Yards Passing: D 11, L 77; Passes (A-C-I): D 4-1-2, L 7-3-2; Punts: D 1-44, L 3-32; Fumbles-Lost: D 4-2, L 1-1; Penalties: D 4-41, L 6-35.

1978:   DeRidder 23 Leesville 6   Series: DHS 5 LHS 0

The Dragons held the upper hand all night in DeRidder on a muggy September night and they extended their lead in the series to 4 – 0.

DeRidder............23
Leesville 6

DeRIDDER — The homestanding Dragons kept their 1978 slate spotless here Friday night as they methodically rolled up a 23-6 win over neighboring rival Leesville.

DeRidder's Mike Jackson picked up two touchdowns on short runs and Larry Simmons chipped in with a 21-yard burst worth six points. The other Dragon points came on a 38-yard field goal by Trey Iles.

The eight points on the Wampus Cat side of the scoreboard were put there by Robert Gains and Rod Simons as they teamed up on a 20-yard aerial strike with Simons throwing and Gains gathering it in.

The Cats trailed in all statistical departments except penalties. The Dragons enjoyed an 11-9 first down edge, 314-201 total offense bulge, but were tagged by the penalty flag nine times for 105 yards. Leesville drew only two whistles for 20 yards.

Offensively the Wampus Cats, now 1-1, were led by Terry Holt with 134 yards on 15 carries while their defensive corps were spearheaded by six solo tackles apiece from Jim Tucker and Scott Harrington.

DeRidder had the top individual ground gainer though as Mike Jackson was credited with 140 yards on 17 tries. Mike Johnson should score tops on the defense with his six unassisted tackles plus one fumble recovery.

DHS's Larry Simons   LHS's Stacy Williams makes the tackle

1979: DeRidder 22   Leesville 14   Series: DHS 6   LHS 0

DeRidder held off a late comeback by the Cats to close out the series on Hooper Trophy II

LEESVILLE—The DeRidder Dragons held on for a 22-14 nondistrict football victory over Leesville here Friday night, with the game-ending tick of the clock catching the Wampus Cats on the Dragon 6.

It was a second win for the unbeaten Dragons while the Cats fell to 0-2.

Greg Hanchey scored on a nine-yard pass from Jim Ambler, Ambler tallied on a one-yard run and then threw a 21-yard touchdown pass to John Gormley. Trey Iles kicked one extra point and a 22-yard field goal.

Scoring for Leesville were Tony Jones on a seven-yard run and Dana Ramono caught a 15-yard pass from Charles Owens.

DHS's Trey Iles   LHS's James Johnson   LHS's Curt Mitchell (32) & Tony Jones (33)

1980:   Leesville 26   DeRidder 15   Series LHS 1   DHS 0

The Cats started Hooper III with a big victory in DeRidder, ending a 10 year non-winning streak in the series.

Joiner, Cats Defeat DeRidder

DERIDDER — Leesville running back Oscar Joiner broke loose for a 77-yard touchdown on a punt return and an 87-yard scoring run from scrimmage during a four minute span of the third quarter Friday night as the Wampus Cats defeated DeRidder for the first time in six years, 26-15.

Joiner, a 5-foot-10, 175-pound sophomore, led Leesville to a 20-7 lead at the 9:12 mark of the third quarter when he pulled in a DeRidder punt on the 23-yard line, broke six tackles and scooted 77 yards for a score. Four minutes later, with 5:13 left in the quarter, Joiner took a pitchout from Wampus Cats quarterback Eddie Barber and flashed 87 yards for his second score and a 26-7 Leesville advantage.

DeRidder totaled 18 first downs to Leesville's 9, but the Wampus Cats took advantage of numerous big plays. Dragon quarterback Ted Harris connected on 13 of 32 passes for 166 yards, but Leesville's Joiner, Charles Owens, and Ernest Bess each intercepted one of his aerials to thwart DeRidder drives.

Leesville struck first, scoring two touchdowns early in the second quarter to open up a 14-0 lead. Barber passed 7 yards to Owens for the first score, and Bess ran two for the second. Harris ran two yards for a touchdown late in the half for DeRidder.

The win improves Leesville's record to 2-0, which equals the total wins by the Wampus Cats last season. DeRidder is now 0-2.

Score By Quarters:
Leesville   0 14 12 0 — 26
DeRidder   0 7 0 8 — 15
Scoring:
L—Charles Owens 7-pass from Eddie Barber. Tom Peavy kick.
L—Ernest Bess 2-run. Tom Peavy kick.
D—Ted Harris 2-run. Tom Peavy kick.
L—Oscar Joiner 77-punt return. Run failed.
L—Oscar Joiner 87-run. Run failed.
D—Andy Sander 7-pass from Ted Harris. Sanders pass from Harris.
Yardstick
(Leesville-DeRidder) First Downs: 9-18. Yds. Rushing: 246-133. Yds. Passing: 78-166. Passes (A-C-I): 5-4-1, 32-13-3. Punts-Avg.: 3-33.0, 3-35.0. Fumbles-Lost: 2-2, 1-1. Penalties-Yds: 8-95, 4-30.

LHS's Earnest Bess   LHS's David Bonner, DHS's Mike Crawford

DHS's Andy Sanders.   DHS's Gerald Bickham & LHS's Oscar Joiner

Hooper Trophy in Leesville after 10 years
Ernest Bess, Michael Deans, Steve Morrison, Charles Owen

1981: Leesville 21   DeRidder 7   Series   LHS 2   DHS 0

The Wampus Cats pulled off a home win and extended their lead in the series.

By Bill Chamberlain

Despite a second quarter downpour that left the playing field as slippery as an eel, running sensation Oscar Joiner broke loose for three long spectacular scoring gallops here last Friday night to help lead the Wampus Cats to a dramatic, 21-7, comeback win over their archrivals, the DeRidder Dragons.

The victory put the Cats back into the running for at least a runnerup-position tie in district 5-AAA and a state playoff berth.

For while Leesville was knocking off DeRidder, West Lake was polishing off Jennings, 27-0 to push the Bulldogs down to a 1-2 district record.

Leesville is now fifth in district, trailing two of the top-ranked triple A teams in the state, Washington of Lake Charles (2-0), and West Lake (2-0), Jennings (2-1), and Sam Houston (1-1).

Lying ahead for the Cats is Sam Houston of Moss Bluff (near Lake Charles), who came from behind a 20-6 halftime deficit Friday to upend Oakdale, 35-28. Leesville is pointing to a game they pulled out last year with a 14-7 victory over the Broncos.

After Sam Houston, the Cats return home for their homecoming game against the number one ranked team in triple A in the state, Washington, who whipped Plaquemine 14-6 Friday in Lake Charles.

Despite what lies ahead, though, for the Wampus Cats, they'll long remember the second licking in a row they gave the Dragons here on a rain-swept, slippery field.

Joiner had put Leesville on the scoreboard in the first quarter, dashing around right end for 24 yards and paydirt standing up.

The 61-yard drive began when Clint Ensley intercepted a Ted Harris pass on the Leesville 15 and returned it to the Cat 39.

Mark Clay, sophomore speedster, took off around left end on the next play, setting up a first and ten at DeRidder's 24 on a spine-tingling 34 yard run.

Henry Dotson, one of the hardest runners faced by the Cats this season got most of the yardage as DeRidder moved the ball down to 18 on 17 hard nosed plays during a driving rainstorm that chased the Dragon band and many spectators to shelter.

At the 18 on a fourth and three Harris lofted a bullseye down the middle to his 6 2, 210 pound end, Andy Sanders, who pulled it down all alone in the end zone.

Following a 5 yard illegal procedure penalty, Daniel Johnson booted the extra point to put DeRidder up front at halftime, 7 6.

Joiner's prelude began in the third quarter, when he cracked a booming, 50-yard punt down to the DeRidder 31 from his own 19 yard line, pulling Leesville out of a hole.

DeRidder was forced to punt, and following a fumble recovery of the punt by Clay, Leesville took off on a 92 yard scoring march, all on the ground, and mostly down the middle on pad-cracking plays against the heavier Dragon defensive line.

With Lester Johnson and David Deans carrying most of the time, Joiner got the call at the Leesville 39.

He swept right end, stopped momentarily and fought his way clear from two defenders, and then cut back to the middle where he found daylight en route to a 39-yard scoring dash.

Moore got the call on the extra point attempt faking a handoff and then turning and squeezing in over right guard for a two point conversion and a 14 7 Leesville lead.

Dazed by the big comeback and spectacular run DeRidder used a 12 yard pass by Harris to advance the ball down to their 42, where a fumble recovery set up a fourth and 19.

The Dragon punt rolled dead on the Leesville six, and once again Joiner punted the Wampus Cats out of danger.

James Walters recovered a Dragon fumble on the ensuing series, giving Leesville possession on its 33 yard line with about three minutes left in the fourth

At that point, Joiner got his call for his first carry of the night. He took a pitchout from quarterback T.J. Moore and sped 24 yards down the right sidelines to score with 5:18 left in the first quarter.

The extra-point kick was blocked, but Leesville had a 6-0 lead.

The show had hardly begun for Joiner, though, who totaled an incredible 192 yards in nine carries, for an average per carry of 21 yards, including touchdown runs of 24, 39 and 68 yards.

In the second quarter, DeRidder cranked up a 77 yard drive from Leesville's 20 down to the three yard line, where a stonewall defense, led by tackle Melvin Maxwell, linebacker Steve Gunn, and defensive end Robert Pynes, cut them off at the three on fourth and goal to go.

Pynes hauled down Harris back on the 10 to halt the lengthy, time-consuming Dragon drive.

On the following series, Joiner got a bad snap from center (the first this season) and got off a 17 yard punt before later redeeming himself by blasting a 50-yarder in the fourth quarter.

After in turn forcing DeRidder to punt, Moore lost possession on a fumble at the DeRidder 18, and the Dragons launched their only scoring drive of the

The yardstick

	DeRidder	LHS
First downs	14	9
Yards rushing	158	332
Yards passing	71	0
Pass. Com . Att . Int	6 19 1	0 1 0
Punts, avg	4 35	4 30-5
Fumbles, lost	7 2	5 2
Penalties, yds	5 45	3 32

Score by quarters
DeRidder 0 7 0 0   7
LHS   6 0 0 15 21

LHS's TJ Moore

A smiling winner

1982: DeRidder 37   Leesville 12   Series: LHS 2 DHS 1

DeRidder took back the trophy in 1982 with a dominating performance

Dragons tame Cats!!!

LHS counts 16 penalties, 178 yards

By Rick Barnickel
Country 105 Sports Director

It was not a pretty sight Friday night when the LHS Wampus Cats left the field after their 37-12 loss at the hands of the DeRidder Dragons.

In fact it was not a pretty sight during the game either.

The Cats were ripped by the one-two running punch of Henry Dotson and Paul Jones, staggered by penalties, and plagued by offensive mistakes. It was a game that Leesville fans would like to forget. With the help of a hypnotist that may be possible.

The Dragons jumped out to a 13-0 lead in the first half on a pair of scoring runs by DeRidder quarterback Jones. His first touchdown came on a four-yard dive that ended a 24-yard drive. The drive was set up by a bad Daniel Aboutabol punt that lost one yard as it hit short and took a funny bounce. The Dragons pushed it over four plays later and had a 6-0 lead.

Leesville dipped into their bag of tricks on their next possession when Aboutabol faked a handoff on a fourth down and scampered 16 yards for a first down. Four plays later the Cats punted and the Dragons had the ball first and ten on their 28. The Cat defense appeared ready to challenge the Dragon when they forced a fumble by Dotson and recovered on the DeRidder 37.

Darren Fowler, in at quarterback, pitched back to starting quarterback T.J. Moore, who fired an option pass incomplete. DeRidder sacked Fowler for a 16-yard loss on the next play and the Cats were forced to punt.

DeRidder took over on their 26 yard line to start the second period and promptly scored on a 74-yard run by Jones. The Cat Defense keyed on Dotson in the first half and Jones burned them for 108 yards on seven carries. He finished the night with 131 yards on 14 carries.

The Cats came roaring back with Steve Gunn rumbling 23 yards to the Leesville 43. Fowler then hit Gunn over the middle for 23 more to the Dragon 27. On second and 13 from the 30 Fowler drifted back to throw a perfect touchdown strike to sophomore Percy Burns. Aboutabol missed the point after and DeRidder led by 13-6.

The Leesville defense, hampered by the loss of linebacker Jimbo Shapkoff, hung tough and kept DeRidder out of the endzone for the rest of the first half. They recovered a fumble at the Dragon 40 but the offense couldn't capitalize.

After an exchange of punts the Dragon defense stiffened, repeatedly sacking Fowler for big losses. They got to him four times for 41 yards in the first half. The Dragons got a break when Chris Robertson couldn't handle the ball on a punt and was tackled in the endzone for a safety. DeRidder led 15-6 at halftime.

The third quarter was the straw that broke the camel's back for the Cats. They recovered a fumble at the Dragon 20 only to fumble it back at the DeRidder 40. Henry Dotson then took off on a 60 yard romp to make it 21-6. The Cats misfortune did not end there as DeRidder came up with another safety on a bobbled punt to make it 23-6.

The Dragons weren't through yet, as they added a two-yard touchdown run by Jones to make it 30-6 with minutes left in the third period.

The Wampus Cat offense was hampered by the loss of running back Mark Clay who went down in the first half along with Shapkoff. The Dragon defense, led by Bennie Sylvest, Jeff Kite, and Thurman Spikes sealed off the middle, forcing the Cats to go wide. They found the going tough there as both Leesville quarterbacks had trouble running the option. When they did get the ball to Gunn and Eric Rhodes they found some room to run. It seemed like every time the Cats would get something going another penalty was called. In their worse performance

SCORE BY QUARTERS

	1st	2nd	3rd	4th	final
Leesville	0	6	0	6	12
DeRidder	6	9	15	7	37

SCORING SUMMARY

DHS...4yd run by Paul Jones (kick failed)
DHS...74yd run by Jones (Mayes kick)
LHS...30yd pass Darren Fowler to Percy Burns (kick failed)
DHS...Safety, punt recovered in endzone
DHS...60yd run by Henry Dotson (kick failed)
DHS...Safety punt recovered in endzone
DHS...2yd run by Jones (Mayes Kick)
DHS...1yd run by Dotson (Mayes kick)
LHS...16 pass T.J. Moore to Burns (run failed)

DeRidder Seniors (Fall of 1982), Class of 1983

DHS Coach Crow

Fans at Cecil Doyle Memorial Stadium

1983: Leesville 37   DeRidder 26   Series: LHS 3   DHS 1

A high scoring contest saw Leesville put a big win. 1983 would be the first season for the Wampus Cats to go back to the playoffs since 1963.

Leesville douses Dragons' fire 37-26

Pete Osborne

AL CAPELLO FIRES THE BALL DOWN FIELD while Eric Rhodes holds off Richard Moore.

The game had it all.

When it came down to it, emotion and an innovative defensive plan carried the day as Leesville High School used a balanced and big play offense to upset arch-rival DeRidder 37-26 in front of an ecstatic, home crowd.

Going in, the defense knew it had to stop the vaunted running attack of the Dragons, and stop it it did. Using a defense which disguised an eight man front and dared DeRidder to pass, the Wampus Cats held the opposition to 125 yards on the ground, all the more impressive considering 50 of those yards came early in the game on a keeper by quarterback Dowd Douglas.

The swarming Leesville defense refused to allow highly touted running backs Mike Mayes and Greg Thomas to break loose at any time Thomas scored on a 93 yard punt return that would make any football follies highlight film and Mayes scored from in close but that was all they got.

Leesville, on the other hand, found the offense that was missing during the Washington game.

All-district candidates Al Capello and Percy Burns hooked up for a 67 yard touchdown on Leesville's fourth play from scrimmage in the first quarter. Burns took the pass on a called slant and outdistanced the DeRidder secondary The point after was no good but Leesville held a 6-0 lead as the fans barely had time to settle into their seats, before they had something to cheer for.

The Leesville game plan on defense hinged on the teams ability to stop option quarterback Douglas.

For a while it looked like the plan was going to fail miserably as Douglas kept the ball on the option on DeRidder's third play from scrimmage and went 50

| LEESVILLE | 6 14 8 9 — 37 |
| DeRidder | 7 0 13 6 — 26 |

Leesville: Percy Burns 67-yard pass from Al Capello (kick failed)
DeRidder: Dowd Douglas 1 yard run (Mayes kick good)
Leesville) Mark Clay 3-yard run (Calvin Dixon pass from Al Capello)
Leesville: Eric Rhodes 53-yard run (kick failed)
DeRidder: Michael Mayes 5-yard run (kick failed)
DeRidder Greg Thomas 92-yard punt return (Mayes kick good)
Leesville: Calvin Dixon 29-yard run (Eric Rhodes run)
Leesville J.R./Dethorn 28-yard field goal
DeRidder: Ricky Anderson 53-yard pass from Dowd Douglas (pass failed)

touchdown and Mayes' successful conversion made it 7 6 DeRidder

As the first quarter drew to a close, the Wampus Cats brought out the big play offense for a second time as Capello connected with Andrew Robinson for a 58 yard gain and a first down on the DeRidder seven.

Two plays later, running back Mark Clay ran in from the three on the first play of the second quarter. Capello's pass to Calvin Dixon on the conversion attempt was good and Leesville moved into a 14-7 lead with just five seconds played in the second quarter.

The Wampus Cats returned to the Pac-Cats of old on the next DeRidder drive, shutting down the running attack completely and forcing the Dragons to punt.

When Leesville took possession back, few expected that a new hero was about to be born. With the ball on the Leesville 47, Capello handed off to Eric Rhodes who scampered 53 yards on an electrifying run for a touchdown which gave Leesville a surprising 20-7 halftime lead

The crowd was buzzing at halftime, expecting the Wampus Cats to roll to an easy victory and take back the Hooper Cup, symbolic of victory in the heated rivalry between the two schools

Leesville wasn't out of the woods yet.

DeRidder found a way to quiet the partisan Leesville fans down They opened the half with two quick scores, the first on a 5 yard run by Mayes and the second on Thomas' long punt return.

The punt return will go down in the books as a 92 yarder but that only tells part of the story. As Leesville ran down to cover the punt, the ball inadvertantly hit Rhodes on the helmet on the Dragon 15. Thomas alertly picked the ball up and raced past the startled Wampus Cat punting team for the touchdown

But traditional rivalries are not won early in the third quarter They are won late in the game and this one was no exception. The character of the Wampus Cats came out at a time when it would have been easy to fold.

Leesville took the ensuing kickoff and Mark Clay and Rhodes took over Then got the ball down to the Dragon 29 where Coach Jack Andre reached down

The scouting report lied. Douglas hit Andrews with a perfect pass, causing many in attendance to wonder why DeRidder doesn't go to the air more often. The two point conversion attempt failed but DeRidder was back within range at 31-26 with just under seven minutes remaining in the game.

After Leesville was forced to punt following the possession after the touchdown, DeRidder took over for their last chance with 3:13 remaining, a five point deficit, and 65 yards of muddy ground in front of them to the Leesville end zone.

The character and emotion of the Leesville defense came through. They stopped the Dragons cold and on fourth down, everyone in the stadium knew what was coming. The fake punt failed miserably as the Wampus Cat defense snowed the punter Andrews under the Leesville took over.

Rhodes capped the game off with his second touchdown of the game from 3 yards out with only 47 seconds remaining in the game. Rhodes rushed for 108 yards on 18 carries in the game.

Character and emotion can win football games. So can a great game plan. Leesville had all this and more Friday night. No matter what happens the rest of the season, this was a game few people in attendance are going to forget or stop talking about. Hats off to the players and to the coaches who put it all together for sixty minutes under the lights of Wampus Cat Stadium.

Jennings is next on the schedule as the Wampus Cats travel to the Bulldogs home turf Friday night. Jennings was stunned 14-6 Friday by Washington and second place in the district and a playoff berth will be on the line when Jennings and Leesville lock horns.

DISTRICT 5-AAA (Overall standings)			
Jennings	6	2	213	62
Wash Marion	5	3	113	123
West Lake	5	3	87	77
LEESVILLE	5	2	158	89

into his bag of tricks.

All season, Andre has used the reverse with his wide receivers and tight ends to keep the defense off balance and it's worked to mixed reviews. In this case, it worked to perfection, as Calvin Dixon took the ball from Capello and went the distance for the touchdown which put Leesville back into the lead for good. Rhodes scored on the two point conversion and the Wampus Cats entered the fourth quarter with a precarious 28-20 lead. It would be up to the defense to save the game for Leesville.

DeRidder quarterback Douglas has to be hurting this weekend after the pounding he took from the Wampus Cat defense. Coach Andre used the week layoff to full advantage as he installed a new defense designed to slow down the DeRidder attack. Chris Williams, normally a defensive back, moved up into a linebacker position. Arnold MacPherson moved from the defensive line to a linebacker position. Leesville showed an eight man front throughout most of the game and yet DeRidder chose not to go to the air until the fourth quarter.

Douglas went to his bread-and-butter in the fourth quarter. Leesville put it back in his face. The Wampus Cat defense rose up as Douglas attempted a pitchout from his own 25. Al East intercepted and the Leesville offense was in business.

For one of the first times all night, the offense couldn't get much going. Clay ran the ball four times. With the ball on the 11, an incomplete pass made it fourth down and in trotted freshman J.R. Dethorn at attempt a field goal which would give the Wampus Cats some breathing room. Dethorn's 28 yard field goal was good and Leesville moved out to a 31-20 lead with just over 8 minutes remaining.

It wasn't over yet. DeRidder coach Larry Crowe suddenly realized that if eight people were on the line stuffing the ball down his runners' throats, there probably weren't many people back defending in the secondary.

Douglas went deep and hit wide receiver Ricky Andrews for a 53 yard touchdown. The scouting report on Douglas said "good run, lame duck pass."

108

LEESVILLE	6	14	8	9	— 37
DeRidder	7	0	13	6	— 26

Leesville: Percy Burns 67-yard pass from Al Capello (kick failed)
DeRidder: Dowd Douglas 1-yard run (Mayes kick good)
Leesville: Mark Clay 3-yard run (Calvin Dixon pass from Al Capello)
Leesville: Eric Rhodes 53-yard run (kick failed)
DeRidder: Michael Mayes 5-yard run (kick failed)
DeRidder: Greg Thomas 92-yard punt return (Mayes kick good)
Leesville: Calvin Dixon 29-yard run (Eric Rhodes run)
Leesville: J.R. Dethorn 28-yard field goal
DeRidder: Ricky Anderson 53-yard pass from Dowd Douglas (pass failed)
Leesville: Eric Rhodes 3-yard run (pass failed)

AL CAPELLO FIRES THE BALL DOWN FIELD
... while Eric Rhodes holds off Richard Moore.

1984:   DeRidder 14   Leesville 12   Series: LHS 3   DHS 2

DeRidder closed the gap in the series in game decided by missed extra points

DeRidder 14
Leesville 12

DE RIDDER — DeRidder's previously winless Dragons pulled perhaps the biggest upset of the high school football season Friday night by defeating ninth-ranked Leesville 14-12.

Leesville's defense shut down the DeRidder attack in the second half, after the homestanding Dragons had built a 14-0 halftime lead. But the Wampus Cats, with one of the state's most potent offenses, couldn't complete drives for scores.

Greg Thomas scored both touchdowns for DeRidder, which had lost its first seven games, four of them in District 3-AAA play.

DeRidder scored on its first possession, going 55 yards in 11 plays and Thomas scoring from the one, following a 27-yard pass from Scott Neace to Dowd Douglas to the Leesville 17.

In the second quarter, Thomas broke a 76-yard touchdown run.

Mike Blankenbaker booted both extra points for the difference.

Leesville's first touchdown was scored by the defense. Craig Pierce picked up the ball, after a DeRidder punt attempt had been smothered, and ran it 15 yards into the end zone.

On its next possession, Leesville drove from its 14 to the DeRidder 5, threatening to take control of the game, but fumbled the ball away there.

Charles Buckley raced 54 yards for a touchdown in the fourth period, but his run for a two-point conversion failed, and DeRidder still led.

With three and a half minutes remaining, Leesville recovered a fumble at the DeRidder 38, but was promptly pushed back, and then lost a fumble at the Dragon 45 with two minutes left.

Jeff Steele led Leesville's ground game with 115 yards on 17 carries, and Buckley added 92 yards on 16 tries, but the Wampus Cats still had their records lowered to 5-2 overall and 2-2 in district.

Thomas was the workhorse for DeRidder. He carried 32 times for 165 yards and the two touchdowns.

Leesville   0   0   6   6 — 12
DeRidder   7   7   0   0 — 14

D—Greg Thomas 1-run (Mike Blankenbaker kick)
D—Thomas 75-run (Blankenbaker kick)
L—Craig Pierce 15-blocked punt (run failed)
L—Charles Buckley 54-run (run failed)

	L	D
First downs	13	14
Yards Rushing	208	202
Yards Passing	32	29
Passes (A-C-I)	12-4-0	14-2-0
Punts/Avg.	4-32	5-31
Fumbles/lost	3-3	2-2
Penalties/Yards	11-110	10-71

DHS's Greg Thomas

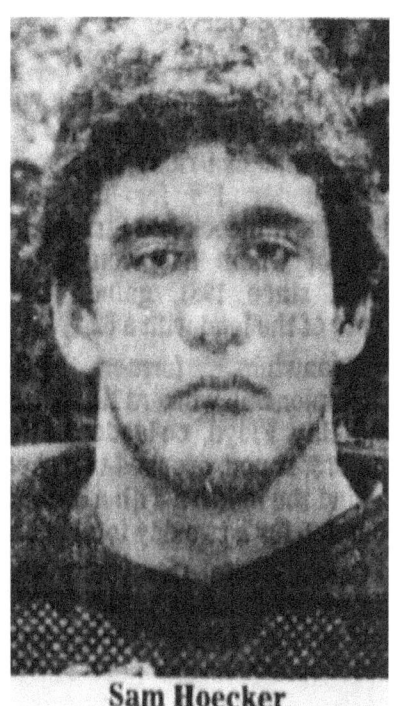
LHS's Sam Hoecker

LHS's Steve Gunn

1985:   Leesville 36   DeRidder 0   Series: LHS 4   DHS 2

The Cats extended their lead in the Hooper III series.   Future LSU start, of "Earthquake" fame, Eddie Fuller, starred for the Cats

Fuller, Leesville Shell DeRidder

LEESVILLE — Eddie Fuller accounted for five touchdowns — three by rushing, one by passing and one by receiving — to lead eighth-ranked Leesville to a 36-0 shellacking of DeRidder in a District 4-AAAA contest Friday night.

Fuller, the state's scoring leader going into the contest, now has 21 touchdowns for the unbeaten Wampus Cats, 5-0 overall and 2-0 in league play. He finished with 81 yards rushing on 18 carries.

He ran back a punt 75 yards for a touchdown and had scoring runs of 5 and 1 yards. He connected with Anthony Burns on a 20-yard halfback option pass for a touchdown, and he had a 19-yard reception from Clint Batteford for another score.

The only score Fuller didn't have a role in was a 31-yard field goal by Jeff Mitcham to open the scoring in a 16-point second period.

A fake punt and run of 36 yards by Arnold McPherson highlighted the Wampus Cats' first scoring drive.

Paul McClurg's interception and 44-yard return to the DeRidder 20 preceded Fuller's scoring strike to Burns with 25 seconds left in the first half.

An onside kick by Leesville to open the second half resulted in a DeRidder fumble and a Leesville recovery to ignite a five-play, 48-yard scoring march.

Greg Thomas led all rushers with 122 yards on 12 carries for DeRidder, which slipped to 2-3 overall and 0-2 in district.

Leesville held DeRidder three times on fourth down inside the Wampus Cats' 20, and cornerback Vincent Fuller (Eddie's brother) stymied DeRidder's best penetration of the night, intercepting a pass in the end zone when the Dragons got as close as the Leesville 7.

DeRidder	0	0	0	0 —	0
Leesville	0	16	13	7 —	36

L — Mitcham 31-field goal.
L — Fuller 75-punt return. (Mitcham kick)
L — Burns 20-pass from Fuller. (Kick failed)
L — Fuller 5-run. (Kick blocked)
L — Fuller 19-pass from Clint Batteford. (Mitcham kick)
L — Fuller 1-run. (Mitcham kick)

	D	L
First downs	15	13
Yards Rushing	205	186
Yards Passing	85	131
Passes (A-C-I)	27-6-2	7-7-0
Punts/Avg.	3-30.1	2-28.1
Fumbles/lost	2-1	4-2
Penalties/Yards	8-90	8-65

LHS's John Westmoreland & Eddie Fuller

1986: Leesville 45   DeRidder 14   Series: LHS 5   DHS 2

Wampus Cat Rush Riddles DeRidder

DeRIDDER — Tony Rush scored two touchdowns and amassed 245 yards on 17 carries to power fourth-ranked Leesville to a 45-14 shelling of DeRidder in District 4-AAAA high school football Friday.

Leesville quarterback Clint Batteford rushed for 51 yards and one TD and passed for 86 yards and two other touchdowns in helping the Wampus Cats stay unbeaten at 5-0 overall, 2-0 in district.

Leesville struck three times in the first half to fashion a 21-0 lead. Sparked by Vincent Fuller's 29-yard sprint to the DeRidder 8, the Cats marched 78 yards on seven plays on the opening series. Rush scored from six yards out and Jeff Mitcham booted the first of six extra points.

Leesville drove 62 yards on eight plays later in the quarter. Batteford plunged the final 2 for the score. In the second quarter, Batteford connected with Demetrius Payton on a 27-yard scoring toss, which climaxed a 70-yard drive, set up by Stan Whatley's inteception.

On the third play from scrimmage in the third quarter, Rush danced and darted 50 yards to put the Cats up 27-0.

DeRidder bounced back with a pair of touchdown drives. DeRidder used 16 plays and three Leesville penalties to go 75 yards. Tailback Raymond Porter dashed in from the 12 and Porter's run on the conversion cut the margin to 28-8. The Dragons added a second TD on quarterback Scott Nease's 1-yard sneak. The key play in the drive was Jesse Johnson's 57-yard run to the Leesville 6.

In the fourth quarter, Leesville drove to the DeRidder 3 and Mitcham booted a 20-yard field goal. The Cats added TDs on Fuller's 7-yard run and a 24-yard pass from Batteford to Anthony Burns.

Leesville captured the Hooper Trophy, symbolic of dominance in the series between the two schools.

Leesville   14 7 7 17 — 45
DeRidder   0 0 14   0 — 14

L—Tony Rush 6 run (Jeff Mitcham kick)
L—Clint Batteford 2 run (Mitcham kick)
L—Batteford to Demetrius Payton 27 pass (Mitcham kick)
L—Tony Rush 50 run (Mitcham kick)
D—Raymond Porter 12 run (Porter run)
D—Scott Nease 1 run (pass failed)
L—Mitcham 20 field goal
L—Vincent Fuller 7 run (Mitcham kick)
L—24 pass Batteford to Anthony Burns (Mitcham kick)

	L.	D
First downs	12	12
Yards Rushing	381	148
Yards Passing	86	65
Passes (A-C-I)	6-4-0	25-6-1
Punts/Avg.	1-34	3-36.6
Fumbles/lost	3-1	1-0
Penalties/Yards	13-123	2-20

LHS's Clint Batteford   DHS's David Cliburn

1987: Leesville 24   DeRidder 14   Series: LHS 6 DHS 2

Leesville captured the Hooper Trophy III with a 10 point win over the Dragos

Lucky Leesville clips DeRidder; Dragons boot chance for upset

DERIDDER — Leesville took advantage of two short DeRidder punts in the fourth quarter to hold off the stubborn Dragons, 24-14, in a District 4-AAAA grudge match Friday.

Early in the final quarter, DeRidder shanked a 1-yard punt, giving Leesville the ball on the Dragon 49. The Wampus Cats drove to the Dragon 1.

DeRidder's goal line defense held on fourth down. The Dragon offense couldn't move the ball and, again, DeRidder shanked the punt, this attempt covering 6 yards.

Four plays later, Vincent Fuller scored from a yard out, clinching Leesville's sixth win against one loss. The Wampus Cats are 1-1 in district.

Fuller finished with 190 yards on 29 carries and two touchdowns. His first touchdown was a 31-yard run in the first quarter.

Kevin Smith sparked the Leesville attack, returning the opening kickoff 84 yards for a touchdown.

Deridder, 1-6, answered with a 72-yard, 13-play drive. Quarterback Scott Lowe called his own number for a 1-yard touchdown.

Derrider took control of the third quarter with an eight minute, 65-yard drive in 15 plays. Milliard Brandford capped the drive with a 2-yard run for a 14-13 lead.

Leesville quickly regained the lead with a 32-yard field by Guintini.

SCORE BY QUARTERS

	1	2	3	4	Final
DeRidder	7	0	7	0	14
Leesville	13	0	3	7	23

SCORING SUMMARY

LHS— Kevin Smith 84 kickoff return; Jason Giutini kick.
DHS— Scott Lowe 1 run; Tim Wilcox kick.
LHS— Vincent Fuller 31 run; kick failed.
DHS— Millard Bradford 2 run; Tim Wilcox kick.
LHS— Giutini 32 field goal.
LHS— Fuller 1 run; Giutini kick.

INDIVIDUAL STATS

RUSHING— DeRidder: Johnny Thibodeaux 5-12; Earl Hadnot 10-60; Derek Knighton 4-21; Scott Lowe 5- -3; Marcus Lee 17-68; Millard Bradford 8-35. Leesville: Chris Davis 6- -7; Vincent Fuller 29-178; Joe Williams 8-78.

PASSING— DeRidder: Scott Lowe 10-5-1-80. Leesville: Chris Davis 8-2-0-31.

RECEIVING— DeRidder: David Simmons 3-54; Maurice Greening 1-21; Charles Thomas 1-5. Leesville: Erwin Brown 1-11; Paul Clay 1-20.

1988: DeRidder 17   Leesville 16   Series: DHS 1 LHS 0

Hooper IV began with a close DeRidder win at Wampus Cat Stadium

Wilcox field goal puts DeRidder by Leesville 17-16

By Glenn Guilbeau
Staff reporter

LEESVILLE — "Dang, we're out of the playoffs," a young Leesville fan said as time expired.

"They're having so much fun now, it's unbelievable," DeRidder Coach Gerald Laughlin said after his team edged Leesville 17-16 on a 25-yard field goal by Tim Wilcox with seven seconds remaining.

The fifth consecutive win for the Dragons, 5-2 overall, ties them with LaGrange for first in District 4-AAAA with 2-0 records. LaGrange beat Barbe Thursday night, 12-0.

Leesville is 0-2 in 4-AAAA and 4-3 on the season after losing its second straight.

"We're pretty much riding in the driver's seat for district," said Wilcox, who beat Mansfield, 23-20, with a last-second field goal three weeks ago.

Leesville Coach Brownie Parmley called a timeout just before Wilcox was going to kick, but the strategy didn't work.

"I just used the time to gather my thoughts," Wilcox said. "Mansfield did the same thing, but they called two in a row."

"I was nervous, though. I'm always a little nervous."

Had missed some

And it's no wonder. Wilcox missed three field goals in a season-opening, 8-7 loss to Westlake.

But that was then.

At a midfield celebration, Laughlin gladly handed Wilcox the shiny new Hooper Trophy, which goes to the DeRidder-Leesville winner each year.

The first-year coach broke DeRidder's three-year losing skid to the Wampus Cats but extended another streak. The last six DeRidder head coaches have beaten Leesville on their first try. DeRidder leads the series, 42-21-3.

"Call the TV station and repeat the score to them twice, 17-16. Make sure they get it right," Laughlin instructed an assistant after the game.

"The kids showed a lot of poise on that last drive," the coach said. "This has to go down as one of my better victories."

Tailback Marcus Lee, who led DeRidder with 86 yards on 14 tries, carried eight times for 53 yards in the Dragons' 15-play, winning drive that covered 73 yards. The drive started on DeRidder's 19 with 7:26 to play.

With 1:30 left in the third quarter, Chip Clark put the Wampus Cats ahead 16-14 with a 31-yard field goal. Those points took away DeRidder's first second half lead over Leesville since 1984, which was the year of the Dragons' last win over the Cats.

Leesville took a 13-0 lead in the first quarter on a 60-yard run by Erwin Brown and on Clark's 36-yard touchdown pass to Jason Brunson. But Jason Giuntini, who kicks conversions for Leesville while Clark handles field goals, missed the extra point.

DeRidder got within 13-7 at halftime on a 5-yard touchdown run by Lee with 3:43 to go in the second quarter.

Halftime dazzle

Then Leesville's band put on a dazzling halftime show. Only the dazzle lasted a bit too long, and the Wampus Cats were penalized 10 yards for delay of game. DeRidder kicked off from 10 yards closer than usual and Leesville started its drive on the 24.

The Wampus Cats, who finished with 10 penalties for 89 yards, failed to get a first down and punted.

DeRidder took over on its 39 and drove 61 yards for a touchdown to take the lead. Maurice Greening caught a 24-yard pass from quarterback Brock Bihm for the score and a 14-13 lead with 5:04 remaining in the third quarter.

"That halftime penalty hurt us," Parmley said. "It gave us worse field position than we could have got."

Leesville's Brown was held to 17 yards on nine carries after his 60-yard run. He finished with 77 on 11 carries as Leesville was held to three first downs in the second half.

Parmley had joked of having to move if he lost to DeRidder prior to the game, but he downplayed the pressure of his job.

"The only pressure on me is the pressure I put on myself," he said.

DeRidder 17, Leesville 16

DeRidder	0	7	3	7	17
Leesville	13	0	3	0	16

L — Erwin Brown 60 run (Jason Giuntini kick)
L — Jason Brunson 36 pass from Chip Clark (kick failed)
D — Marcus Lee 5 run (Tim Wilcox kick)
D — Maurice Greening 24 pass from Brock Bihm (Wilcox kick)
L — Clark FG 31
D — Wilcox FG 25

	D	L
First downs	15	7
Rushes-Yds	47-174	32-134
Yds. Passing	88	69
Passes (C-A-I)	6-11-1	4-9-0
Punts-Avg	4-36.2	6-37.8
Fumbles/lost	2-1	0-0
Penalties/Yds	5-55	10-89

LHS's Chip Clark   DHS's Altheus Thomas

1989: DeRidder 14   Leesville 7   Series: DHS 2 LHS 0

The Dragons extended their lead in the series with a one score victory.

DeRidder never lost faith in its offense

Two 3rd quarter TDs lead Dragons to 14-7 win over Leesville

By David West
Staff reporter

DERIDDER — Even after a scoreless first half, DeRidder's Dragons never lost faith in their offense.

And that faith paid off when the Dragons scored two touchdowns in the third quarter and held on to beat Leesville 14-7 in a high school football game Friday night.

DeRidder, 4-5, 2-1 in district, won its second straight district game and needs a win next Friday against LaGrange to get a play-off spot.

"We were confident at halftime," said Dragon running back Herbert Roberts. "We knew it was just a matter of time. They said all week they were going to stop me, but the offensive line opened up some holes for me."

Roberts won the showdown with Leesville running back Erwin Brown by a landslide. Roberts had 24 carries for 147 yards and one touchdown. Brown was held to 10 yards rushing on 18 carries.

Leesville, 4-5, 1-2, had just 88 yards total offense.

"This was the most frustrating game of the season for me," said Leesville coach Brownie Parmley. "We just let them drive the ball on us."

Roberts scored the winning touchdown on a 5-yard run with 4:54 to go in the third quarter. On first and goal, Roberts leaped over the line, regained his balance and went in for the score. Chris Mogridge's kick pushed the Dragon lead to 14-7.

Roberts set up the touchdown with a 15-yard carry to the 5 on third-and-short.

Leesville best chance to tie came early in the fourth quarter when the Wampus Cats drove to the Dragon 24. But Kevin Smith was stopped short of a first down on a fourth-and-two, giving the ball back to DeRidder.

Played solid defense

"We played solid defense in the second half," said DeRidder coach Gary Feaster. "We're starting to gang tackle. We just decided in the second half that we were going to win no matter what."

Roberts score broke a 7-7 tie created when both teams scored within 16 seconds.

The Dragons took a 7-0 lead and the Wampus Cats answered when Kevin Smith fielded Mogridge's kick at the 1, busted through the wedge at the 25 and went down the left sideline for a 99-yard kick return.

Ellis Garner's kick tied the game 7-7.

"We thought we had gotten the momentum when we got that kick return," said Parmley. "But we let them get it right back. We just made too many mistakes."

DeRidder scored on its first possession of the second half. The Dragons went 53 yards in 7 plays led by Roberts. Roberts had 46 yards on 4 carries on the drive including a 13-yard carry to the Wampus Cat 1. Venturella scored on a sneak on first and goal.

"We felt good at halftime," said Feaster. "Last week we were behind and came back. We said we were going take the opening kickoff and take it in. And the kids felt we would do that."

Neither team mounted a serious scoring threat in a scoreless first half. DeRidder's best opportunity in the first half came on the Dragons' first possession when they moved to the Wampus Cat 24.

But Leesville's defense stiffened and forced Venturella to throw incomplete on fourth-and-five at the Wampus Cat 24. Leesville moved into DeRidder territory on their next drive moving to DeRidder's 41. On a second down, Wampus Cat quarterback Ellis Garner made a bad pitch to Brown who gave ground and was trapped for a 23-yard loss to the Leesville 34.

The two teams exchanged fumbles around the Dragon 35 late in the first half.

DeRidder 14, Leesville 7

Leesville	0	0	7	0 — 7
DeRidder	0	0	14	0 — 14

D—Darrell Venturella 1 run (Chris Mogridge kick)
L—Kevin Smith 100 kickoff return (Scott Clark kick)
D—Herbert Roberts 5 run (Mogridge kick)

	L	D
First downs	7	13
Rushes-Yds.	44-87	49-257
Yds. Passing	1	6
Passes (C-A-I)	1-3-0	1-5-0
Punts-Avg.	3-34	2-26
Fumbles/lost	3-3	5-2
Penalties/Yds.	7-55	4-41

Herbert Roberts

Erwin Brown

1990 Leesville 15   DeRidder 0   Series: DHS 2   LHS 1

Leesville pitched a shutout in a year that saw its return of a former coach who had taken the team to significant achievement a few years previousl.

Leesville beats DeRidder in District 4-AAAA game

By David West
Staff reporter

LEESVILLE — Leesville's John Brown hadn't got many chances to return kickoffs. Unfortunately for DeRidder, he got one chance Friday night.

Brown took the second half kickoff 82 yards to lead Leesville to a 15-0 win over DeRidder in a District 4-AAAA high school football game.

The win gives Leesville (3-6, 2-1 in district) possession of the Hooper Trophy which goes to the winner of the annual game between the two arch-rivals. DeRidder falls to 4-5 overall and 1-2 in district. Leesville broke a two-game losing streak to the Dragons.

Brown had returned two punts for touchdowns this season and broke the game open for the Wampus Cats when he put Leesville ahead 9-0. Halfback Ray Mason threw a key block to take out the last defender at midfield. The point after was no good.

Key block important

"They did a good job of blocking up front and Ray gave me the key block and I accelerated," said Brown. "They've been kicking away from me a lot. I was glad I got a chance to return a kick."

Leesville got the ball right back when the ensuing kick hit a Dragon upback and Adam Jackson recovered for Leesville at the DeRidder 38. Leesville was unable to get a first down and had to punt.

The Wampus Cats got their final touchdown on a 4-yard Ellis Garner run with 10:08 to go in the fourth quarter.

Leesville held DeRidder to 48 yards rushing and 80 yards passing, most of which came after the game had been decided.

"We never could generate any kind of drive against them," said DeRidder coach Gerald Laughlin. "We had five kids out. We haven't been the same team since Ruston beat us."

Leesville coach Jack Andre said taking away DeRidder's power sweep was the key for his defense.

"We knew we had to stop their power sweep. Once we did that, we knew they would have to do some things they didn't want to do," said Andre. "They had to go to their passing game and they hadn't had much success with it."

Heggie Reynolds led Leesville on the ground, getting 80 of their 168 rushing yards. Ellis Garner had 52 yards on 17 carries.

Mike Allen had six carries for 28 yards to lead DeRidder.

The Wampus Cats held a shaky 3-0 lead at halftime despite a 2-to-1 advantage in time of possession in the first half. Leesville had he ball for 16 minutes and ran 32 plays to 16 for the Dragons in the first half.

Leesville got its first half points on a 24-yard field goal by Richard Brennan with 39 seconds to go in the first half.

Drive stalled

The Wampus Cats were stalled on their drive but got a break when Danny Cain fielded a punt at the Dragon 47 and retreated to his 30 and fumbled.

Leesville had a first and goal at the DHS 2, but Garner was thrown for an 8-yard loss on first down and Reynolds was thrown back another yard on second down. Reynolds got five yards back to the 6, forcing the field goal.

In the first quarter, the Wampus Cats got to the DHS 5, but Garner was sacked twice, pushing Leesville back to the 20. Brennan came in to attempt a 37-yard field goal, but Garner couldn't field a bad snap and Brennan was brought down at the 28.

DeRidder was in Wampus Cat territory briefly in the first half. Kenric Stevenson carried for 23 yards to the Leesville 45. The Dragons had a chance to pick up a first down at the 25 on third and long but Jason Kelly couldn't hold a Marcus Epperson pass at the 25.

Leesville 15, DeRidder 0

DeRidder	0	0	0	0—	0
Leesville	0	3	6	6—	15

L—FG Richard Brennan 24
L—John Brown 82 kickoff return (Kick failed)
L—Ellis Garner 4 run (Run failed)

	D	L
First downs	8	13
Rushes-Yds.	27-48	42-168
Yds. Passing	80	12
Passes (C-A-I)	8-15-0	1-7-1
Punts-Avg.	6-31	3-35
Fumbles/lost	2-1	2-0
Penalties/Yds.	5-30	4-26

Jack Andre

Gerald Laughlin

DHS's Kimojah Brooks

LHS's John Brown

1991: DeRidder 26 Lesville 12   Series: DHS 3 LHS 1

DeRidder extended its lead in the series with a two score, early season win

DeRidder cleans up against Leesville, 26-12

By David West
Town Talk correspondent

DERIDDER — A change of clothes changed the game for the DeRidder Dragons Friday night. DeRidder changed out of their muddy uniforms at halftime into clean pants and jerseys and blew past Leesville for a 26-12 win at Cecil Doyle Memorial Stadium.

DeRidder, 1-0, trailed 12-7 at halftime and completely dominated Leesville in the final two quarters. Leesville ran just 16 offensive plays in five second half offensive series. DeRidder held Leesville to minus-1 yard offense in the second half.

"Maybe the uniforms helped us," said DeRidder coach Gerald Laughlin. "We weren't as heavy footed and felt like we were starting over."

Actually, having running Kenric Stevenson was a bigger help. Stevenson, a senior, had 22 carries for 215 yards and four touchdowns. Stevenson scored on runs of 65, 39, 10 and 10 yards.

Stevenson gave DeRidder's run dominated offense something it hasn't had in recent years: big play speed.

DeRidder completed one pass for 26 yards while running for 266 yards.

"The offensive line blocked well and gave me some big holes. I used my speed," said Stevenson. "We just played together in the second half."

Leesville, 0-1, saw its chances fade in the first half when the Wampus Cats failed to score on two opportunities deep in Dragon territory.

A Keith Dove fumble gave LHS the ball at the DHS 29 early in the first quarter. Late in the second quarter, a muff by Maurice Bynum gave Leesville the ball at DeRidder's 34 but the Wildcats failed to score. The Wampus Cats could have led 28-7 but instead were up 12-7.

"We didn't convert and kept them in the game," said Leesville coach Danny Smith. "Then we gave up the big play to them and that's what we didn't want to do."

Stevenson gave DeRidder the lead, 13-12 on a 39-yard cutback run with 5:32 to go in the third quarter. The try for two was no good.

Later, he went over the left side from the 10 with 5:39 left to put the game out of reach at 19-12.

Against DeRidder's defense, a seven-point deficit was insurmountable for Leesville's offense which was reduced to three downs and out. Leesville failed to get a first down in the second half and finished with 138 yards total offense.

"We didn't do anything much different," said defensive end Doug Scott. "We tightened up and played well."

Stevenson scored from the 10 in the final minute for the final touchdown.

Leesville led 12-7 after a 11-play, 75 yard drive. Quarterback Davis went the final five yards on a keeper with 8:59 to play in the second quarter.

1st Quarter
Leesville: Ellis Garner 20 yard run (PAT failed)

2nd Quarter
DeRidder: Kenric Stevenson 66 yard run (PAT good)
Leesville: Corey Davis 5 yard run (PAT failed)

3rd Quarter
DeRidder   Stevenson 40 yard run (PAT failed)
DeRidder   Stevenson 8 yard run (PAT failed)

4th Quarter
DeRidder   Stevenson 9 yard Run (PAT good)

LHS's Tyrone Smith; DHS's Steve Graves

DHS's Kenric Stevenson

1992: Leesville 13   DeRidder 12   Series: DHS 3 LHS 2

The Cats pulled out their second win of the Hooper IV series

B-4 Saturday, September 5, 1992 — The Town Talk, Alexandria-Pineville, La.

Stars shine on Leesville as DeRidder falters

By John Marcase
Staff reporter

LEESVILLE — What a difference a year makes.

Last season Leesville couldn't catch a break. Friday night the Wampus Cats capitalized on five DeRidder mistakes and several crucial Dragons' penalties as the Cats defeated DeRidder 13-12 before a packed stadium.

"Lady luck shined down upon us," said Leesville coach Danny Smith. "Last year she didn't at all."

For a while Friday, it looked as if she wouldn't shine at all as a steady rain fell upon Wampus Cat Stadium prior to kickoff, but then the sun came out and Leesville soaked it up.

Leesville mounted its winning drive as the beginning of the fourth quarter after DeRidder punted.

Heggie Reynolds capped the 13-play, 70-yard drive with his second 1-yard plunge of the night. The drive was aided by a DeRidder personal foul penalty, just one of the Dragons' many mistakes they comitted.

DeRidder lost three fumbles and had several long plays called back by penalties.

The most crucial mistake came on DeRidder's last possession when Dragon quarterback Mike Williams threw deep to Fred Mango who had three steps on the Leesville secondary. Williams' pass was on the target, but slipped through Mango's hands.

A few plays later, Quinton Conner intercepted Williams' final pass of the game to give Leesville its first victory in two years, and Smith his first at Leesville.

"Our kids defensively stepped up and did a super job," Smith. "Our defense was a big question mark coming into the game."

Leesville, depsite being outsized at almost every position, held DeRidder to 97 total yards.

And yet, Smith's first victory seemed in doubt as DeRidder received the second-half kickoff, trailing 7-0.

Tom Issac's kick skidded along the turf, coming to a stop on the one-foot line. Jarrette Acker picked up the ball, found a seam and returned the kick to Leesville's 10-yard line before Issac could stop him.

DeRidder scored on the next play as Williams connected with Keith Dove in the endzone. After the missed PAT, DeRidder trailed 7-6.

DeRidder took the lead 12-7 two minutes later as Dove ran in from the 14 as the Dragons capitalized on a bad snap from center on a punt that gave them the ball at the Leesville 14.

Last season Leesville might have folded the tent and packed it in, but this is a new season and the Cats' have a new attitude according to Smith.

"We told the kids all week and at halftime that somehow, someway, we were gonna find a way to win."

Friday night, they finally did.

"It's a tough way to start out," said first year Dragon coach John Storer. "Anytime you have a loss like this, its disheartening.

"We played hard but had a couple of crucial turnovers."

Leesville 13, DeRidder 12

Visitor   0 0 12 0 — 12
Home   0 7   0 6 — 13

L—Heggie Reynolds 1 run (Tom Issac kick)
D—Keith Dove 10 pass from Mike Williams (kick failed)
D—Dove 14 run (run failed)
L—Reynolds 1 run (kick failed)

	D	L
First Downs	6	10
Rushes/Yds.	29-87	45-76
Yds. Passing	10	69
Passes (C-A-I)	1-6-1	6-10-0
Punts/Avg.	3-37	4-37
Fumbles/lost	3-3	1-0
Penalties/Yds.	9-64	7-31

The 1992 DeRidder Dragon offensive line has six returning starters

Mawae

Celebration time
Members of the Leesville Wampus Cats football team hold the Hooper Trophy high moments after winning it back from DeRidder by a 13-12 margin. The Wampus Cats will go to Vivien for a 6:30 p.m. game Friday against the Southwood Cowboys.

1993:   Leesville 24   DeRidder 14   Series: DHS 3   LHS 3

Leesville closed the gap in the series with a 10 point win at Cecil Doyle stadium

Dragons beat Cats via the turnover

By David West
Town Talk correspondent

DERIDDER — DeRidder took advantage of four Leesville turnovers to pick up a 24-14 District 4-4A win Friday in high school football.

The win kept DeRidder (5-2, 1-1) in the district race after last week's loss to Crowley, and gave DeRidder possession of the Hooper Trophy. Leesville fell to 3-4 overall and 1-1 in district.

"Turnovers. Need I say more," said Leesville coach Danny Smith. "We played hard for 48 minutes but we made the little mistakes at crucial times."

Two turnovers in the final two minutes of the first half gave DeRidder a 17-0 halftime cushion.

Trailing 7-0, Leesville was on the move in Dragon territory when Leesville quarterback Corey Davis was intercepted by his counterpart Fred Mango at the Dragon 37 and Mango went the distance to give DeRidder a 14-0 lead with 1:58 left in the first half.

DeRidder got the ball back two plays later when James Collins fumbled and Joseph Boudrant recovered for the Dragons at the Wampus Cat 35.

Joe Schaller booted a 33-yard field goal with nine seconds left in the half, increasing DeRidder's lead to 17-0.

Leesville got back into the game on a short drive set up when the Wampus Cats partially blocked a Dragon punt, setting up Leesville at the Dragon 41. Cecil Collins scored from the two to get the Wampus Cats on the board at 17-7 with 1:46 left in the third quarter.

After a roughing the kicker penalty on DeRidder. The Wampus Cats successfully ran an onside kick, recovering the ball at the Dragon 35. Leesville drove inside the DeRidder 10 when Cecil Collins fumbled at Mango recovered.

"We made some big plays on defense at some big times," said DeRidder coach John Storer. "We weren't intense enough in the second half but we played some tough defense."

Cecil Collins had 22 carries for 125 yards. The Wampus Cats outgained DeRidder on offense 280 to 174.

Brad Bradford got a late touchdown on a 36-yard run for DeRidder. Davis hit Lawrence Powell on a pretty 15-yard scoring pass in the final seconds to close out the scoring.

Chuck Long

DeRidder 24, Leesville 14

Leesville   0 0 7 7 — 14
Deridder   7 10 0 7 — 24

D—Brad Radford 3 run (Joe Schaller kick).

D—Fred Mungo 63 interception return (Schaller kick).

D—FG Schaller 33.

L—Cecil Collins 2 run (Tom Issac kick).

D—Radford 36 run (Schaller kick).

L—Lawrence Powell 15 pass from Corey Davis (Issac kick).

Leesville Daily Leader, Friday, Oct. 22, 1993 P. 7A

Hooper Trophy presentation
Leesville High School Principal Billy Crawford (third from left) presents DeRidder High School Principal Stan Levy with the Hooper Trophy following last week's 24-14 victory by the Dragons. Joining Crawford in the presentation are (from left): Roger Rolon, LHS curriculum director; Curtis Clay, LHS vice principal; and Tom Neubert, LHS vice principal and athletic director.

BRING HOME THE HOOPER

1993 DeRidder High School Dragons

DeRidder Dragons vs. Leesville Wampus Cats

Friday
October 15, 1993
at
Cecil Doyle
Memorial Stadium
☆Go Dragons☆

1994: Leesville 28   DeRidder 0   Series: DHS 3   LHS 4

The Wampus Cats shut out the Dragons as the Cats took a one game lead in the series

Collins, Leesville beat DeRidder 28-0

By Jeffrey Nixon
Staff reporter

LEESVILLE — Before Friday night's game, DeRidder's cheerleaders hung a sign that asked Leesville's star running back Cecil Collins "Cecil ... Does It Hurt?" Another sign asked "Cecil Who?"

Collins answered both questions on the first play from scrimmage.

Collins broke a multitude of tackles to score on an 80-yard run on the first play from scrimmage.

That set the tone as Collins scored two other touchdowns to lead Leesville to the 28-0 District 4-4A win over visiting arch-rival DeRidder.

Leesville improves to 5-2 and 2-0 while DeRidder falls to 2-5 and 0-2.

Collins hurt his ribs in the third quarter of Leesville's win over Washington-Marion a week earlier. There was a possibility he would miss the DeRidder game.

But, on the first run, Collins swept left, broke two tackles, stiff-armed another, broke one final tackle and was gone.

"The first run was good blocking," Collins said. "I saw the hole, headed for it, then headed for the end zone."

"That answered in a hurry if he was ready to play," cracked Leesville coach Danny Smith.

Collins admitted his ribs gave him a little discomfort, but "I knew I was going to play." He finished with 254 yards on 22 carries.

Leesville as a team rushed 38 times for 423 yards.

Collins later added a 53 and 19-yard touchdown runs to bring his TD total for the season to 20. Wampus Cat quarterback Andre Middlebrooks scored on an 81-yard quarterback sneak for Leesville's other touchdown.

But it was Leesville's defense that stood out.

Four times, Leesville's offense turned the ball over inside its 40. DeRidder drove inside the Leesville 20 four times and the 10 twice, but the Wampus Cat defense kept DeRidder out of the end zone each time for Smith's first career shutout.

Leesville also had to deal with 13 penalties for 120 yards.

Leesville's defense has played two straight games without giving up a touchdown. Washington-Marion scored its six points on an interception return.

"Our guys are playing with a lot of confidence," Smith said. "We didn't play a real good game offensively, but our defense bowed-up and kept them out of the end zone."

The defensive tone was set in the first quarter. With Leesville leading 7-0, Collins lost a pitch from Middlebrooks. Three plays later, the Dragons had first-and-goal from the Leesville 9.

DeRidder pushed it to the 6 on first down, but Clarence Jones and Remone Richardson stopped Ray Peters for a one-yard loss on second down.

On third down, Jones and Robert Robinson dropped Titus Latchison for a one-yard loss, setting up a fourth-and-goal from the 8.

Dragon quarterback Albert Weinnig overthrew his receiver in the end zone to end the threat.

One player who especially stood out was Leesville linebacker Greg Rone. Rone was in on five tackles for losses and had three sacks, several times going untouched to DeRidder quarterback Weinnig.

"Those were called stunts and blitzes," Smith said. "We were able to utilize his speed and get him back there then he made the play."

Leesville 28, DeRidder 0

```
DeRidder     0 0 0 0 -  0
Leesville    7 7 7 7 - 28
```
L- Cecil Collins 80 run (Joseph Culic kick)
L- Collins 53 run (Culic kick)
L- Andre Middlebrooks 81 run (Culic kick)
L- Collins 19 run (Culic kick)

	D	L
First downs	9	13
Rushes-yards	40-60	38-243
Passing	74	3
C-A-I	7-18-1	1-3-1
Punts	4-32	1-16
Fumbles-Lost	0-0	4-4
Penalties-Yards	5-30	13-120

INDIVIDUAL STATISTICS
RUSHING-Deridder, Omar Lynch 11-46, Titus Latchison 9-36, Ray Peters 11-30. Leesville, Collins 22-254, Middlebrooks 5-87, Matt Glasper 10-72.
PASSING-Deridder, Albert Weinnig 7-18-1 74. Leesville, Middlebrooks 1-3-1 3.
RECEIVING-Deridder, Angelo Melvin 4-48. Leesville, Lawrence Powell 1-3.

1995: Leesville 29   DeRidder 0   Series: DHS 3   LHS 5

For the second year in a row, the Cats shut down the Dragons, mostly on the legs of "Mr. Football" Cecil Collins.   Leesville pulled ahead in the Hooper IV Series with the win

Alexandria Daily Town Talk — HIGH SCHOOL

Collins hits 2,000
Leesville star helps Cats stop Dragons, 15-6

Town Talk sports services

DERIDDER — Third-ranked Leesville staved off a late DeRidder drive to hold on for a 15-6 win Friday night to clinch the District 4-4A title outright.

Leesville closed out the regular season 9-1 and 5-0 in district. The Wampus Cats will host a wildcard next Friday in the first round of the state playoffs. The opponent will be announced Sunday by the LHSAA. DeRidder closes at 6-4 and must hope for on the 12 wildcards.

"It was a typical Leesville-DeRidder game," said Wampus Cats coach Danny Smith. "They were ready."

Cecil Collins led Leesville with 153 yards rushing on 31 carries and both Wampus Cats' touchdown. Collins ended the regular season with 2,022 yards and 29 touchdowns. Collins also added one huge tackle.

DeRidder opened the game with a fumble on its 22. It took Collins four plays to score his first touchdowns of the night on a 2-yard run with 8:18 left in the first quarter.

The Dragons answered with a nine-play, 72-yard drive. Chris Ashworth capped the drive with a 7-yard run. The two-point conversion failed as Leesville still led, 7-6.

Leesville's ensuing possession was halted when Jason Green's screen pass was picked off by Marlon Woods at the Leesville 40.

Woods took off for the end zone in a sprint. Collins ran him down from the opposite side of the field, making a diving tackle at the half-foot line.

Leesville's defense then completed a goal line stand, stopping DeRidder for a 1-yard loss on fourth down.

Green was once again picked off on the Wampus Cats' next possession, but DeRidder turned the ball over back the Cats.

Collins made sure Leesville didn't waste this opportunity, capping a 40-yard drive by scoring from the 4. Greg Rone then added the two-point conversion for a 15-6 halftime lead.

DeRidder tried to mount a potential game-tying drive gaining two first downs, but Marlon Woods was sacked and then misfired on fourth down to end the threat.

Leesville 15, DeRidder 6

Leesville	7 8 0 0	– 15
DeRidder	6 0 0 0	– 6

L-Cecil Collins 2 run (Josh Dill kick).
D-Chris Ashworth 7 run (pass failed).
L-Collins 4 run (Greg Roan run).

	L	D
First downs	8	9
Rushes-yards	40-178	31-103
Passing	56	31
C-A-I	2-5-2	2-6-1
Punts	3-26	2-25
Fumbles-Lost	1-0	2-2
Penalties-Yards	12-105	1-5

INDIVIDUAL STATISTICS

RUSHING-Leesville, Collins 31-153, Ryan Buckner 5-30. DeRidder, Jody Boudurant 4-46, Derrick Peters 6-28.
PASSING-Leesville, Jason Green 2-5-2 56. DeRidder, Marlon Woods 1-5-1 15, Boudurant 1-1-0 16.
RECEIVING-Leesville, Jerry Haynes 2-56. DeRidder, Ray Peters 2-31.

1995:   Leesville 29   DeRidder 0

For the second time in series history, the two schools met in the LHSAA State Playoffs. The Cats came away with a big win, evening the score in playoff wins.   The first playoff event between the schools was in 1963, and the Dragons took a 34-19 victory.

Cats make semis
Collins hits for 245 yards in 29-0 win

By John Marcase
Staff reporter

DERIDDER— In its storied program's history, the Leesville football team had never made it to the state semifinals.

Until Friday night.

Cecil Collins ran for 245 yards and four touchdowns on 28 carries while the Wampus Cat defense pitched a shutout in a 29-0 romp over arch-rival DeRidder before a capacity crowd of 4,500 Cecil Doyle Memorial Stadium in the Class 4A quarterfinals.

Leesville improves to 12-1 on the season and will host Breaux Bridge in the semifinals next week for the right to go the Superdome Classic and play for the state title. The 12 wins is a new school record. DeRidder, after finishing just 2-8 a year ago, ends its season at 7-4.

"The defense stepped up a whole lot," said Leesville senior defensive back Robert Robinson. "The last time we gave them six points. We weren't going to do that tonight."

Friday night's meeting was the second in four weeks, with Leesville taking a 15-6 win over the Dragons in the regular season finale.

"The defense, they played well," said Leesville coach Danny Smith. "Throughout the playoffs, you have to play good defense. You have to be able to play defense and do it consistently.

The shutout was the second for the Leesville defense in three playoffs games. The Wampus Cats tossed a 30-0 shutout over Opelousas in round one, but gave up 28 last week in a 30-28 win at Carroll.

Collins staked Leesville to an early 7-0 lead with a 35-yard scamper on the game's fourth play from scrimmage. He would add his second score 40 seconds before halftime by plunging in from the 1 on fourth-and-goal. His score was set up by a 48-yard pass from Jason Green to Marcus Thurman.

In the second half, Collins turned it loose, running for 165 yards, scoring from 18 yards and 51 yards out. He now has 96 career rushing touchdowns.

"In the first half, they were doing a good job of containing me," said the senior, who now has rushed for nearly 7,500 yards in his remarkable career. "Coach told me to get outside and run and the offensive line did a good job."

On Collins' 51-yard score, that came with 5:49 remaining, one thought went through DeRidder coach John Storer's mind: "When he made his last touchdown, I thought, 'he can make all he wants. They won't have him next year'."

While the defense limited DeRidder to just 136 yards and seven first down. The Dragons' only scoring threat of the game came on their second drive of the game. DeRidder quarterback Jody Bondurant hit Sheaun Hooper for a 23-yard gain down to the Leesville 13.

The Dragons proceeded to lose a yard on their next four plays and turned the ball over on downs when Bondurant's completion to Derrick Peters on fourth down was two yards short.

"They have a good defensive unit," said Storer. "Their defense has been consistent all year. They have quickness and (on offense), they have the ability to score many points. By doing that, the defense can play with a lot of emotion. It's a combination of good quickness and being inspired.

Smith said getting the team inspired for DeRidder a second time was no problem.
■ Please see CATS, B-4

High School Football SCOREBOARD

Leesville 29	DeRidder 0
DeQuincy 20	Mamou 6
Ferriday 21	Lake Charles-Boston 0
West Monroe 6	Natchitoches Central 13

Leesville 29, DeRidder 0

Leesville	7	8	0	14	— 29
DeRidder	0	0	0	0	— 0

L-Cecil Collins 35 run (Josh Dill kick).
L-Collins 1 run (Greg Rose run).
L-Collins 18 run (Dill kick).
L-Collins 51 run (Dill kick).

	L	D
First downs	13	7
Rushes-yards	272	87
Passing	48	59
C-A-I	1-2-0	5-12-0
Punts	5-40	6-30
Fumbles-Lost	0-0	2-0
Penalties-Yards	4-29	1-14

INDIVIDUAL STATISTICS
RUSHING-Leesville, Collins 28-245.
PASSING-Leesville, Jason Green 1-2-0 48.
DeRidder, Jody Bondurant 5-12-0 59.

1996: DeRidder 25   Leesville 7   Series: DHS 4 LHS 5

The Dragons took the Cats down with a strong win, ending a 3 year and 4 game losing streak.   The series in Hooper IV was tied after this game.

DeRidder spoils Leesville hopes

Town Talk sports services

LEESVILLE — Mistakes and poor tackling Friday night may have knocked Leesville out of the playoff picture as DeRidder beat the rival Wampus Cats 25-7 in District 4-4A competition.

The loss evened both teams' records at 5-5 overall and 2-3 in district play. The LHSAA announces final playoff pairings Sunday.

"We'll find out Sunday if we are in," DeRidder coach John Storer said. "There are enough 5-5 teams out there."

Leesville coach Danny Smith saw the same thing he has the last several weeks: key turnovers and poor tackling.

"Two big (fumbles)," Smith said of two first half fumbles that stalled drives. "Then we are going in for another (score) and we get a clipping. Mistakes. We're not a good enough football team to overcome those mistakes. Give DeRidder credit. They took advantage of them."

Leesville's second fumble resulted in a Dragon touchdown as Quartez Buckley scored a 14-yard run with 10:08 remaining in the first half.

After Leesville was forced to punt on the next possession, Storer dipped into his bag of tricks for a halfback option the Dragons turned into a touchdown. Buckley hit Justin Governale on a 46-yard pass to give DeRidder a 12-0 lead. The Dragons later added a one-yard scoring run by James Greening to take an 18-0 halftime lead.

Leesville's Dustin Smith led the Wampus Cats on a 97-yard scoring drive capped when Xavier Burrell went in from five yards out with 4:47 to play in the third quarter. Burrell finished with 180 yards on 24 carries to lead all rushers.

The Cats had a chance to get back into the game when DeRidder fumbled away its next possession, but Leesville was unable to capitalize and the Dragons essentially sealed the game with a six-minute drive that ended with Johnny Storer's 14-yard run.

"Our kids always seem to play up for this game," Storer said. "We had a good effort tonight, good enough to win."

Steve Levy   Adam Housley   Xavier Burrell

	Q1	Q2	Q3	Q4	Final
Leesville	0	0	7	0	7
DeRidder	0	18	0	7	25

2nd Quarter
DeRidder   Quartez Buckles, 14-yard run (kick failed)
DeRidder   Buckles, 46-yard pass Justin Governale (kick failed)
DeRidder   James Greening, 1 yard run (kick failed)

3rd Quarter
Leesville   Xavier Burrell, 5-yard run (Stan Catron kick)

4th Quarter
DeRidder   Johnny Storer, 15 yard run (PAT good)

HOOPER TROPHY   1996   25-7

1997: DeRidder 14   Leesville 12   Series: DHS 5   LHS 5
                                                DeRidder Wins Hooper IV

DeRidder nips Leesville

By Bruce M. Viergutz
Staff reporter

LEESVILLE — DeRidder banked on its defense through most of the game and since Leesville's Wampus Cats couldn't cash in on a late break, the Dragons were able to escape with a victory Friday night.

Leesville senior Stan Catron missed a 41-yard field goal with 32 seconds left and the Dragons held on for a 14-12 victory in District 4-4A prep football action at Wampus Cat Stadium.

DeRidder improves to 5-1 and Leesville evens its record to 3-3.

"We played good defense," said DeRidder coach John Storer. "They scored right away and we settled down after that. We stopped the run pretty good."

DeRidder held the Wampus Cats to just 83 yards rushing on 36 attempts.

"You've got to be able to run the football," said Leesville coach Danny Smith. "The strength of their defense is their run defense. In the first half we had some success, but we were playing against an eight-man front and we felt we had to open it up."

The Wampus Cats did just that.

Trailing 14-6 with 3:40 left in the game, Leesville drove 76

■ Please see NIPS, B-5

Leesville quarterback Dustin Smith keeps the ball for a short gain on fourth down to give the Wampus Cats a first down near the DeRidder end zone in the final minutes of the first half. Leesville lost the ball on a fumble on the ensuing play.

Nips

■ Continued from B-1

yards in eight plays to pull within two points. Wampus Cat quarterback Dustin Smith completed 5 of 7 passes on the drive. Smith finished the game connecting on 14 of 29 for 198 yards.

Keith Smith ran around the left side for four yards and extended the ball over the goal on the score with 2:02 remaining.

The Wampus Cats lined up for a two-point conversion, but Derek Mayo jumped offside to put the ball back on the eight. Smith then rolled right but couldn't connect with wide receiver Greg Burns for the conversion.

The Wampus Cats got a huge break when DeRidder quarterback Ryan Temple fumbled the ball and Leesville defensive lineman Renard Brown recovered at the Dragon 46 with 1:07 left.

"We called a naked bootleg with a new quarterback so it was probably a coaching error — not thinking that he would just take two hands and run around the end if (the pass) wasn't there," said Storer. "He had the ball and was trying to make some yards with one hand (on the ball). Leesville knocked the ball down and it was a good play by them."

DeRidder, despite being assessed a 10-yard holding penalty on first down, only let Leesville drive 12 yards on a pass from Smith to Demond McNeely. On fourth-and-10, Catron attempted his field goal but it was short and right.

"It was a hard-fought game," said Storer. "Leesville has a great team and they did a great job."

The Dragons took a 14-6 lead on James Greening's 1-yard blast with 3:41 to go in the third. The touchdown was set up on a 37-yard pass from Temple to Andy Smith.

DeRidder blew a golden opportunity to score when they reached the Wampus Cat five on its first offensive possession of the second half. But a 10-yard penalty and three straight passes that gained a minus-two yards stifled the threat.

Leesville also blew a scoring opportunity late in the first half. The Wampus Cats drove from their own 21 to the Dragon seven before Keith Smith fumbled the ball at the nine, where defensive tackle Willie Farrow recovered it with 55 seconds left. Leesville recorded 15 plays on the drive that consumed nearly seven minutes.

"That was a big drive and we came up empty," said coach Smith. "When you get into big ballgames, a turnover here or there or a breakdown in the kicking game can make a big difference.

"But I'm not going to point my finger at one particular thing," said Smith. "We gave ourselves a chance at the end and we didn't make the play.

"But that (fumble) hurt," Smith continued. "If we score or get three points, it really puts the pressure on DeRidder because we get the ball to start the second half."

DeRidder took a 7-0 lead on a 4-yard TD run by Johnny Storer (the coach's son) midway through the second quarter. John Weinnig booted the PAT which eventually proved crucial.

Leesville scored on its first possession when Keith Smith raced in from nine yards. Catron's conversion kick went wide left.

"This is a big district win and it's a rivalry, too" said coach Storer. "All of our district games from here on out are going to get bigger and tougher every week."

DeRidder 14, Leesville 12

	D	LV
DeRidder	0 7 7 0	— 14
Leesville	6 0 0 6	— 12

LV-Keith Smith 9 run (kick failed)
D-Johnny Storer 4 run (John Weinnig kick)
D-James Greening 1 run (Weinnig kick)
LV-K. Smith 4 run (pass failed)

	D	LV
First downs	9	21
Rushes-yards	36-98	36-83
Passing	75	198
Comp-Att-Int	4-10-0	14-29-0
Punts-Avg.	5-37	3-27
Fumbles-Lost	1-1	4-1
Penalties-Yards	10-122	6-50

INDIVIDUAL STATISTICS
RUSHING–D, Eric Mazyck 11-48, Storer 9-36. LV, Keith Smith 14-22, Markese Steward 4-20, Deshun McNeely 9-19, Dustin Smith 7-18.
PASSING–D, Ryan Temple 4-10-0 75. LV, Dustin Smith 14-29-0 198.
RECEIVING–D, Andy Smith 2-51, Greening 1-22, Daniel Housely 1-2. LV, Keith Smith 5-81, Ronnie Robinson 4-43, Demond McNeely 2-

DHS Fans in Leesville

1998: Leesville 36 DeRidder 34   Series: DHS 0   LHS 1

Leesville took an early lead in the Hooper V

Leesville takes wild 36-34 overtime win from DeRidder in 4-4A

By Bruce M. Viergutz
Staff reporter

DERIDDER —Leesville coach Danny Smith celebrated his 40th birthday on Wednesday and Thursday night at DeRidder, his Wampus Cats had their coming-out party.

Leesville (2-4, 1-0) gave Smith a birthday present by squeezing past DeRidder 36-34 in overtime in District 4-4A action at Cecil Doyle Memorial Stadium.

"I am so proud of these kids," said Smith, who received several handshakes and hugs as the Wampus Cats enjoyed a wild celebration on the field. ""We could have folded tonight because the last few weeks we haven't had a lot of things go our way. We needed this victory bad."

It didn't look as if the Wampus Cats would win after falling behind 28-13 at halftime. But Leesville got second-half touchdowns from senior tailback Deshun McNeely to force the game into overtime.

▶ LEESVILLE 36, DERIDDER 34

The Dragons didn't score in overtime until quarterback Daniel Housley hit Andy Smith on fourth down from the three. Housley first faked a hand-off into the line, but pulled it out and ran to his right.

DeRidder then tried for the same play on the two-point conversion attempt, but Andy Smith was covered and Housley threw an incomplete pass.

"I thought (Leesville) might have had a lineman go offside in the neutral zone, but the refs didn't call it," said a disappointed DeRidder coach John Storer. "We just gave (Leesville) some breaks the second half after having the lead and it swung the momentum their way. We had some breakdowns at crucial times, and that's what's so disappointing."

The overtime loss was the second in a row for the Dragons, who fell to Washington-Marion in an extra period last week.

Leesville 36, DeRidder 34

Leesville   7 6 8 7 8—36
DeRidder   13 15 0 0 6—34

D—Curtis Harris 4 run (John Weinning kick)
D—Harris 10 run (kick failed)
L—Deshun McNeely 8 run (Jason Whitfield kick)
D—Roosevelt Moore 10 pass from Daniel Housley (Housley run)
L—McNeeley 7 run (kick failed)
D— Housley 5 run (Weining kick)
L— McNeeley 1 run (Sam Scott pass from Dustin Smith)
L— McNeeley 33 run (Whitfield kick)
L— McNeeley 1 run (McNeely run)
D— Andy SMith 3 pass from Housley (pass failed)

INDIVIDUAL STATISTICS

RUSHING—Leesville, McNeely 23-151, Oliver Cook 3-8, Dustin Smith 12-(-4). DeRidder, Eric Mayzck 21-183, Curtis Harris 11-67, Daniel Housley 10-67, Moore 10-23.
PASSING—Leesville, Smith 9-19-0-155 DeRidder, Housley 5-12-0-80, Mayzck 0-1-1-0
RECEIVING—Leesville, McNeely 2-55, Keith Smith 3-39, Sam Scott 2-37, Demond McNeely 2-24. DeRidder, Andy Smith 3-63, Moore 1-10, Mayzck 1-7

DHS's Daniel Housley   LHS Coach Danny Smith

1999: Leesville 30 DeRidder 8   Series: DHS 0 LHS 2

Leesville took a 2-0 lead in the Hooper V Series.   Long time LHS Coach Danny Smith started a tenure in DeRidder in the 1999 season.

Cats race past DeRidder

By Daniel Green
Sports Editor

DeRIDDER — For one half, it looked as if the contest between Leesville and DeRidder might go down to the wire.

But a kickoff return for a touchdown by Justin Brown to open the second half, along with a five-yard run from quarterback Sam Scott, broke open a close game as Leesville posted a 30-8 victory over the Dragons Friday at Cecil Doyle Memorial Stadium.

With the win, Leesville (3-4, 1-1) moved out to a 2-0 lead over the Dragons (1-6, 1-1) in the Hooper Trophy V Series.

"DeRidder really got after our butts in the first half," said Wampus Cat head coach Jerry Foshee. "They gave us all we wanted, but the kickoff return knocked them out and the touchdown later in the quarter also helped."

Following a 10-play drive by DeRidder that ended with a punt, Leesville went to work.

Scott connected with Derek Beebe for a 28-yard gain on the first play of the drive and Anderson gained 26 yards on the ensuing play to move the Cats from their own 24 to the Dragon 22.

After Ashley Deans and Anderson rushed for a total of three yards on the next two plays, Scott picked up 11 yards and a first down, getting to the DeRidder six.

SEE CATS P. 4B

Continued from page 1B

However the drive stalled at that point and the Cats had to settle for a 23-yard field goal by Jason Whitfield to take a 3-0 lead.

Again, DeRidder went to the ball control offense, plugging their way upfield from their own 25 to the Cat 33 in nine plays. On the 10th play of the drive, Billy Ortagus attempted a 50-yard field goal but it landed 15 yards short of the uprights and Leesville took over at their own 20.

The Cats were unable to move the ball on that possession, being forced to punt the ball away.

Mark Dowden got away a 33 yard punt but DeRidder's Kevin Akins returned it 22 yards, back to the Leesville 30.

But the Dragons were unable to capitalize on the good field position as a bad snap on a 29-yard field goal attempt caused DeRidder to lose 16 yards giving the Cats the ball at their own 28.

However the Cats were forced to punt again and DeRidder was content to run the clock out, going in at the half down by a 3-0 score.

"We played about as well as we have all season in the first half," said DeRidder head coach Danny Smith. "But we didn't capitalize on the opportunities we had then and that hurt us."

And it hurt even more when the opening kickoff of the second half was returned 87 yards by Brown for a touchdown and a 10-0 Leesville lead. For Brown, it was his third kick return for a touchdown this season, the other two coming on punt returns.

"That kickoff return was a big play," Foshee said. "In my opinion, that was the play that broke the game open."

DeRidder was able to pick up one first down on the ensuing drive but stalled out at their own 43 and had to punt the ball back to the Cats.

Leesville responded with an 11-play drive for a touchdown, but not without some trouble.

On the second play of the drive, Anderson fumbled but Dowden recovered the ball for a gain of four, leaving the Cats with a third and one situation.

Leesville dodged another bullet on the following play when senior offensive tackle Lamond Lesure recovered a Deans fumble for a gain of 10 yards and a first down.

Three plays later Scott gained 15 yards and a first down to the Dragon 37. Two plays later, Scott again broke free, this time for a gain of 29 yards.

The drive ended as Scott scored from five yards out. With the Whitfield extra point, Leesville held a 17-0 lead with 1:41 to go in the third quarter.

But once again, the Dragons went on a long drive only to come away with nothing. DeRidder covered 50 yards on a 13-play drive but turned the ball over on downs at the Leesville 18.

The Cats followed up with a seven play, 82 yard drive to take a 24-0 lead. The big play of the drive was a 47-yard pass play from Scott to Brown, which took the ball down to the DeRidder one.

Scott scored on the next play to put the Cats in control of the game.

But DeRidder refused to die, going 59 yards on five plays to score their first touchdown of the game and only their third of the year. Josh Miers connected with Jared Barmore for a 15-yard scoring strike to break into the scoring column.

Miers found Carl Hubbard for the two-point conversion making the score 24-8.

Leesville added a late touchdown by Deans to account for the final margin.

The Wampus Cats will host the Washington-Marion Charging Indians Friday at 7 p.m. in another District 4 4A matchup.

It is homecoming night as well for Leesville.

DeRidder takes to the road next week as they will face the district-leading Eunice Bobcats.

2nd Quarter
Leesville   Jason Whitfield, 23-yard field goal

3rd Quarter
Leesville   Justin Brown 87-yard kickoff return (Whitfield kick)
Leesville   Sam Scott 5-yard run (Whitfield kick)
Leesville   Sam Scott 1 yard run (Whitfield kick)
DeRidder   Justin Miers 15-yard pass to Jared Barmore (Miers pass to Carl Hubbard 2 pt)

4th Quarter
Leesville   Ashley Deans 1 yard run (kick failed)

LHS's Sam Scott

LHS's Ashley Deans

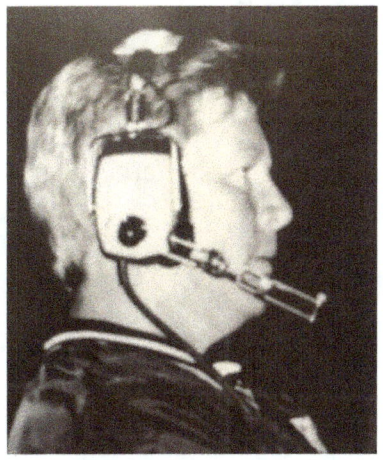

DHS Coach Danny Smith

2000: Leesville 40 DeRidder 0					Series: DHS 0 LHS 3

The Cats took one of their biggest wins in the series in 2000.

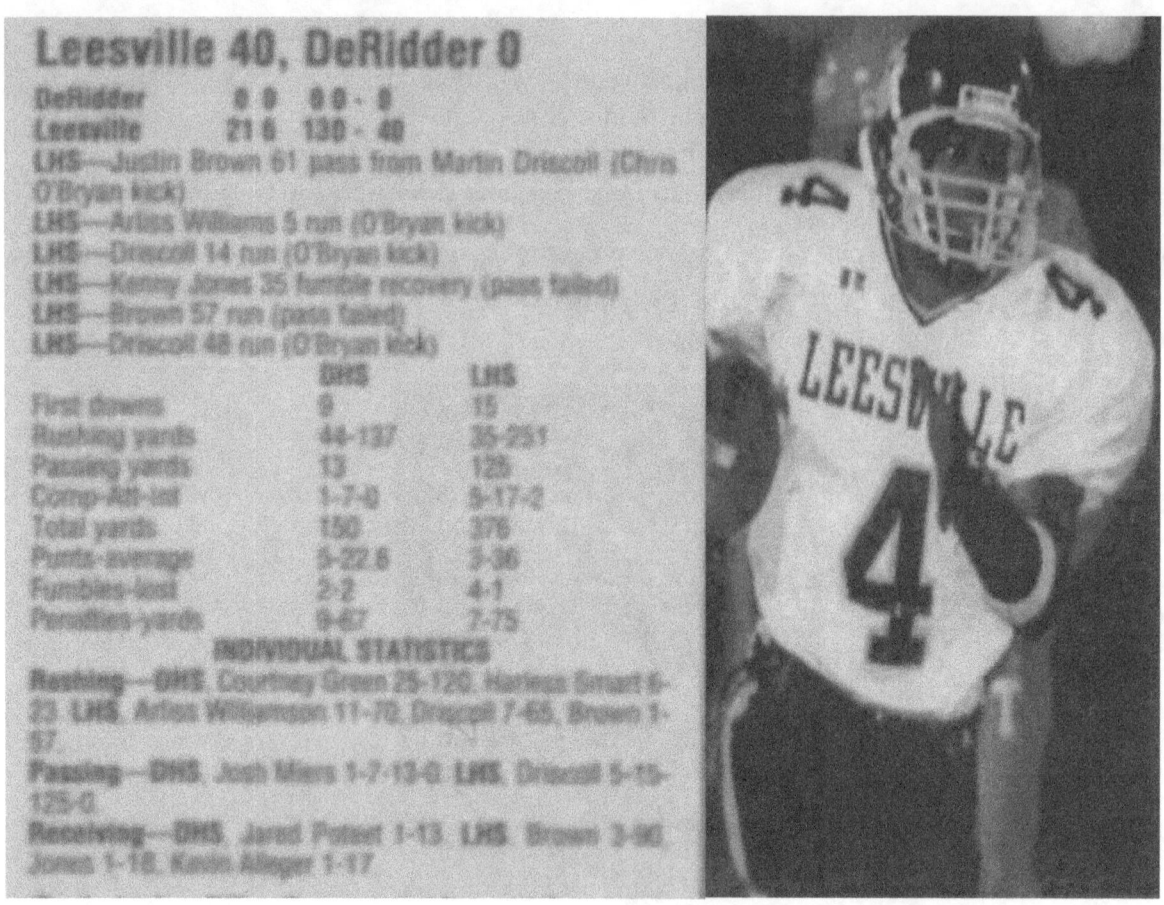

Justin Brown

LEESVILLE 40, DERIDDER 0

Quarterback Martin Driscoll threw a 61-yard touchdown pass to Justin Brown and had TD runs of 14 and 48 yards to lead Leesville to the win.

The Wampus Cats (3-4, 1-1 in District 4-4A) rushed for 251 yards in the game. DeRidder (2-5, 1-1) was held to 150 yards of offense.

Brown also had a 57-yard TD run for Leesville, while Arliss Williams added a five-yarder and Kenny Jones returned a fumble 35 yards for a score.

2001:   Leesville 14   DeRidder 3   Series: DHS 0   LHS 4

The Wampus Cats extended their winning streak in the series to four games.

Leesville 14, DeRidder 3

DeRidder	3	0	0	0—3
Leesville	0	0	7	7—14

D—Christian Dunn 24 FG.
LV—Chris Nash 1 run (Michael Coode kick).
LV—Nash 1 run (Coode kick).

	DHS	LHS
First downs	6	18
Rushes-yards	21-31	56-204
Passing	92	15
Total Offense	123	219
Comp-Att-Int	5-20-0	1-7-0
Punts-Avg	7-35.6	3-37.7
Fumbles-Lost	0-0	3-2
Penalties-Yards	4-45	4-30

INDIVIDUAL STATISTICS

RUSHING—DHS, Ryan Miller 4-15, Brian Ashworth 11-10, Eric Cooper 6-6. LHS, Nash 24-112, Derek Williams 17-83, Martin Driscoll 3-11, Courtney Booth 1-5, Roderick Lawhorn 3-5.
PASSING—DHS, Cooper 5-19-0—92, Donnie Tellis 0-1-0—0. LHS, Driscoll 1-3-0—15, Justin Goins 0-4-0—0.
RECEIVING—DHS, Brandon Clinton 2-33, Tellis 1-25, Robbie Hooks 1-22, Ashworth 1-12. LHS, Keith Alleger 1-15.

LEESVILLE 14, DERIDDER 3

Chris Nash gained 112 yards on 24 carries and had a pair of 1-yard second-half touchdown runs to headline Leesville's District 4-4 win.

The Wampus Cats (4-3, 1-1) held DeRidder (1-6, 0-1) to 123 yards, including 31 rushing yards on 21 carries.

Derek Williams added 83 yards on 17 carries for Leesville.

2002:   Leesville 14   DeRidder 6   Series: DHS 0 LHS 5

The Wampus Cats won their fifth consecutive game in the series. Future, two time LSU national champion Keith (Alleger) Zinger starred in the contest

DeRidder	6	0	0	0–6
Leesville	0	0	7	7–14

DHS-- Derrick Taylor 33 run (pass failed).
LHS-- Keith Alleger 14 pass from Justin Goins (Michael Coode kick).
LHS-- Issac Grant fumble recovery in end zone (Coode kick).

	DHS	LHS
First Downs	11	10
Rushes-Yards	41-105	36-150
Passing Yards	24	64
Total Offense	129	214
Passes (C-A-I)	7-13-1	4-7-0
Punts	5-30.2	3-39.0
Fumbles-Lost	4-1	1-0
Penalties	11-73	6-35

INDIVIDUAL STATS
RUSHING — DeRidder, Derrick Taylor 12-61; Donnie Tellis 6-41; Kenneth Nance 6-9, James Oliver 2-3, Eric Cooper 15-(-9). Leesville, Jason Leacock 20-86, Chris Nash 5-40; Justin Goins 7-18; Courtney Booth 3-7, Keith Alleger 1-(-1).
PASSING — DeRidder-- Eric Cooper 7-12-1, Donnie Tellis 0-1-0. Leesville, Justin Goins 4-7-0.
RECEIVING — DeRidder, Kenneth Nance 2-7, Donnie Tellis 2-6, Derrick Taylor 2-3, Roger Mayes 1-8. Leesville, Keith Alleger 2-36, Michael Toney 2-28.

DHS's Marcus Scott

LHS's Keith (Alleger) Zinger

2003:   Leesville 21   DeRidder 14   Series: DHS 0 LHS 6

Leesville continued its longest winning streak in the history of the Hooper Trophy with a one score win at home.   The Cats also closed out the Hooper V Series and retained the trophy.

Leesville 21, DeRidder 14

DeRidder	6	0	8	0—14
Leesville	0	21	0	0—21

D: Derrick Taylor 63 run (kick failed)
L: Kenyon Martin 4 run (Josh Quayhagen kick)
L: Bernardo Henry 75 pass from Justin Goins (run failed)
L: Tommy Neubert 15 pass from Goins (Neubert pass from Goins)
D: Eric Cooper 3 run (Taylor run)

INDIVIDUAL LEADERS
RUSHING—DeRidder, Derrick Taylor 28-187, Eric Cooper 11-47, Kenneth Nance 1-5, James Porter 5-23. Leesville, Kenyon Martin 12-50, Justin Goins 3-4, Bernardo Henry 6-38, Quentiza Scott 11-38, Ibraham Kaba 1-2, Josh Quayhagen 2-(minus 1).
PASSING—DeRidder, Eric Cooper 3-6-0—15, Donnie Tellis 0-1-1—0. Leesville, Justin Goins 5-13-0—114.
RECEIVING—DeRidder, Donnie Tellis 3-15. Leesville, Tommy Neubert 2-20, Bernardo Henry 2-86, Kenyon Martin 1-8.

LEESVILLE 21 DERIDDER 14

LEESVILLE – Justin Goins passed for two touchdowns, and Kenyon Martin ran for another, all in the second quarter, to lead Leesville in its last tuneup for District 3-4A competition that begins next week.

Goins had a 75-yard touchdown pass to Bernardo Henry and a 15-yard scoring strike to Tommy Neubert. Martin, who gained 50 yards on 12 carries, scored on a 4-yard run.

Derrick Taylor rushed for 187 yards on 28 carries and scored on a 63-yard scamper to lead DeRidder (2-3). The Dragons had four turnovers, including three lost fumbles.

DHS's Calvin Davis

LHS's Bernardo Henry

2004: Leesville 46 DeRidder 7   Series: DHS 0 LHS 1

The Hooper VI series began with a decisive LHS win in DeRidder.

Leesville 46, DeRidder 7

Leesville	14	6	6	20–46
DeRidder	0	0	0	7–7

LV—Casey Vinson 4 run (Daniel Eaves kick).
LV—Bernardo Henry 25 pass from Justin Goins (Eaves kick).
LV—Henry 21 pass from Goins (run failed).
LV—Vinson 2 run (kick failed).
LV—Justin Ford 1 run (Eaves kick).
D—Reggie Hoard 10 pass from Micah Harrington (Casey Burks kick).
LV—Ford 55 run (kick failed).
LV—Justin Ford 58 interception return (Eaves kick).

LEESVILLE 46, DERIDDER 7

DERIDDER – The Wampus Cats (4-1) rushed for 310 yards to steamroll the Dragons (2-3).

Leading the Wampus Cats' was Edwin Ivory, who rushed for 108 yards. Justin Ford added 99 yards and two scores and Kenyon Martin 71 yards.

The Dragons were held to 138 yards and committed seven turnovers.

INDIVIDUAL STATISTICS
RUSHING–LV, Edwin Ivory 14-108, Kenyon Martin 14-71, Henry 3-16, Goins 1-0, Vinson 5-16, Ford 8-99, Darren Holbrook 1-6. DHS, Hoard 11-29, Boyd Mayers 2-10, James Porter 5-4, D.J. Jackson 1-(-3), Harrington 7-(-9), Michael Canady 1-(-7).
PASSING–LV, Goins 8-15-0-138. DHS, Harrington 9-15-2-114.
RECEIVING–LV, Marquis Williams 3-53, Tommy Neubert 1-12, Henry 2-60, Darryl Joiner 2-23. DHS, Hoard 5-90, Canady 3-19, Jerome Gipson 1-5.
Records: Leesville, 4-1-0; DeRidder, 2-3-0.

LHS's Edwin Ivory

DHS's Brandon Thomas

2005: No game was played in 2005.   Southwest Louisiana had been devasted by the landfall from Hurricane Rita and the game had to be cancelled.

2006:   Leesville 33   DeRidder 7 　　　　　　　　　　　　　　Series: DHS 0   LHS 2

Leesville won its eight straight game in the series and built a two game lead in the Hooper VI.

LEESVILLE 33, DERIDDER 7

DeRidder — Michael Ford ran for 111 yards and two touchdowns on just seven carries as Leesville pounded DeRidder.

Ford scored on a 2-yard run in the second quarter and a 46-yard run in the fourth quarter.

Leesville 33, DeRidder 7

Leesville	0	12	14	7—33
DeRidder	0	0	0	7—7

LHS—Michael Ford 2 run (kick failed).
LHS—Josh Cryer 26 run (kick failed).
LHS—Justin Ford 12 run (kick good).
LHS—Cryer 1 run (kick good).
LHS—M. Ford 46 run (kick good).
DHS—Danny Williams 15 run (Casey Burk kick).

INDIVIDUAL STATISTICS
RUSHING—DeRidder, Williams 20-55, Darius Bruce 11-31, Stuart Peterson 1-8, Vance Worthen 1-6, Hunter Bardin 5-4, Burks 1-(-10). Leesville, Michael Ford 7-111, Cryer 13-81, Tyson Ingram 4-37, Justin Ford 5-24, Djuan Taylor 2-20, Tyrell McTear 3-5, Norman Allen 1-(-6).
PASSING—DeRidder, Bardin 2-9-0--13. Leesville, Allen 6-7-0--55; Chris Brown 0-1-0--0.
RECEIVING—DeRidder, Tate O'Neal 1-8, Peterson 1-5. Leesville, Travante Stallworth 3-28, Allen Muse 1-14, Cryer 1-7, Taylor 1-6.

LHS's Norman Allen

2007:   Leesville 43   DeRidder 13   Series: DHS 0   LHS 3

Leesville took a convincing win at home to make the Hooper VI series 3-0 and extend the overall winning streak to 9

LEESVILLE 43, DERIDDER 13

LEESVILLE — Wampus Cats' quarterback Travante Stallworth was the star, scoring on three touchdown runs and passing for two more. He would finish with 209 yards passing and 134 rushing. Allen Muse, who scored the game's opening touchdown, finished with 106 yards on six receptions.

Devin Moran contributed another 158 rushing for Leesville (2-3), who racked up 518 yards of offense in the blowout.

David Detz & Michael Harris

Leesville 43, DeRidder 13

DeRidder   0   0   6   7—13
Leesville   18   12   0 13—43

LHS — Allen Muse 39 pass from Travante Stallworth (Kick blocked)
LHS — Stallworth 23 run (Pass failed)
LHS — Devin Moran 65 run (Pass failed)
LHS — Stallworth 1 run (Run failed)
LHS — Stallworth 85 run (Kick failed)
DHS — Shadrick Taylor 5 run (Kick failed)
LHS — Demetrius Mark 18 pass from Stallworth (Tiashun Burnett kick)
DHS — Tevon Steward 1 run (Sam Durham kick)
LHS — David Detz 83 fumble return (No PAT attempt)

INDIVIDUAL STATISTICS

RUSHING—DeRidder, Shadrick Taylor 14-76, Stephen Richmond 3-29, Tevon Steward 5-27, Vance Worthen 1-23, Clinton Willis 4-13, Danny Williams 5-10, Samuel Peterson 1-5, Ronald Acker 1-3, John Schlag 8-(-15). Leesville, Devin Moran 19-158, Travante Stallworth 12-134, DeJuan Taylor 2-15, Chris Brown 2-6, Eddie McTear 3-(-4)

PASSING—DeRidder, John Schlag 4-15-2-42. Leesville, Travante Stallworth 10-13-0, 209, Chris Brown 0-2-1-0

RECEIVING—DeRidder, Tate O'Neal 2-28, Vance Worthen 1-8, Anthony Cooper 1-6. Leesville, Allen Muse 6-106, DeJuan Taylor 3-85, Demetrius Mark 1-18

LHS's Travante Stallworth, DHS's Justin Victor

2008: Leesville 68   DeRidder 29   Series: DHS 0 LHS 4

The Wampus Cats kept the Dragons at bay for a full decade with a big win 2008.   The 2008 contest would be the highest scoring game in the series' history.

High-powered Leesville offense routs DeRidder

By Brian Trahan
For The Town Talk

DERIDDER — What began as a blowout quickly turned into a shootout before No. 4 Leesville finally put a stubborn DeRidder team away 68-29 Friday night in a battle for the Hooper Trophy.

Leesville (4-1) built an early 34-9 lead but had to survive a furious DeRidder rally in the second quarter before holding the Dragons scoreless in the second half.

It was the Leesville offense that again put up huge numbers. The state's leading rusher, Michael Ford, carried 28 times for 274 yards and scored three touchdowns, but he was far from the Wampus Cats' only weapon. Quarterback Travante Stallworth rushed for four touchdowns and added another passing TD to help the Cats put up 534 yards of offense.

Despite the offensive fireworks, Leesville coach Terence Williams was unhappy with the 29 points his defense surrendered in the second quarter.

"It was truly a tale of two halves," he said. "Numbers are exciting, but I am not pleased with the way we played in the first half.

"We got the team in the locker room and challenged them to come out and play Wampus Cat football in the second half. We definitely have some things we need to get ironed out on defense."

Ford, who eclipsed the 1,000-yard mark for the season with 136 rushing yards in the first half, set the tone with an early touchdown, but Stallworth did most of the damage on the scoreboard.

It was the third consecutive game that Leesville scored at least 50 points.

Stallworth added two one-yard plunges and a five-yard TD gallop in the first half, while also hitting sophomore receiver Levander Liggins for a 33-yard TD strike. Momentum swung in DeRidder's favor in the second quarter, however, behind the play of junior quarterback Samuel Peterson.

He threw touchdown passes of 55, 15 and 21 yards to cut into the Leesville lead and when he scampered for a 27-yard TD run just before halftime, Leesville's lead seemed precarious at 41-29 at the break.

Peterson nearly set up another DeRidder score in the third period, faking a punt and running for 52 yards into Leesville territory. However, he was injured when Cassetti Brown made the TD saving tackle and Peterson never returned to the game.

Ford iced the game with touchdown runs of 53 and 19 yards before the junior varsity came in to finish the fourth quarter.

His 274-yard performance marked the third time this season Ford rushed for 200 yards or more in a game. Stallworth added 88 yards on 13 carries. Freshman Diontay Thurman ended the scoring with a one-yard plunge in the fourth quarter.

Peterson threw for 158 yards and rushed for 116 to lead DeRidder before leaving the game. Liggins led the Cats with four catches for 65 yards.

Leesville will open district play Friday night at home against Grant, while DeRidder will take on LaGrange.

Leesville 68
DeRidder 29

2008 – continued

Leesville 68, DeRidder 29

Leesville	20	21	14	13-68
DeRidder	0	29	0	0-29

LHS-Michael Ford 7 run. Allen Perry kick.
LHS-Travante Stallworth 1 run. Kick failed.
LHS- Stallworth 1 run. Perry kick.
DHS-Safety Punter stepped out of endzone.
DHS-Ronald Acker 55 pass from Samuell Peterson. Sam Durham kick.
LHS-Stallworth 5 run. Perry kick.
LHS-Levander Liggins 33 pass from Stallworth. Perry kick.
DHS-Alvais Coronel 15 pass from Peterson. Durham kick.
LHS-Ford 53 run. Perry kick.
DHS-Clinton Willis 21 pass from Peterson. Durham kick
DHS-Peterson 27 run. Pass failed.
LHS-Ford 19 run. Perry kick.
LHS-Devin Moran 37 punt return. Perry kick.
LHS-Stallworth 13 run. Perry kick.
LHS-Diontay Thurman 1 run. Kick failed.

DHS's Clinton Willis

Even in new era, Wampus Cats haven't forgotten old rivals

By Will Tubbs
wtubbs@thetowntalk.com
(318) 487-6367

When Terence Williams took over the Leesville football program, he made no secret about his intentions.

He wanted to bring a state championship to Vernon Parish and everything, from the way the Wampus Cats worked in the offseason to how they prepared for and executed during regular season games, was going to be a stepping stone on the way to the Superdome.

Regular season games were no longer to be viewed as anything more or less than a necessary step on the way to a Class 4A championship.

Williams, whose slogan for the Cats has always been the Muhammad Ali inspired "As a Champion," has been steadfast in his stance that all games are treated as equals, even when that game is for the Hooper Trophy.

The Hooper Trophy, West Central Louisiana's answer to the Morgan Walker Spirit Bell game (Alexandria Senior High versus Bolton), is the prize that Leesville and DeRidder vie for once a year in a rivalry game that has, of late, been dominated by the Wampus Cats.

As his team prepares for a Friday night trip to the Dragons' stadium, Williams said he was confident his team would not lose focus.

"It is still a huge game for both communities," Williams said. "As a football program, we understand the significance of the game for this town and DeRidder, but it's just another step. I expect the same thing from my players this week as I would any week."

In the last three weeks, whether Williams expected it or not, the Wampus Cats (3-1) have trounced their opponents, putting up an average of 52.3 points per game.

Although the Wampus Cats have dominated the Dragons in recent years and won the last nine Hooper Trophy games, Williams said he had no idea what his offense would be able to do against DeRidder.

"We don't like to look at numbers," Williams said. "The thing I always preach to the kids is execution. If we execute the way we should for four quarters, the numbers will be in our favor."

One player who has had little trouble in producing big numbers is senior running back and LSU commitment Michael Ford, who has already rushed for more than 900 yards and is fresh off a 248-yard, four-touchdown performance against La-Grange.

And, while he missed last year's Hooper Trophy game with an injury, he owned the Dragons in 2006, rushing for 111 yards and two scores on just seven carries in a game Leesville won 33-7.

"There's no secret to his success, just hard work," Williams said. "There's no magic fairy dust that makes him the player that he is, he just works hard and not just from August to December. He's in here working from January all the way through the summer. All of our kids are. I think that's being proven through their success on the field."

2009: DeRidder 37   Leesville 18   Series: DHS 1 LHS 4

The Dragons snapped a 10-game losing streak and clobbered Leesville at Wampus Cat stadium.

By Faimon Roberts

DERIDDER—For the first time this millennium, the Hooper Trophy is returning to Beauregard Parish.

The DeRidder Dragons capitalized on mistakes and made a few big plays of their own on their way to reclaiming the trophy in this rivalry, getting a 37-18 win over the rival Leesville Wampus Cats Friday night at Wampus Cat Stadium in Leesville.

After a scoreless first quarter, the Dragons got it going in the second. After holding Leesville to a three and out, the Wampus Cats' Allen Perry dropped back to punt for the third time in the game.

DeRidder had the punt block called, and when the snap came high to Perry, it gave the defenders time to get in on him, and his punt was blocked and scooped up by Sean Freeman, who scored easily to give the Dragons an early seven point lead.

But Leesville responded, going on an 11-play drive capped by a Robert Bush 17-yard touchdown run.

Leesville's Levander Liggins had the two big plays of the drive, a 24-yard run and the next play a 17-yard reception that put the Wampus Cats deep in Dragon territory.

The extra point was blocked, and DeRidder's lead was just 7-6.

On DeRidder's ensuing possession, Samuel Peterson dropped back and let fly a deep ball that fell perfectly into the arms of a streaking Sean Freeman who hauled it and was dragged down at the Wampus Cat six-yard line for a gain of 50 yards.

Four plays later, on fourth and goal from the one, Samuel Peterson took a quarterback sneak around left end for the Dragons second score, the lead extended to eight.

Leesville had further problems on special teams, when a low snap went between Perry's legs and out of the back of the end zone, giving DeRidder a safety and a ten-point lead with just 1:53 to go in the half.

But the Dragons weren't finished. Thanks to a 40-yard scamper by Peterson, the Dragons had another first-and-goal with less than 20 seconds to go in the half.

After a spike, Peterson gave the ball to Antonio Palmer, who plowed ahead for the score with just 12 seconds remaining the half, and DeRidder up 23-6.

Leesville wasn't done fighting, though.

The Wampus Cats opened the second half with an onside kick recovered by the Dragons. But two plays later, Palmer fumbled and the Wampus Cats went on another scoring march, this time Liggins running it in from five yards out.

But the Dragons again responded, this time when Palmer atoned for his mistake by busting a weaving, dodging 44-yard touchdown run to again put the Dragons up by 18.

Bot teams added scores in the fourth, Peterson scrambling for a 13-yarder and Leesville's Tiashaun Burnett getting a five-yard score with less than two minutes to go, and the Dragons claws firmly gripping the Hooper Trophy.

"Right now, all I can think of is Hooper's Home," said Dragon coach Eric Parmley afterward. "The kids worked their tails off, and they deserve it," he added.

Parmley singled out Palmer for praise.

"Antonio, because he has been out of football, is just now getting to where he can see the things he needs to do, and I was real proud of him tonight."

Palmer finished with 141 yards on 20 carries and two scores in the absence of starting tailback Stephen Richmond, who hurt his ankle last week against Westlake.

For Leesville, the loss drops them to 1-4 on the season, while DeRidder moves to 5-0. Both teams will begin District play next week, with DeRidder traveling to Lake Charles to take on St. Louis on Thursday night and Leesville traveling to take on Peabody.

2010:   Leesville 24   Deridder 17   Series: DHS 1   LHS 5

Leesville got back on the winning track in a regular season win over the Dragons. The teams would meet in the playoffs later in the season.

Wampus Cat defense huge in victory over DeRidder

By Brian Trahan

"If you're good at throwing the ball, you're as good as the weather. If you're good at running the ball, you're as good as your running backs. If you're good on defense, you're good all the time." Those were David Feaster's words to the media following a huge 24-17 Hooper Trophy win over DeRidder Friday night.

He was alluding to the play of his defense, which keyed the victory after going through a maturation process through the first four weeks of the season. The Cats came up big with a third-quarter goal line stand which completely changed the outlook of the game in front of a packed crowd at Cecil Doyle Memorial Stadium. That stand preceded a 99-yard drive by the Leesville offense which virtually put the game out of reach and allowed the Cats to take back the Hooper Trophy after losing at Wampus Cat Stadium in 2009.

It was a moment to shine for a defense which was put behind the proverbial eight ball during a difficult early-season schedule. Facing teams such as West Monroe, Sam Houston, Sulphur and Washington-Marion, the defense was allowing 380 yards and 44.5 points per game. The offense carried the Cats through those four games with a 2-2 record. Friday night was a coming of age performance.

DeRidder scored one offensive touchdown, which came late in the game. The Dragons could only muster 17 points and 244 yards of offense. Leesville forced three turnovers and held DeRidder tailback Eddie Meridith to just 72 yards on 20 carries one week after he gashed Westlake for 191 yards rushing.

"You know, we returned only a handful of guys from last year and we had to endure the early part of the season," Leesville defensive coordinator Robert Causey said. "But we have the right kind of guys on defense and they kept believing in what we're doing. They stuck together and hats off to our kids."

Sticking together seems to be a common thread for the defense, even while rumblings and grumblings circulated amongst the fan base due to the gaudy numbers put up by the first four opponents.

The players, however, weren't having it on this night. "That goal line stand was our way of showing what we're made of," junior defensive end Daniel Winfield said. "We got in there, took our shots and got out."

"We have an attitude of never surrendering," junior Adam Woods said. "It's Wampus Cat pride. Coach Causey and coach (Sedric) Clemons kept telling us to stick together and that's what happened on that goal line stand. It was a total team effort." DeRidder did manage to get into the endzone late on offense, but the only other score came on a fumble return. Dragon quarterback Jared Holmes was sacked six times and they managed only 3.35 yards per carry the entire night. Leesville's season-low total of 134 rushing yards allowed came on the heels of giving up four straight 200-yard rushing games and four straight running backs going for more than 100 yards. It's not a shock this performance gives the Cats a well-rounded team heading into district play. Leesville has won three straight after dropping road games to West Monroe and Sam Houston to start the season.

"We're excited about our three-game streak," Feaster said. "It gives us confidence going into district. Peabody beat us a year ago, so we're looking forward to the next challenge this week at home."
If this week's game comes down to a goal line stand, don't bet against the Wampus Cats. When you have 11 guys with their backs to the wall, good things can happen.

	Q1	Q2	Q3	Q4	Final
Leesville	10	7	7	0	24
DeRidder	0	3	7	7	17

DHS's Deshazor Everett and LHS's Levander Liggins.   Both athletes would go on to letter 4 years in the NCAA and Everett would play in the NFL for the Washington Redskins

2010: Leesville 34 DeRidder 20

For the third time in the rivalry, the Cats and Dragons met in the playoffs. Leesville won in a score similar to the first match up in 1963 (34-19).

Liggins leads Leesville over DeRidder

By Raymond A. Partsch III
rpartsch@thetowntalk.com
(318) 487-6353

LEESVILLE — Levander Liggins put on another lights out performance as Leesville defeated DeRidder, 34-20, in the opening round of the Class 4A playoffs.

The score was tied 20-20 after DeRidder's Jace Morein scored on a eight-yard run early in the fourth quarter. Despite being the higher seed, the No. 11 seed Wampus Cats had struggled to put away the No. 22 seed Dragons. Leesville needed a big play and they got one from their playmaker Liggins. The senior star returned the ensuing kickoff 88 yards for a touchdown giving Leesville the lead for good.

Liggins would finish the game with 86 yards on 17 carries, four receptions for 21 yards and scored all five of the team's touchdowns.

"It may be cliché but big time players make big time plays," said Leesville coach David Feaster.

Before Liggins took the game over late in the fourth quarter, it was a back and forth battle. Leesville's offense had problems with putting together consistent scoring drives. DeRidder (6-5) was able to pressure Leesville quarterback Zack Squyres forcing him into making short throws. Squyres completed 13 of 19 passes for 174 yards with one touchdown and one interception.

Leesville got on the scoreboard first after Liggins scored a nine-yard touchdown run. DeRidder responded as Deshazor Everett scored on an eight-yard run. DeRidder took the lead after Jared Holmes scored on a quarterback sneak. Leesville tied up before the half when Squyres hit Liggins in the corner of the end zone for a two-yard touchdown pass.

"They punched us in the mouth and then we punched them in the mouth," said Liggins. "I told the guys at halftime that we had to come together as a family."

Liggins wasn't the only one that stepped up with big plays. Leesville's defense was staunch in the second half. Defensive back Demetrius Atwater picked off Jared Holmes in the fourth quarter but the Wampus Cats were not done. After blocking a punt, DeRidder was driving deep into Leesville territory when Thomas Medina picked off Everett's pass at the 14-yard line and returned it 65 yards. Liggins would cap the game with a five-yard touchdown run.

"There offense played much better," said Feaster, whose team defeated DeRidder 24-17 earlier in the season. "Fortunately for us our defense was better."

Leesville advances to the second round of the playoffs and will travel to face No. 6 seed Franklinton next Friday.

"We are going to find out just how good we are," said Feaster.

LHS's Zach Squyres   DHS's Jared Holmes

2011: DeRidder 42 Leesville 14   Series: DHS 2 LHS 5

The Dragons stayed in contention for the series, taking a 28 point win in an early season contest

> **DERIDDER 42, LEESVILLE 14:** Leesville (0-1) committed seven turnovers in a 42-14 home loss to DeRidder on Friday night.
>
> DeRidder (1-0) took advantage of the turnovers (4 interceptions, 3 lost fumbles) by scoring four touchdowns off of them. Hunter Lewis recovered a fumble in the end zone in the first quarter, Delano Stenson returned an interception back 50 yards for a score, Draye Allen returned another 20 yards for a score, and Chris Crosley returned a fumble back 96 yards for a score in the fourth quarter.
>
> Leesville quarterback Zach Squyres completed 12 of 25 passes for 113 yards, one touchdown and four interceptions. Clinton Thurman led Leesville in rushing and receiving with 79 yards on 17 carries and 6 receptions for 37 yards.

DeRidder   7 7 14 14—42
Leesville 0 14 0 0—14

Scoring summary
DeRidder: Hunter Lewis 30 run (Noah Coronel kick).
DeRidder: Lewis fumble recovery in endzone (Coronel kick).
Leesville: Derrick Blackshire 11 run (Colton Honeycutt kick).
Leesville: Kole Smith 4 pass from Zack Squyres (Honeycutt kick).
DeRidder: Eddie Meridith 8 run (Coronel kick).
DeRidder: Delano Stenson 50 interception return (Coronel kick).
DeRidder: Chris Crosley 96 fumble return (Coronel kick).
DeRidder: Draye Allen 20 interception return (Coronel kick).

Individual statistics
Rushing: DeRidder — Jared Holmes 5-57; Eddie Meridith 16-56; Demarrious Jackson 12-40; Hunter Lewis 2-29; Andre Lovely 1-8; Sam Ford 1-5; Vinny Ventruella 1-0. Leesville — Clinton Thurman 17-79; Zack Squyres 9-28; Derrick Blackshire 8-24; Jeremiah Cross 5-5; Marshall Smith 1-1.
Passing: DeRidder — Jared Holmes 2-6-0—9; Vinny Ventruella 0-2-0—0. Leesville — Zack Squyres 12-25-4—113.
Receiving: DeRidder — Eddie Meridith 1-9; Andre Lovely 1-0. Leesville — Clinton Thurman 6-37; Adam Woods 4-67; Gary McCoy 1-5; Kole Smith 1-4.

DHS's Savion Ashworth tackles LHS's Clinton Thurman

2012 DeRidder 49 Leesville 0   Series: DHS 3 LHS 5

The Dragons throttled the Wampus Cats, in the second most lopsided game in the series' history

DRAGONS WIN BIG - By Alix Kunkle

DeRIDDER – A return to Cecil Doyle Memorial Stadium wasn't enough for the Leesville Wampus Cats to regain possession of the Hooper Trophy, as the De-Ridder Dragons ran over the Wampus Cats, 49-0. It is the first time DeRidder defeated Leesville on their home turf since 1993, when DeRidder beat Leesville, 24-14, and the largest margin of victory for either team since DeRidder defeated Leesville, 50-0, in 1975.

Leesville was plagued with turnovers, as the Wampus Cats threw four interceptions and lost two fumbles. One fumble was returned for a touchdown, and an interception was initially returned for a touchdown, but was negated due to offsetting penalties and Michael Alleva fumbling the ball into the end zone, resulting in a touchback.

'We didn't play well,' Leesville head coach Jimmie Adams said. 'We made some mistakes, but we'll get them fixed.' The first quarter was a defensive stalemate, and the Wampus Cats entered the first half down just 14-0. The only two scores came from 36- and 33-yard runs by DeRidder junior running back Jamon Bradford, who ran for a total of 223 yards. Bradford had a total of 100 in the first half, nearly two-thirds of DeRidder's offense. Leesville tallied just 62 yards, and advanced to the DeRidder 45 on their first drive, but were forced to punt three times. 'For one half, our defense played well,' Adams said.

In the second half, however, DeRidder exploded for 28 points. After the kickoff, Sam Ford capped a eight play drive with a 21yard touchdown run. After an interception by Alleva, Bradford capped a short drive with a five-yard touchdown run to make the score 28-0. Four plays later, J.J. Faciane recovered a Matthew Hoecker fumble 16 yards for a touchdown, and with less than a minute remaining in the third, Bradford scampered in from two yards out to make it 42-0. Bradford added a 28yard touchdown run in the fourth quarter to cap the scoring for the Dragons. Leesville was led in the rushing department by Devail Lewis, who gained 54 yards on 16 carries. Jessie St. Clergy added four yards for the Wampus Cats, and Kaplan Rolon had two yards. DeRidder was led by Bradford's 223 yards and five touchdowns, and D'Angelo Reder added 69. Kole Smith had two receptions for 30 yards for the Wampus Cats, and Bryce Parker added a 16 yard reception. Overall, the Wampus Cats were 4-14 in the passing department for 48 yards, but Adams reiterated that the Wampus Cats are not a passfirst team this year.

'We're going to be a running team,' he said. 'And we're going to get better.'

The Dragon football team and coaching staff would like to thank all of the Dragons fans for their support.

The Wampus Cats continue their earlyseason road trip to face the Sam Houston Broncos at 7 p.m. on Sept. 7, and DeRidder will travel to face Natchitoches Central at 7 p.m. on Sept. 7.

Scoring Summary: First quarter (none)

Second quarter
DR – Jamon Bradford 36-yard run (Broussard PAT good)
Third quarter
DR – Sam Ford 20yard run (Broussard PAT good)

DR – Jamon Bradford 5-yard run (Broussard PAT good)
DR – J.J. Faciane 16-yard fumble recovery return (Broussard PAT good)
DR – Jamon Bradford 2-yard run (Broussard PAT good)
Fourth quarter
DR – Jamon Bradford 28-yard run (Broussard PAT good)

Leesville Leaders Rushing yards: Leesville: Devail Lewis 16-54, Jessie St. Clergy 5-4, Kaplan Rolon 1-2, Dontrell Lewis 1-1, Matthew Hoecker 11-0. DeRidder: Jamon Bradford 20-223-5, D'Angelo Reder 10-69, Sam Ford 4-26-1, Drew Victor 3-17, D'Andre Bellamy 3-8, Vinny Ventrella 2-(2).
Passing yards: Leesville: Kory Jones 3-10-0-2, 23 yards; Matthew Hoecker 1-4-0-2, 25 yards. DeRidder: D'Andre Bellamy 1-2-0-0, 28 yards; Vinny Ventrella 1-2-0-0, 0 yards.
Receiving yards: Leesville: Kole Smith 2-30-0, Bryce Parker 1-16. DeRidder: D'AngeloReder2-28

2013:   DeRidder 36   Leesville 7   Series: DHS 4   LHS 5

In a game that drew the series to within a single contest, the Dragons thrashed the Cats for the third year in a row

WAMPUS CATS FALL TO DERIDDER – from the Leesville Daily Leader
The DeRidder Dragons did not let up Friday night as they picked up their fifth consecutive win and first district 3-4A victory, defeating longtime rival and district Leesville, 36-7, to keep the Hooper Trophy in DeRidder for another year.

With the win DeRidder improved to 5-1 overall and 1-0 in district play on the season, while the Wampus Cats fell to (0-6, 0-1) still looking for their first win.

The first 10:30 minutes of the game proved to be a defensive stalemate, until DeRidder quarterback Tyler Herring hit sophomore Holden Hoerner on a 56 yard touchdown pass, followed by a Jacob Cornel kick, to take an early 7-0 lead with 1:21 remaining in the first quarter.

Just about the time you thought it was going to be a one-touchdown game going into halftime, DeRidder's D'Angelo Reder broke the game open with a 12 yard touchdown run and a Cornel kick extending the Dragon lead to 14-0 at halftime.

The Dragon defense allowed the Wampus Cat offense a mere 46 yards in the first half. Quentin Coleman led the Cats in the first half with 21 yards on 12 carries.

DeRidder on the other hand had 168 total first half yards, with 126 yards on the ground and 62 passing yards. D'Andre Bellamy led the Dragons ground attack with 44 yards, while Reder had 39 yards and Jamon Bradford finished the half with 32.

Hoerner led the Dragon receiving core in the first half with 56 yards.

It did not take the Dragons long to pick up where they left off, with Drew Victor finding paydirt from the 2 yard line with 6:15 remaining in the third quarter, and a Cornel kick extended their lead to 21-0.

Moses Tolbert gave the Wampus Cat fans something to cheer about with 1:19 left in the quarter, breaking several DeRidder tackles and taking the ball 39 yards for the Cats' first and only touchdown of the game, trailing DeRidder at that point 21-7.

DeRidder sealed the game and the Hooper Trophy in the fourth quarter, adding 15 more points to the scoreboard, off two Reder touchdowns. His first came from 2 yards out with a Copeland Zaunbrecher to Hoerner PAT. His third and final TD of game came from 12 yards out, and a Cornel kick capped the scoring at 36-7.

"Our kids played extremely well in a big game," said DeRidder coach Eric Parmley.

Reder led all receivers with 115 yards on 17 carries for three TDs, while Moses Tolbert led the Cats with 72 yards on 15 carries and a touchdown.

Herring passed for 62 yards and a touchdown, completing three of his seven passes. Hoerner led all receivers with 56 yards and a TD.

Next week Leesville will travel to Grant on Friday, while Deridder will host Bolton in their homecoming game.

DERIDDER 36, LEESVILLE 7

DeRidder	7	7	7	15 —	38
Leesville	0	0	7	0 —	7

First Quarter
D— Holden Hoener 58 pass from Tyler Herring (Jacob Coronel kick)

Second Quarter
D— D'Angelo Reder 12 run (Coronel kick)

Third Quarter
D— Drew Victor 2 run (Coronel kick)
L— Moses Tolbert 39 run (Solomon Cross kick)

Fourth Quarter
D— Reder 2 run (Hoener pass from Copeland Zaunbrecker)
D— Reder 10 run (Coronel kick)

	D	L
First downs	13	7
Rushes-yds	37-248	49-68
Passes (C-A-I)	3-7-0	0-3-0
Passing yds	62	0
Total offense	310	68
Fumbles-lost	0-0	3-1
Punts-avg	5-35.6	5-31
Penalties-yds	7-85	5-50

INDIVIDUAL STATISTICS
RUSHING — DeRidder, Victor 7-29; Jamon Bradford 6-47; Reder 17-115; Leesville, Talbert 15-72; Caden Wheeler 7-33
PASSING — DeRidder, Herring 3-7-0-62; Leesville, Wheeler 0-3-0
RECEIVING — DeRidder, Hoener 1-58; Leesville, None

2014: Leesville 21 DeRidder 6					Series: DHS 4 LHS 6

Leesville snapped a 3 game losing streak and secured the Hooper VI Series

Posted Oct 13, 2014 at 12:30 PM

DERIDDER — The Leesville Wampus Cats stunned the DeRidder Dragons on Friday night at Cecil Doyle Memorial Stadium, claiming a 21-6 victory to win the Hooper Trophy Series VI.

DeRidder's only break of the game came early in the first quarter when the Wampus Cats muffed a snap and the Dragons took over on the Cats 23.

Dionte Johnson scored the Dragons' lone touchdown of the game on the ensuing play from scrimmage, taking an early 6-0 lead.

Moses Tolbert and Cory McCoy, who combined for 224 yards rushing a pair of touchdowns, helped spark the Leesville offense, which got off to another slow start.

"It took a little while for offense to wake up and I am just glad it did not come back to bite us in the tail," said Wampus Cat coach Tommy Moore.

Tolbert got the Cats on the scoreboard on their sixth offensive series, capping a 48-yard drive with a 13-yard touchdown run. Sophomore Jacob Adams nailed the PAT kick to give the Wampus Cats a 7-6 lead at the halftime intermission.

DeRidder won the first half on paper with 178 total yards of offense, including 150 of them on the ground. The Wampus Cats netted just 64 total yards of offense, with 62 on the ground.

The Dragons might have won the first half, but it was all Leesville in the second, pounding the ground for 155 yards and 14 points.

McCoy scored the Cats first points of the second half off a 4-yard run. Adamsn nailed to extra point to extend the Leesville lead to 14-6 with 8:35 left in the fourth quarter.

Wampus Cat quarterback Caden Wheeler made the win a little bit sweeter scoring just three minutes later on a 1-yard run, knocking off their District 3-4A rival, 21-6, and taking the Hooper Trophy VI back to Leesville.

"Our coaching staff did a great job getting the kids ready this week and they responded well tonight," Moore said.

McCoy led all rushers with 114 yards on 27 carries and a TD, while Tolbert came in with 110 yards on 22 carries and a touchdown.

DeRidder's D'Angelo Reder and Johnson finished with 87 yards each, while Johnson scored the Dragons' lone touchdown.

Dragon quarterback Jimmie Wilson finished with 43 yards passing, completing 3-of-8 passes with an interception, while Jaylen Heath led all receivers with 28 yards.

Next week, the Wampus Cats host Grant, who lost Friday to Peabody, in the annual Leesville homecoming game, while the Dragons travel to Bolton to face the 0-1 Bears, who fell to Tioga in its 3-4A opener on Friday.

LEESVILLE 21, DERIDDER 6

Leesville	0	7	0	14	— 21
DeRidder	6	0	0	0	— 6

SCORING SUMMARY
First Quarter
D—Dionte Johnson 23 run (kick fail)
Second Quarter
L—Moses Tolbert 13 run (Jacob Adams kick)
Fourth Quarter
L—Cory McCoy 4 run (Adams kick)
L—Caden Wheeler 1 run (Adams kick)

TEAM STATISTICS

	LHS	DHS
First downs	15	12
Rushing yds	217	184
Passes (C-A-I)	1-3-0	3-8-1
Passing yds	2	43
Total offense	219	227
Fumbles-lost	0-0	2-1
Punts-avg	5-39.0	6-28.7
Penalties-yds	5-35	5-31

INDIVIDUAL STATISTICS
RUSHING: Leesville, Cory McCoy 27-114, Moses Tolbert 22-110, Caden Wheeler 4-4; DeRidder, Dionte Johnson 26-87, D'Angelo Reder 10-87, Deonte Wright 1-9, CJ Anderson 1-2, Jimmie Wilson 4-(-1).
PASSING: Leesville, Caden Wheeler 1-3-0-2; DeRidder, Jimmie Wilson 3-8-1-43.
RECEIVING: Leesville, Amone Tolbert 1-2; DeRidder, Jaylen Heath 1-28, CJ Anderson 2-15.

DHS's Dionte Johnson   LHS's Cory McCoy

2015: DeRidder 56 Leesville 20   Series: DHS 1 LHS 0

The Dragons mangled the Wampus Cats in a season ending contest at Wampus Cat Stadium

By Steven Iles

Posted Nov 10, 2015 at 10:00 AM

Coming off a loss last year at Cecil Doyle Memorial Stadium, the DeRidder Dragons (7-3, 3-2) entered Friday nights Hooper Trophy contest looking for revenge.

The Leesville Wampus Cats (3-7, 0-5) were playing for much more than a trophy as they were vying for a spot in the playoffs.

But it wasn't meant to be as the Dragons reclaimed the Hooper Trophy on Friday night, taking a 56-20 victory over the Wampus Cats.

Things started off great for the Wampus Cats as leading rusher Cory McCoy took the ball 66 yards on their second play for the first points of the ball game, leading 7-0, with 11:11 left in the first quarter.

DeRidder's Daniel Crosley answered for the Dragons, racing 54 yards, while Tommy Duong added the extra point, knotting things up, 7-7, with 10 minutes left in the quarter.

The Dragon defense, led by the duo of Daniel and David Crosley, stopped the Wampus Cats offense after the first series, with the Dragon offense taking full advantage of the miscues.

Landon Taylor scored the Dragons' next points off along touchdown run of 54 yards, giving the Dragons a 14-7 lead with 3:53 left in the quarter.

Crosley scored a pair of touchdowns on runs of 25 and 13 yards to push the DeRidder lead to 28-7 with 6:49 left in the first half.

The Wampus Cats briefly came back to life just before halftime when Caden Wheeler scored on a 2-yard touchdown run, cutting the Dragon lead to 28-13.

However, Crosley still had a little bit of steam left in him as he scored his fourth touchdown of the game on a 84-yard dash, giving the Dragons a 35-13 lead going into the locker room.

DeRidder scored on its first possession of the second half on a Camron Clark 1-yard touchdown run, increasing the lead to 42-13 with 7:40 left in the third quarter.

Mckenzie Jackson took the ensuing kickoff 60 yards for the Wampus Cats third and final touchdown of the game, cutting the deficit to 42-20 with 7:31 left in the third.

DeRidder added 14 more points to the scoreboard, first on a 51-yard bomb from Robret Lewis to Holden Hoerner before sealing the victory with a 46-yard touchdown run, accounting for the final margin of victory, 56-20.

"We faced a very tough athletic team tonight who got the best of us," said Wampus Cat coach Tommy Moore.

Daniel Crosley led all rushers in the game with 329 yards and four touchdowns off 25 carries, while Cory McCoy finished with 167 yards off 23 carries and one touchdown for Leesville.

With the win, DeRidderwill play a first-round playoff game on the road at Edna Karr in the New Orleans area, while Leesville was eliminated from playoff contention.

DHS's Daniel Crosley   LHS's Caden Wheeler

BOX SCORE:

RUSHING

DERIDDER – Daniel Crosley 25-329, 4TD, Landon Taylor 3-96, 2TD,Camron Clark 14-71. LEESVILLE – Cory McCoy 23-167, 1TD, Caden Wheeler 9-64, 1TD.

PASSING

DERIDDER – Robert Lewis 1-1-0 51yds 1TD. LEESVILLE – Wheeler 7-16-0 34yds.

RECEIVING

DERIDDER – Holden Hoerner 1-51, 1TD. LEESVILLE – Trevon Lewis 1-12, Skylar Beabout 1-9, Brady Westerchil 2-8, EJ Ane 1-7.

2016:   Leesville 42   DeRidder 28   Series: DHS 1 LHS 1

The Wampus Cats evened the Hooper VII Series with a 2 score win in DeRidder

DERIDDER — A late Friday evening surge lifted the Leesville Wampus Cats past the DeRidder Dragons, 42-28, not only bringing home the Hooper Trophy, but also clinching a share of the District 3-4A title.

"I am extremely proud of our kids tonight as they came out and played hard for 48 minutes," first-year Wampus Cat head coach Robbie Causey said. With the victory, the Wampus Cats improved to 6-4 overall, finishing district play with a mark of 4-1, tying with LaGrange and Rayne for the crown. DeRidder finished the regular season with a record of 2-8 overall, 1-4 in the league

After an uneventful first half Friday night at Cecil Doyle Memorial Stadium, both the Dragons and Wampus Cats went into the locker room with the score knotted at 0-0. The Wampus Cats defense opened up the second half with an interception from Andrew Croker, taking over with excellent field position at the DeRidder 20. A couple of plays later, quarterback Theron Westerchil found DaQuan Davis on a 27-yard touchdown pass. Jacob Adams connected on the extra point to give Leesville a 7-0 lead with 10:53 left in the third quarter.

DeRidder answered on the ensuing drive with sophomore quarterback Lane Armer connecting with Dre Bagley on a 41-yard bomb. Tommy Doung added the kick to tie things up at 7-7. It didn't take Westerchia and his offense long to put seven more points on the scoreboard, hitting Croker on a 30-yard TD pass. With Adams kick, Leesville was back out by a touchdown. DeRidder senior Zac Pursley answered right back for the Dragons as toted the ball 21 yards down the left sideline for the touchdown. Doung's point after tied it back up at 14-14.

Once again, Leesville, behind a long touchdown run by Davis, silenced the DeRidder crowd with an 83 yard sprint to the endzone, lifting his team to a 21-14 lead with three quarters in the books. Opening the fourth quarter, DeRidder managed to tie things back up at 21-21 when Pursley and Armer teamed up for a 41-yard touchdown pass with 10:43 left in the game.

Leesville put together back-to-back impressive drives with Westerchil finding pay dirt on a 1-yard touchdown run and Cory McCoy on a 7-yard dash to the end zone, opening things up for the Cats as they took a 35-21 lead with 6:17 to go. DeRidder answered with a score of its own off a 61-yard touchdown pass from Armer to Bagley, pulling the Dragons within a touchdown with 4:35 left in the game.

Westerchil sealed the Cats' victory and clinched a share of the district crown for his team on a 2-yard touchdown, 42-28. Davis led all rushers in the game with 125 yards off 13 carries with a touchdown, while tMcCoy wasn't far behind finishing with 119 yards off 21 carries and a score. Westerchil completed 6-of-10 passes for 136 yards and two touchdowns, connecting once with Davis and once with Croker.T

he Dragons were led on the ground by Deauntrae Mays with 74 yards off 16 carries, while Torrin Bouvia had 47 yards off 12 carries. Armer completed 6-of-8 passes for 154 yards and two touchdowns. Bagley led all receivers with 102 yards off an impressive two receptions

While the Dragons season came to an end Friday night the Wampus Cats lived to fight another day. All indications are pointing to the Cats either finishing the season as the No. 17 or 18 team in Class 4A, which will put them on the road in the first week of the playoffs.

	Q1	Q2	Q3	Q4	Final
Leesville	0	0	21	21	42
DeRidder	0	0	14	14	28

3rd Quarter
Leesville   Theron Westerchil, 27 yard pass to Daquan Davis (Jacob Adams Kick)
DeRidder   Lane Armer, 41 yard pass to Dre Bagley (Tommy Doung kick)
Leesville   Theron Westerchil, 30 yard pass to Andrew Croker (Jacob Adams Kick)
DeRidder   Zac Pursley, 21 yard run (Tommy Doung kick)
Leesville   Daquan Davis, 83 yard run (Jacob Adams kick)

4th Quarter
DeRidder   Lane Armer, 41 yard pass to Dre Bagley (Tommy Doung kick)
Leesville   Theron Westerchil, 1 yard run (Jacob Adams kick)
Leesville   Cory McCoy, 7 yard run (Jacob Adams kick)
DeRidder   Lane Armer, 68 yard pass to Dre Bagley (Tommy Doung Kick)
Leesville   Theron Westerchil, 2 yard run (Jacob Adams kick)

DHS's Lane Armer   LHS's Theron Westerchil

2017:   Leesville 27   DeRidder 0   Series: DHS 1 LHS 2

The Cats pitched a shutout in the 2017 contest and took a one game lead in Hooper VI

By Chris Schoonover - Leesville Daily Leader

The Leesville defense was fast and physical up front, leading the Wampus Cats to the win, keeping the Hooper Trophy in Leesville.

Leesville held DeRidder to 75 total yards, including -4 rushing yards, in its 27-0 victory Friday night.

DeRidder had just five first downs and were 0-for-10 on third downs.

"The kids just played hard," Leesville coach Robert Causey said. "I don't think we did anything differently than we had done in the other weeks. We had to play four quarters because of what they do. DeRidder is a very talented football team, so we had to play four quarters of football.

"We're quick up front. We do some things to cover up for our weaknesses. We have strengths and weaknesses too."

The Wampus Cats racked up 432 yards of offense with 236 coming through the air and 196 on the ground.

"They were the better team tonight, and did a better job of playing football tonight than we did," DeRidder head coach Brad Parmley said.

"They just played better than us. They didn't do anything special. They just played better football."

Dragon quarterback Lane Armer was picked off by Leesville corner McKenzie Jackson on their second possession, setting up a 24-yard touchdown pass from quarterback Chris Vargas to running back Andrew Croker as time expired in the first quarter.

Croker ran for 83 yards on 17 carries and caught 9 passes for 84 yards.

"I just told (Croker) to go play and have fun and don't do anything that you're not capable of doing," Causey said. "Sometimes kids press, but he stayed inside his skill set and played hard. All of them did. Every kid across that white line gave the best effort. That was the best kickoff coverage we've had all year, and we made every extra point and field goal."

With 6 minutes, 34 seconds remaining in the second quarter, Leesville sophomore running back Dante Gallashaw ran it in from 11 yards out to make it 14-0. The Wampus Cats added a field goal from Xavier Reyes to make 17-0 headed into halftime.

Gallashaw finished with 88 yards on 13 carries.

DeRidder opened up the second half with two three-and-outs, and Reyes added another field goal to take a 20-0 lead.

At the 4:43 mark in the fourth quarter, Vargas executed a 1-yard quarterback sneak for the game's final score.

Vargas was 16-for-30 through the air for 236 yards and a touchdown.

"I put all my trust in Chris," Croker said. "We have a great team and great athletes. I believe Chris plays with a chip on his shoulder because people say he's too small and he likes to shut the doubters up."

Torrin Bouvia led DeRidder with 21 rushing yards, and Dre Bagley had 56 receiving yards on 3 catches.

Causey hopes playing in the high intensity, rivalry game will benefit his guys come playoff time.

"You try to teach the kids that the season means more than just two games," Causey said. "But it does mean something. You always have to have a rival, because that's a playoff atmosphere. That's a playoff game."

With the win, the Hooper Trophy belongs in the Leesville trophy case for another year.

"It's a great feeling," Croker said. "It's bragging rights for another year, then it starts over."

	Q1	Q2	Q3	Q4	Final
Leesville	7	10	3	7	27
DeRidder	0	0	0	0	0

DHS's Jemarcus Evans (32) & Nakeya Blake (6) and LHS's Andrew Croker

2018: Leesville 26 DeRidder 7   Series: DHS 1   LHS 3

Leesville defeated DeRidder in a late season, Homecoming contest, a rarity for the series

WAMPUS CAT WIN ON HOMECOMING -- Leesville Leader

LEESVILLE – In one of the oldest rivalries in the state, defense was the key for Leesville as it kept the Hooper Trophy north on Highway 171.

The Wampus Cats held DeRidder to 59 total yards as Leesville defeated the Dragons 26-7 Friday night at Wampus Cat Stadium.

"I'm pleased," Leesville head coach Robert Causey said. "The community came out and supported us. Our kids fought and were resilient. We struggled, but we never quit or gave up. The game played out how we thought it would play out. We knew they would be well-coached and schemed up. For us to do what we did against a quality opponent like that, it's pleasing. We're growing and improving."

The DeRidder defense made plays, as well, holding Leesville almost 10 points under its season average.

"It was a hard-fought game until the end," DeRidder head coach Brad Parmley said. "Our kids played their tails off, and credit to Leesville, they took away what we do, offensively. Our defense played their tails off. On defense, we did enough to win, but on offense, we have to move the ball. We will. Our kids are growing up before our eyes. I was proud of their effort. We gave them a fight."

Leesville got on the board first with a 15-yard touchdown on a throw from Jacob Mount to tight end Noah Allain with 5:16 to play in the first quarter.

Allain, who started the season in a quarterback battle with Mount, caught four passes for 70 yards, but three of his four catches picked up a first down on third or fourth down or recorded a touchdown.

"We preach being unselfish, and we talked about serving other people," Causey said. "It's hard, because you're dealing with teenage boys. You preach to them to serve others because you don't know when it's going to be someone else's turn to play and who are you here trying to make better? Our kids are buying into that.

"Noah just wants to do well. He plays wherever you put him, and he gives you great effort."

The Wampus Cats (8-0, 3-0) and Dragons stayed out of the end zone for the rest of the first half, but Leesville got back on the board in the third quarter on a 15-yard run by running back Darius Sawyer.

Sawyer recorded 94 receiving yards and scored on his line carry of the game.

"Penalties hurt us," Causey said. "We would get down there and there would be a flag. It's hard to call when you're on the 5 and next thing you know, it's third-and-goal from the 15."

With 4:17 left in the third, Mount hit Sawyer for a 5-yard touchdown to put Leesville up 20-0.

On DeRidder's next possession, quarterback KJ Gooden rolled out to his left and found a wide-open Ashton Broussard for a 25-yard touchdown on the first play of the fourth quarter.

The Dragons (4-4, 0-2) picked off a pass on the ensuing possession but were forced to punt deep in their own territory.

Leesville capitalized with a 9-yard touchdown run by D'Ante Gallashaw for the game's final score. Gallashaw finished with 58 yards, and Caleb Gallashaw had a game-high 122 yards on 21 carries.

Jalyn Thurman finished with 25 yards on seven carries for DeRidder, while Damian Latham ran for 18 yards on eight carries.

"(Leesville is) so athletic up front," Parmley said. "They were able to get some penetration, early on especially, and we could never really get into a rhythm, offensively. We couldn't get a big play and made us earn everything we got. They're a good football team."

Leesville is back in action Friday night to take on Tioga to claim an outright district title, and DeRidder takes on Buckeye at home to try and end its three-game losing streak.

Leesville 26   DeRidder 7

Scoring
Leesville: Allain, 5 Yard Pass from Mount (PAT Good)
Leesville: Sawyer, 5 Yard pass from Mount (PAT Good
Leesville: Sawyer, 15 Yard Run (missed PAT)
DeRidder: Gooden, 25 Yard Pass from Gooden (PAT Good)
Leesville: Gallashaw, 9 Yard Run (missed PAT)

Leesville	7	7	6	6
DeRidder	0	0	7	0

LHS's Jakob Feliciano (24), Tyler Brady (43) and

Christian Patterson; DHS's KJ Gooden

2019:   DeRidder 24 Leesville 21   Series: DHS 2 LHS 3

The Dragons snapped a 3 game losing streak and took the trophy back home!

Beauregard Daily News

DERIDDER – For the first time since 2015, the Hooper Trophy will reside in DeRidder.

The Dragons kept the ball out the hands of the hands of the explosive Leesville offense, en route to a 24-21 win Friday night at DeRidder High School.

"It feels great," DeRidder head coach Brad Parmley said. "Tonight is a great night to be a Dragon. These kids played their tails off. The community came out tonight and supported us.

"It's a big ball game. This game has been played for a long, long time. It was a great atmosphere tonight. It was a good Louisiana high school football game."

The loss marks the second in a row for the Wampus Cats, and head coach Robert Causey wants to see his team learn from the defeats.

"It was just execution," he said. "They did, and we didn't. There were too many turnovers again. Defensively, we didn't fit on the run. They went to something that they showed just a little bit of and stayed in it all game. They were smart. Coach Parmley is a great coach.

"I told them that it's just life. Bad things happen to good people, and you don't know why. You just have to keep plugging away. To me, that's the lesson. Our season isn't defined by the DeRidder ball game. It's defined on how we handle each week. I'm looking to see how we lead."

DeRidder kept the ball on the ground, and its running backs ran behind the big offensive line all game. "They're explosive on offense, so limiting possessions gives them less chances to score," Parmley said. "We kept throwing body blows. Finally, it paid off in the fourth quarter." Leesville ran just 40 plays compared to 68 plays from DeRidder.

"Our offensive is explosive at times, and they don't need a whole lot of plays anyway," Causey said. "I didn't thing that effected us. It just put more pressure on the defensive side of the ball, because we didn't fit right. They found the mismatches and went right at them."

The Dragons leaned on running back Jalyn Thurman, who carried the ball 37 times for 213 yards in the win. "He's a warrior," Parmley said. "He's the kind of kid you want to coach. He's a yes, sir-no, sir kind of kid. He comes to practice every day and is a great teammate. He had a heck of a night." After a scoreless first quarter, Leesville got on the board first with a 2-yard keeper by quarterback Jacob Mount to go up 7-0.

With 2:28 left in the half, Thurman scored on a 10-yard run to tie it up, and as time expired in the second quarter, Jose Mijares kick a 39-yard field goal to give DeRidder a 10-7 lead at the break.

In the third quarter, Mount hit tight end Noah Allain with an 18-yard touchdown pass to retake the lead.

DeRidder quarterback KJ Gooden reclaimed the lead for DeRidder with a 1-yard sneak on the 1-yard line.

"It's hard to find the right the answers, sometimes," Causey said. "When you do have the answers, can your kids execute? That's what it boils down to, and that's my fault. I told them when we win, the kids get the credit, but when we lose, it's my fault."

With 6:58 to play and facing a fourth and 11, Gooden hit wide receiver Ashton Broussard in the back corner of the endzone in double coverage for a 22-yard touchdown.

Leesville (5-2, 0-2) pulled within a 3 after a 7-yard touchdown by Caleb Gallashaw with two minutes left on the clock. DeRidder (5-2, 2-0) recovered the onside kick, and facing a fourth-and-4 with under 1:30 to play, Parmley rolled the dice to put the game away. The Dragons lined up in their big S.W.A.T. package, and Josiah Henry picked up the first down to give his team the win.

"We weren't going to try and trick anybody," Parmley said. "We've been running that formation since August. The kids are comfortable and confident in it. "You put the ball on the 40 or 20, it doesn't matter. They are too explosive." Gooden went 8-for-11 for 78 yards and rushed for 47 yards on 13 carries.

Gallashaw led Leesville with 91 yards on 12 carries, and Darius Sawyer pulled down three passes for 81 yards. Mount went 9-for-13 for 147 yards and a touchdown.

DeRidder is now tied at the top of the District 3 with Tioga at 2-0.

"No. 1, it's a big ball game because it's DeRidder-Leesville," Parmley said. "No. 2 it's a big district win, and No. 3, they were top-five in the Power Rankings. This game was huge, and I'm so proud of our kids for trusting and believing what we've been teaching them about getting better. We want to line up, play a physical brand of football and play good football."

DHS's Jose Majeris (45)

2021 Game Result
LHS 49 DHS 41

      The Leesville Wampus Cats and DeRidder Dragons met for the 100th time in 2021 in Leesville and the game was one of the most exciting in the storied history of the rivalry. Leesville retrieved the Hooper Trophy and added to its lead in Hooper series. The game was a back and forth contest that saw plenty of action on both sides of the ball and on special teams. Anyone who attended the game witnessed a truly great high school game at Wampus Cat Stadium.

      The contest began with a 100-yard kick-off return by DHS's Daniel Crosby. One of the stars of the Southwest Louisiana rushing scene, Crosby gathered up a deep Caden Catron kick and raced down the west sideline to give the Dragons a lead right out of the gate. On the ensuing kickoff, the Dragons recovered an onside kick and were back in business at the Cat 35. A few plays later, DeRidder's Darien Castille found the end zone and LHS found themselves down 14-0.

      Leesville responded when they finally got the ball on a 65-yard run by senior Caleb Gallashaw. The touchdown by the Cats' star would be the first of 6 on the night and back and set the tone for the back and forth nature of scoring on the night. DeRidder would put up three more scores in the first half, two through the air; Dragon quarterback Ethan Maples would hit Castile on a 10-yard scoring strike and Crosby on a 60 yarder as the half was coming to a close. Gallashaw found the end two more times and quarterback Parker Maks picked up a score on the ground, as well in the first half. The teams went into the locker room with DeRidder in the lead 34-28.

      The Cats got the ball in the second half and were driving to tie the game. Big runs by Gallashaw put Leesville in a first and goal, with a chance to tie or take the lead but a fumble ended the effort. DeRidder took the ball and drove the length of the field, yet again. A 3 yard run by Alex Archield, extending the lead again to a two-score margin.

      But the Cats kept fighting back. Two plays after receiving the DHS kick, Gallashaw took a shovel pass from Maks and raced 65 yards for a score, closing the gap to 41-34. Leesville executed a successful onside kick on the ensuing kickoff and the Cat offense was set up inside Dragon territory. A quick drive got the Cats in the end zone again, with Leesville taking the lead for the first time on the night. Leesville went ahead 42-41 on Gallashaw's fifth score of the evening.

      The Wampus Cat defense struggled to stop DeRidder's explosive veer offense in the first half, but adjustments in the locker room turned the tide in the 2nd stanza. The Cats stopped the 3-man combo of Crosby, Castile and Archield on the next series and the Dragons were forced to punt. Leesville got the ball at the DeRidder 25 and began what some hoped would be a time-sustaining drive late in the 3rd to extend the one-point lead. The drive was not short, however, as Parker Maks found a streaking Gallashaw down the middle of the field and the duo teamed up for the second TD pass of the night. The 75 yarder and the ensuing point after touchdown would end the scoring for the night, 49-41.

      DeRidder had the ball several times in the fourth quarter, but Coach Robert Causey's defense stiffened on each occasion. A tide-turning interception by Derek BeeBee with 4 minutes to go near the end zone halted a Dragon drive that could have led to a tying score. The Cats burned almost 3 minutes of clock before turning the ball back over to the Dragons at their own 35. With a 1:41 to go in the game, DeRidder's last gasp drive ended with a fumble on a double reverse as the Cats covered up the miscue. Linebackers Frank Ford, Caden Bealer and

Nathan Mawae had big nights in tackling statistics, with all three in double figures. Kicker Caden Catron was 7 for 7 on the night in extra points.

The game was truly one for the ages. In the 100th meeting between the two schools, the teams played valiantly. Caleb Gallashaw's six touchdowns (4 on the ground, 2 via pass) on the night broke the series record of five scores by LHS's Malcolm Smart in the 1938 contest. Gallashaw picked up 271 yards on the ground and 152 through the air, for 423 total yards from scrimmage. With his 271 rushing yards, Gallashaw eclipsed the 1,000 barrier for the season, and pushed his career total to 3,504, with 51 touchdowns on the ground. Caleb moved past his brother D'Ante Gallashaw and LHS legend Vincent Fuller in all-time rushing yards with his performance on the night. Young Gallashaw's 3,504 total yards leave him behind only Cecil Collins (7,843), Michael Ford (4,971) and Cory McCoy (4,111) on the all-time rushing leaders for the black and gold.

With his 161 yards through the air, first-year starting quarterback Parker Maks eclipsed the 1,000 yard barrier for the season, making him only the ninth Wampus Cat ever to go over 4 digit barrier. On the season, Maks has now thrown for 1,003 yards with 10 touchdowns and only 2 interceptions.

For the Hooper: The Cats now lead Hooper VII 4-2 and the trophy returns to Leesville. In the series since the Hooper was created (1962), Leesville leads 34-25. Since the teams first met in 1910, DeRidder leads 55-41-4.

Caleb Gallashaw, Leesville: Gallashaw accounted for 423 yards and six touchdowns in the Wampus Cats' 49-41 win over DeRidder. He rushed for 271 yards and four touchdowns on 25 carries and caught four passes for 152 yards and two touchdowns.

2022 Game Result

LHS 24 DHS 15

Leesville bested Deridder 42-15 at Wampus Cat Stadium to retain the Hooper Trophy. For the 101st time, Leesville and DeRidder met on the gridiron and the hometown crowd was not disappointed. Xavier Ford picked up over 170 yards on the ground and scored 5 of the 6 Cat touchdowns on the night. Quarterback Parker Maks who was also near 100 yards on the night on the ground scored the other Cat TD. Defensive backs Jeremiah Lee and Stefan James led a swarming Cat defense on the night, stifling the Dragons' highly prolific ground attack the entire game.

As of game 101, All-time records were: DeRidder 54, Leesville 43, with 4 ties. In the Hooper Trophy, the Cats took their 33rd game in the series. The Dragons have won 24 and there has been a single tie. Hooper Trophy VII is at 5 wins for Leesville and two for the Dragons.

There was a great crowd at the game. The 2022 game also marked the 60th anniversary of the Hooper Trophy series. Son of former DHS coach Cecil Doyle (David---and a player in the 62 contest), former LHS standout Louis Magee, and nephew of Buck and Agnes Hooper, David Lewis, met at midfield for a pre-game celebration.

L-R: Samuel Staples Lewis, David Doyle, Louis Magee
Hooper Trophy 60th Anniversary Commemoration

2023 Hooper Trophy Game: LHS 28 DHS 22

October 13, 2023.   By Rodrick Anderson, Lake Charles American Press

Leesville running back Xavier Ford scored twice in the fourth quarter to help the Wampus Cats beat DeRidder 28-22 on Friday at Cecil Doyle Stadium. (Rodrick Anderson / American Press) DERIDDER — Leesville gave up 15 points in the third quarter, but the Wampus Cats made big plays in the fourth quarter to beat DeRidder 28-22 for the Hooper Trophy on Friday at Cecil Doyle Stadium. "We didn't play perfect," Leesville head coach Robbie Causey said. "We had a lot of unforced mistakes, mental mistakes. "Special teams, we are still struggling there. The kids responded. I talked to them about that in pregame. You are never going to be anything. You have to go earn it, and you got to rise above every time you get knocked down."

Down 22-14 after being stopped inside the red zone on their previous drive, the Wampus Cats (4-3, 2-0) got the ball back and scored on their next two possessions. Junior running back Xavier Ford scored both touchdowns, but the biggest was the last with 5:59 left in the game. The Wampus Cats were faced with a 3rd-and-1, but Ford ripped off a 51-yard run and scored the two-point conversion for a six-point lead. Ford ran for 231 yards on 26 carries. "I got to watch the film on that one," Causey said. "I didn't get to see it, but I am happy. "I was over there trying to figure out how to stop them (DeRidder), and I just heard the crowd and I smiled and said we have to find a stop somewhere. I am happy for the kid. When people think what he is a football player, he is 100 times a better person, and that is what makes him special. He is such a good person. "The run is a credit to everybody on offense doing what they are supposed to do when they are supposed to do it and at a very adverse time. They (DeRidder) played great defense, and they got after us and made us work for it. It was just a great team win for these kids." Then it was the Wampus Cats' defense's turn. The Dragons (4-3, 1-1) got a 20-yard kickoff return from Reed Williams to their 40-yard line and went 47 yards in eight plays. They got some help from a horse collar penalty to reach the Wampus Cat 13-yard line, but Leesville stopped Reed behind the line of scrimmage twice and stopped Javaughn Fairley well short of the goal line as time expired. "Wasn't that fun? That was exciting," Causey said. "Everybody got their money's worth on that one. "(It is) just the kids responding. These are high school kids, and they make a memory. To have that memory here for this game is special. You look at high school football, this senior class, you are only guaranteed 10 (games). In other sports, you get 25 or 30. They play forever. "Football, all you are guaranteed is 10, and I tell them to make the most of your 10 you get because you are not guaranteed many. And I was proud of the way our kids responded in the red zone." DeRidder came out in the second half strong, holding the ball for the first 7 minutes, 10 seconds. Reed scored the second of his three touchdowns on a 15-yard run on 3rd-and-9, and Kenias St. Romain added the 2-point conversion for the Dragons' first lead, 15-14.

DeRidder gambled with an onside kick after a 15-yard Leesville penalty, and Ja'Tari Harris recovered it on the Wampus Cat 34-yard line. That turned into a 4-yard touchdown run by Williams and a 22-14 lead, the Dragons' largest of the game, with 4:50 left in the third quarter. The Dragons took another gamble late in the third quarter when they went for it on 4th-and-1 from their 20-yard line, but the Wampus Cats made the stop, setting up the first of Ford's two fourth-quarter touchdowns. Williams led DeRidder with 84 yards on 17 carries. Leesville's Izaiah Farley had seven receptions for 96 yards, including a 48-yard touchdown in the fourth quarter that gave the Wampus Cats a 14-7 halftime lead.

 Leesville 28 DeRidder 22

SCORE BY QUARTERS Leesville 7 7 0 14 — 28 DeRidder 0 7 15 0 — 22
SCORING SUMMARY
L: Corbitt Robbins 12 run (Matthew Andress)
D: Reed Williams 9 run (Tucker Williams kick)
L: Izaiah Farley 48 pass from Robbins (Andress kick)
D: Williams 15 run (Kenias St. Romain run)
D: Williams 4 run (Tucker Williams kick)
L: Xavier Ford 4 run (pass failed)
L: Ford 51 run (Ford run)

INDIVIDUAL LEADERS RUSHING — Leesville: Xavier Ford 26-231, Corbitt Robbins 3-18, Izaiah Farley 2-11. DeRidder: Javaughn Fairley 17-56, Dylan Vines 18-60, Uriah Wade 6-9, Jayden Aswell 1-6, Reed Williams 17-84.
PASSING — Leesville: Robbins 9-14-0—102. DeRidder: Wade 3-9-1—27.
RECEIVING — Leesville: Farley 7-96, Deandre Herron 1-5, Boston Manci 1-1. DeRidder: Semont Fairley 1-1, Javaughn Fairley 2-26.

DeRidder vs. Leesville
All Time Scores

DeRidder Leads Series 54 – 44 – 4
Leesville Won Hooper Trophy I, III, V, VI and VII
DeRidder Won Hooper Trophy II and IV

1910: DeRidder 35, Leesville 0
1913: DeRidder 24, Leesville 0
1915: DeRidder 6, Leesville 0
1920: Tie, DeRidder 6, Leesville 6
1921: DeRidder 19, Leesville 7
1921: DeRidder 49, Leesville 0
1922: DeRidder 53, Leesville 0
1929: DeRidder 13, Leesville 0
1930: DeRidder 13, Leesville 0; at Leesville
1931: Leesville 7, DeRidder 6; at DeRidder
1932: Tie, DeRidder 19, Leesville 19
1933: DeRidder 13, Leesville 0; at DeRidder
1934: Leesville 25, DeRidder 13
1935: DeRidder 25, Leesville 0
1936: Leesville 7, DeRidder 0; at Leesville
1937: Tie, DeRidder 7, Leesville 7; at DeRidder
1938: Leesville 49, DeRidder 0; at Leesville
1939: DeRidder 33, Leesville 0; at DeRidder
1940: DeRidder 39, Leesville 0; at Leesville
1941: DeRidder 14, Leesville 6
1942: Score not found; 6 Nov 1942
1943: DeRidder 13, Leesville 7; at DeRidder
1943: Leesville 7, DeRidder 6
1945: DeRidder 61, Leesville 7
1945: DeRidder 27, Leesville 7
1946: DeRidder 53, Leesville 0; at DeRidder
1947: DeRidder 25, Leesville 0; at Leesville
1948: DeRidder 20, Leesville 6; at DeRidder
1949: DeRidder 20, Leesville 19; at Leesville
1950: DeRidder 7, Leesville 6; at Leesville
1951: DeRidder 28, Leesville 7; at DeRidder
1952: DeRidder 39, Leesville 0; at DeRidder
1953: Leesville 18, DeRidder 7; at Leesville
1954: DeRidder 12, Leesville 6; at DeRidder
1955: DeRidder 32, Leesville 6; at Leesville
1956: DeRidder 34, Leesville 7; at DeRidder

1957: Leesville 33, DeRidder 6; at Leesville
1958: DeRidder 14, Leesville 0; at DeRidder
1959: DeRidder 7, Leesville 6; at Leesville
1960: DeRidder 13, Leesville 12; at DeRidder
1961: DeRidder 47, Leesville 7; at Leesville
1962: DeRidder 12, Leesville 0; at DeRidder --- Hooper Trophy Begins
1963: Leesville 28, DeRidder 6; at Leesville
1963: DeRidder 34, Leesville 19; at Leesville (Playoff Game)

1964: DeRidder 39, Leesville 13; at DeRidder
1965: DeRidder 13, Leesville 0; at Leesville
1966: Leesville 21, DeRidder 7; at Leesville
1967: Leesville 21, DeRidder 0; at DeRidder
1968: Leesville 26, DeRidder 20; at Leesville
1969: Leesville 25, DeRidder 0; at DeRidder
1971: DeRidder 21, Leesville 6; at Leesville
1972: DeRidder 14, Leesville 0; at DeRidder
   Leesville Wins Hooper I
   DHS forfeit of game---ineligible player (official score recorded as 2-0)
1973: tie, DeRidder 6, Leesville 6; at Leesville
1974: DeRidder 28, Leesville 6; at DeRidder
1975: DeRidder 50, Leesville 0; at Leesville
1976: DeRidder 42, Leesville 6; at DeRidder
1977: DeRidder 6, Leesville 0, OT; at Leesville
1978: DeRidder 23, Leesville 6; at DeRidder
1979: DeRidder 22, Leesville 14; at Leesville
   DeRidder Wins Hooper II
1980: Leesville 26, DeRidder 15; at DeRidder
1981: Leesville 21, DeRidder 7; at Leesville
1982: DeRidder 37, Leesville 12; at DeRidder
1983: Leesville 37, DeRidder 26; at Leesville
1984: DeRidder 14, Leesville 12; at DeRidder
1985: Leesville 36, DeRidder 0; at Leesville
1986: Leesville 45, DeRidder 14; at DeRidder
1987: Leesville 23, DeRidder 14; at DeRidder
   Leesville Wins Hooper III
1988: DeRidder 17, Leesville 16; at Leesville
1989: DeRidder 14, Leesville 7; at DeRidder
1990: Leesville 15, DeRidder 0; at Leesville
1991: DeRidder 26, Leesville 12; at DeRidder
1992: Leesville 13, DeRidder 12; at Leesville
1993: DeRidder 24, Leesville 14; at DeRidder
1994: Leesville 28, DeRidder 0; at Leesville
1995: Leesville 15, DeRidder 6; at DeRidder

1995: Leesville 29, DeRidder 0; at DeRidder (Playoff Game)

1996: DeRidder 25, Leesville 7; at Leesville
1997: DeRidder 14, Leesville 12; at Leesville
    DeRidder Wins Hooper IV
1998: Leesville 36, DeRidder 34, OT; at DeRidder
1999: Leesville 30, DeRidder 8; at DeRidder
2000: Leesville 40, DeRidder 0; at Leesville
2001: Leesville 14, DeRidder 3; at DeRidder
2002: Leesville 14, DeRidder 6; at Leesville
2003: Leesville 21, DeRidder 14; at Leesville
    Leesville Wins Hooper V
2004: Leesville 46, DeRidder 7; at DeRidder
2005: Did Not play due to Hurricane Rita
2006: Leesville 33, DeRidder 7; at DeRidder
2007: Leesville 43, DeRidder 13; at Leesville
2008: Leesville 68, DeRidder 29; at DeRidder
2009: DeRidder 37, Leesville 18; at Leesville
2010: Leesville 24, DeRidder 17; at DeRidder
2010: Leesville 34, DeRidder 20; at Leesville (Playoff Game)

2011: DeRidder 42, Leesville 14; at Leesville
2012: DeRidder 49, Leesville 0; at DeRidder
2013: DeRidder 36, Leesville 7; at Leesville
2014: Leesville 21, Deridder 6, at DeRidder
    Leesville Wins Hooper VI
2015: DeRidder 56, Leesville 20, at Leesville
2016: Leesville 42, DeRidder 28, at DeRidder
2017: Leesville 27, DeRidder 0, at DeRidder
2018: Leesville 26, DeRidder 7, at Leesville
2019: DeRidder 24, Leesville 21, at DeRidder
2020: No Game—COVID
2021: Leesville 49, DeRidder 41, at Leesville
2022: Leesville 42, DeRidder 15, at Leesville
2023: Leesville 28, DeRidder 22, at DeRidder
    Leesville Wins Hooper VII

DeRidder Dragons: All-State Players

1951 End: Bob Hamilton

1952 Guard: W.D. Goodeaux

1955 Tackle: Melvin Branch

1956 Guard: Robert Welborn

1959 Guard: George Bass

1961 Tackle: Shirley Smith

1963 Guard: John Moses

1963 Back: Tommy Allen

1966 Tackle: Jerry Craig

1976 Running Back: Theron McClendon

1989 Linebacker: Brandon Meno

1991 Guard: Jason Laughling

1993 Guard: Rawleigh Fisher

2009 Linebacker: DeShazor Everett

2012 Defensive Lineman: Chris Crosley

2013 Running Back: D'Angelo Reder

2013 Defensive Lineman: Daniel Crosley

2014 Defensive Lineman: Daniel Crosley

2015 Defensive Lineman: Daniel Crosley

2015 Linebacker: David Crosley

Leesville Wampus Cats: All State Players

1951 Tackle: Ted Paris
1958 Back: Robert Pynes
1984 Linebacker: Steve Gunn
1984 Running Back: Charles Buckley
1985 Running Back: Eddie Fuller
1986 Tackle: Brian Estep
1986 Lineman: Robert Jenkins
1987 Tackle: Raymond Smoot
1987 Running Back: Vincent Fuller
1988 Offensive Lineman: Kevin Mawae
1988 Punter: Chip Clark
1994 Guard: Andrew Mageo
1994 Running Back: Cecil Collins
1995 Tackle: Dennis Fetting
1995 Running Back: Cecil Collins
1995 Linebacker: Greg Rone
1998 Defensive Back: Keith Smith
2000 Athlete: Justin Brown
2001 Tight End: Keith Alleger (Zinger)
2002 Tight End: Keith Alleger (Zinger)
2007 Athlete: Travante Stallworth
2008 Running Back: Michael Ford
2008 Defensive Back: Devin Moran
2010 Return Specialist: Levander Liggins
2011 Wide Receiver: Clinton Thurman
2018 Offensive Lineman: Matthew Anderson

Research: Sources and Methods

This book was compiled via a number of routes and sources. The personal collection of the Lewis and Hooper Family in DeRidder provided the bulk of material related to Buck and Agnes Hooper. Samuel Staples Lewis was the researcher and author of this information.

The information about the football games and the gridiron rivalry was discovered through research in archived and hard copy newspapers, including the Beauregard Daily News, the Leesville Leader, and through digital versions of statewide newspapers. Digital newspapers were accessed primarily through Newspapers.Com and the Vernon Parish Library. Archived yearbooks from both Leesville High School and DeRidder High School were important sources of information, as were the private collections of individuals in both cities. Charles Owen compiled and pieced together the information on the football games and series. 2007 LHS graduate Clayton Iles of Leesville edited the book.

The good work of former Leesville Daily Leader Editor Brian Trahan got this work started in 2014. Over the course of a number of years, Brian Trahan and Daniel Green, former Sports Editor at the Leader and Daily News did much of the legwork early in compiling the records related to the series. Mr. Howard Coy of the Leesville Leader provided unfettered access to the Vernon Parish Library and the institution's important, archived materials. Special thanks to Vincent Labue, Elona Weston and the City of DeRidder, Louis Magee, David O'Neal, Sedric Clemons, Jimmy Lestage, TJ Moore, David O'Neal and Sam Fertitta are also in order.

Benefactors and Sponsorship

The purpose of this book is two-fold: (1) To tell the story of the Hooper Family and the century-old football rivalry between the high schools in DeRidder and Leesville; and (2) To raise funds for DeRidder High School and Leesville High School.

The football rivalry between the two schools has been a pivot point and a day of emphasis for the two cities for many years. The generosity and benevolence of Buck and Agnes Hooper to establish the trophy and codify the rivalry with an award of note will always be remembered. This book illuminates the lives and contributions of the fine couple who loved the two schools so much. The chronology of the games through pictures and news stories from the time of the games documents what has happened and will hopefully be a treasure for fans everywhere.

In a resource constrained environment, public schools are in a constant struggle to maintain sufficient resources to maintain day to day operations. All profits generated from these books will be transmitted directly to the two high schools, on a semi-annual basis. These proceeds will come directly from the book's publisher.

The design and publication was made possible by Mr. Tim Temple, a 1988 graduate of DeRidder High School. The Temple family has been a constant and civic-minded presence in Beauregard Parish for many years and their love for the communities extends to this day.

INDEX: BY LAST NAME

Abner	Wiley	37
Abney	Allen	37
Abney	Marion	37
Aboutaboul	Daniel	106
Acker	Jarrette	121
Acker	Ronald	142
Acker	Ronald	145
Adama	Jimmie	153
Adams	John	94
Adams	Mike	94
Adams	Gary	95
Adams	John	96
Adams	Jacob	157
Adams	Jacob	160
Adams	Jacob	161
Adams	Jacob	162
Adams	Bert	44
Adamson		44
Akins	Kevin	134
Alford	Buddy	82
Allain	Noah	165
Allain	Noah	166
Allain	Noah	167
Alleger (Zinger)	Keith	136
Alleger (Zinger)	Ketih	137
Alleger (Zinger)	Keith	138
Allen	Tommy	29
Allen	Tom	47
Allen	Edward	59
Allen	Tommy	67
Allen	Tommy	72
Allen	Tommy	73
Allen	Tommy	75
Allen	Tommy	77
Allen	Mike	117
Allen	Norman	141
Allen	Draye	151
Alleva	Micahel	153
Alston	Rickey	80
Alumni Association	LHS	14
Ambler	Jim	101
Anderson	Ward	37
Anderson		43

Anderson	Peter	46
Anderson	Paul	47
Anderson		59
Anderson	Kennety	66
Anderson	Ricky	108
Anderson	CJ	158
Andeson	P	48
Andre	Jack	108
Andre	Jack	117
Andre	Jack	118
Armer	Lane	161
Armer	Lane	162
Armer	Lane	163
Armes	James	84
Armes	James	84
Arnold	J.C.	40
Ashfield	Jack	85
Ashfield	Jack	87
Ashworth	Murphy	59
Ashworth	Chris	127
Ashworth	Brian	137
Ashworth	Savion	152
Atwayer	Demetrius	150
Ayala	Daniel	85
Baden	Ira	37
Baden	Marvin	37
Bagents	John	40
Bagley	Drew	161
Bagley	Drew	162
Bailes	Thad	80
Bailey	Jerry	67
Bailies	Dickie	80
Banks	Ronald	80
Banks	Gerald	80
Barber	Eddie	102
Bardin	Hunter	141
Barmore	Jared	134
Bass	Leo	57
Bass	Leo	58
Bass	George	63
Bass	Geroge	65
Bastedo	Rochard	98
Batteford	Clint	112
Batteford	Clint	113
Beard		43
Beaubout	Skylar	160
Bedell	Dick	62
Beebee	Derek	134

Beeson	W.H.	40
Bellamy	D'Andre	153
Bellamy	D'Andre	155
Bellamy	D'Andre	154
Bennett		45
Berry	Dick	57
Bess	Ernest	102
Bickham	Gerald	103
Bilbo	Porter	38
Black	Ronnie	67
Blackshire	Derrick	151
Blake		59
Blake	Nakeya	164
Blakes	Tommy	61
Blankenbaker	Mike	110
Blue	Sheldon	38
Bolgiano		54
Bolton	George	40
Bonner	David	102
Booth	Courtney	137
Booth	Courtney	138
Bos	Earl	92
Bosway	Randy	95
Bosway	Mike	96
Boudrand	Joseph	123
Boudreaux		54
Boudurant	Jody	127
Boudurant	Jody	128
Bouvia	Torrin	163
Bradford	Brad	123
Bradford	Jamon	153
Bradford	Jamon	156
Brady	Tyler	166
Branch		41
Branch	Melvin	59
Brandford	Milliard	114
Breaux	Roland	80
Brennan	Richard	117
Brinkley	Carl	36
Brister		59
Brock		41
Brooks	Overton	22
Brooks	Kimoja	118
Broussard		153
Broussard	Ashton	167
Brown		49
Brown	Lewis	58
Brown	Bennie	62

Brown	Michael	93
Brown	Erwin	115
Brown	Erwin	116
Brown	John	117
Brown	John	118
Brown	Renard	131
Brown	Justin	134
Brown	Justin	136
Brown	Chris	142
Brown	Cassetti	144
Bruce	Darius	141
Brumley		54
Brunson	Jason	115
Bryan	Mac	54
Bryan	Hank	70
Buckley	Charles	110
Buckley	Quartez	129
Buckner	Ryan	127
Bullock	Coach	29
Bunch	Aubrey	46
Burby	Robert	92
Burdish	John	70
Burks	Casey	140
Burnett		44
Burnett	Tiashun	142
Burnett	Tiashuan	147
Burns	Percy	106
Burns	Percy	108
Burns	Anthony	112
Burns	Greg	131
Burrell	Xavier	129
Bush		41
Bush	Norris	46
Bush	Norris	47
Bush	Robert	146
Bynum	Maurice	119
Byrd	Sonny	57
Byrd	Ronnie	65
Byrd	Ronnie	66
Byrd	David	93
Cabra	Percy	40
Cabra		41
Cade	Darrell	92
Cagle		59
Cagle	Don	59
Cagle	Don	61
Cagle	Steve	79
Cagle	Steve	80

Cain	Henry	36
Cain	A.B.	40
Cain	Danny	117
Caldwell	Larry	81
Canady		140
Capano	Nick	80
Capano	Nick	82
Capello	Al	108
Carlock	Bill	47
Carr	Larry	80
Carroll	Lola	15
Carter		45
Carver	Eveitt	14
Carver	Mike	67
Carver	Keith	71
Carver	Keith	76
Carver	Keith	78
Carver	Keith	79
Carver	Keith	80
Casarez	Lionel	93
Castillio	Teddy	47
Catchings	Danny	71
Catchings	Danny	76
Catron	Stan	129
Catron	Stan	131
Causey	Rodger	34
Causey	Rodger	80
Causey	Rodger	81
Causey	Robert	148
Causey	Robert	161
Causey	Robert	163
Causey	Robert	165
Causey	Robert	167
Cavanaugh	Wayne	80
Cecil	Doyle	148
Chaisson	Malcom	90
Chaisson	Jeremy	91
Chaisson	Raymond	93
Chelette	Ronald	80
Chison	Malcom	89
Clark		54
Clark	Jerry	64
Clark	Jimmy	64
Clark	Chip	115
Clark	Camron	159
Clark	Camron	160
Clay	Mark	104
Clay	MarkS	106

Clay	Mark	108
Clay	Paul	114
Clay	Curtis	124
Clemons	Cedric	34
Clemons	Sedric	148
Cliburn	David	113
Cline	Dennie	80
Clinton		41
Clinton	Brandon	137
Coburn		57
Coburn	James	58
Cohen	Mike	80
Coleman	Quentin	155
Collins	James	123
Collins	Cecil	123
Collins	Cecil	125
Collins	Cecil	127
Collins	Cecil	128
Colquette	Ernest	63
Colquette	Gary	70
Colvin	Jack	40
Conner	Quenton	121
Coode	Michael	137
Coode	Michael	138
Cook	Oliver	133
Cooley	Dan	58
Cooley		59
Cooley	Tommy	80
Cooper		59
Cooper	John	94
Cooper	John	96
Cooper	Eric	137
Cooper	Eric	138
Cooper	Eric	139
Cooper	Anthony	142
Cordeau	Ducky	40
Cordeau		41
Cornel	Jacob	155
Corney	Jacob	156
Coronel	Alvais	145
Coronel	Noah	151
Craft		44
Craft	Ira	46
Craft	Carson	47
Craft	Bobby	80
Craig	Jerry	80
Craig	Jerry	82
Crawford	Mike	102

Crawford	Billy	124
Creamer	Doug	89
Creamer	Doug	90
Creamer	Doug	92
Crider	Mac	69
Crider	Mac	70
Crocker	Rush	37
Crocker	Sid	37
Crocker	George	37
Crocker	Sid	38
Croker	Andrew	161
Croker	Andrew	163
Croker	Andrew	164
Crosley	Chris	151
Crosley	Daniel	159
Crosley	David	159
Crosley	Daniel	160
Cross	Jeremiah	151
Crow	David	107
Crowe	Gary	59
Crowe		59
Cryer		45
Cryer	Harvey	59
Cryer	Josh	141
Culpepper		49
Daldwell	Larry	80
Davis		59
Davis	Darwin	80
Davis	Don	80
Davis	Darwin	84
Davis	Chris	114
Davis	Corey	119
Davis	Corey	123
Davis	DaQuan	161
Davis	Daquan	162
Day		59
Dean	James	91
Deans	David	104
Deans	Ashley	134
Deans	Ashley	135
Dees	Mark	88
Delia	Frank	50
Delia	Frank	51
Detz	David	142
Dick	Eugene	36
Dickerson	Jack	47
Dietzel	Paul	59
Dixon	Calvin	108

Doane	Homer	37
Donald		41
Donald		41
Donald		45
Dotson	Henry	104
Dotson	Henry	106
Douglas		108
Douglas	Dowd	110
Dove	Keith	119
Dove	Keith	121
Dowden	J.B.	46
Dowden	Mark	134
Downs		59
Doyle		59
Doyle	Cecil	69
Doyle	Cecil	71
Doyle	Cecil	72
Doyle	Cecil	73
Doyle	Cecil	78
Doyle	Milton	80
Doyle	Cecil	119
Doyle	Cecil	128
Doyle	Cecil	133
Doyle	Cecil	134
Doyle	Cecil	153
Doyle	Cecil	159
Doyle	Cecil	161
Doyle	David	29
Driscoll	John	87
Driscoll	Dennis	92
Driscoll	Dennis	94
Driscoll	Martin	136
Driscoll	Martin	137
Droddy	Jack	47
Dryden	Don	80
Dudley	Mike	84
Dummeier	E.F.	36
Dunlap	W.L.	40
Dunn		49
Dunn	Christian	137
Duong	Tommy	160
Duong	Tommy	161
Durand		59
Durham	Bobby	92
Durham	Peterseon	145
East	Al	108
Eaves	Daniel	140
Edwards	Charlie	84

Ensley	Clint	104
Epperson	Marcus	117
Ernest	Crocker	38
Erwin	Brown	114
Eubanks		59
Evans	Jemarcus	164
Everett	Deshazor	149
Everett	Deshazor	150
Faciane	JJ	153
Farrow	Willie	131
Faulks	Larry	63
Feaster	Gary	116
Feaster	David	148
Feaster	David	150
Feliciano	Jakob	166
Ferguson	Danny	46
Ferguson	Robert	47
Ferguson	R	48
Fertitta	Sam	31
Fertitta	Anthony	31
Fertitta	Samuel	31
Fertitta	RJ	31
Fertitta	Ronald	31
Fertitta	Fatty	31
Fertitta	Anthony	40
Fertitta	Sam	40
Fertitta	Anthony	40
Fertitta		41
Fertitta		43
Fertitta		44
Fertitta	RJ	71
Fertitta	RJ	75
Fertitta	RJ	77
Fertitta	Allen	80
Fertitta	Ronald	89
Fidler		43
Fisher	George	40
Fisher		57
Ford	Roy	36
Ford	Jessie	53
Ford	Justin	140
Ford	Michael	141
Ford	Justin	141
Ford	Michael	145
Ford	Sam	151
Ford	Sam	153
Fort	Howard	46
Fort	Michael	144

Fortier	Lewis	20
Foshee	Jerry	105
Foshee	Jerry	134
Foster	John	40
Fowler	Darren	106
Franklin	Louie	36
Franklin	Ernest	46
Franklin	Ernest	47
Franklin		48
Frazar	Lether	9
Frazar	Lily	9
Frusha	Johnny	80
Frushe	Johnny	82
Fuller	Gary	93
Fuller	Eddie	112
Fuller	Vincent	112
Fuller	Vincent	113
Fuller	Vincent	114
Funderburk	Jimmy	80
Gaines	Robert	100
Gallashaw	D'Ante	163
Gallashaw	D'Ante	165
Gallashaw	Caleb	165
Gallashaw	Caleb	166
Gallashaw	Caleb	167
Galloway	James	97
Gamblin		41
Gardnier	Jack	38
Garner	Pat	80
Garner	Ellis	116
Garner	Ellis	117
Garner	Ellis	119
Gendron	Joe	80
Gibson	Lloyd	38
Gill	Donnie	80
Gill	Donnie	84
Gipson	Jerome	140
Glasper	Matt	125
Goins	Justin	137
Goins	Justin	138
Goins	Justin	139
Goins	Justin	140
Goldsby	Doug	87
Goodeaux		59
Gooden	KJ	165
Goodsen	KJ	166
Gormley	Jack	73
Gormley	Jack	74

Gormley	John	101
Governale	Justin	129
Grade		44
Granger	Johnny	80
Granger	Tommy	80
Grant		54
Grant	Issac	138
Gravel	Camile	11
Graves	Steve	120
Green	Winfred	37
Green	V.E.	37
Green	Milford	38
Green	Bill	66
Green	Wayne	71
Green	Wayne	80
Green	Bobby	80
Green	Jason	127
Green	Jason	128
Green	Courtney	136
Greening	Maurice	114
Greening	James	129
Greening	James	131
Gross	Jack	80
Guidry		44
Guintini	Jason	114
Guintini	Jason	115
Gunn	Steve	104
Gunn	Steve	106
Gunn	Steve	111
Hadnot	Buddy	40
Hadnot		41
Hadnot	Jack	80
Haley	James	90
Hall	John	61
Hamilton		54
Hamilton	Bob	55
Hammersly		44
Hanchey	Greg	101
Hanchy		59
Harbison		59
Harmon		45
Harper	Darrell	80
Harrington	Micah	140
Harris	Mike	85
Harris	Frankie	89
Harris	Tim	94
Harris	Ted	102
Harris	Ted	104

Harris	Curtis	133
Harrison		44
Harrison		45
Harrison	R	48
Hayes	Ronnie	80
Haymon	Jimmy	67
Haynes	Terry	97
Haynes	Terry	98
Haynes	Jerry	127
Hays	Steve	87
Hays	Steve	88
Heath	Jaylen	157
Heath	Jaylen	158
Heisman	Tom	80
Henderson	Wayburn	50
Hennigan	Bobbie	89
Henry	Bernardo	139
Henry	Bernardo	140
Hernandez		45
Hernandez	Bobby	75
Hernandez	Bobby	78
Herring	Tyler	155
Herring	Tyler	156
Herrington		43
Herrington	Scott	100
Hess	John	80
Hickman	Bill	81
Hicks	Jack	40
Hicks		45
Hicks		54
Hillman		44
Hines	Robert	92
Hinson		59
Hoard	Reggie	140
Hodge		59
Hoecker	Sam	111
Hoecker	Matthew	153
Hoecker	Matthew	154
Hoener	Holden	156
Hoerner	Holden	155
Hoerner	Holden	159
Hoerner	Holden	160
Holmes	Jared	148
Holmes	Jared	150
Holt	Terry	100
Hooker		44
Hooks	Robbie	137
Hooper	LS "Buck"	3

Hooper	Agnes	3
Hooper	Louis Sylvester	4
Hooper	Catherine Agnes	4
Hooper	Buck	5
Hooper	Walter	5
Hooper	Buck	8
Hooper	L.W.	9
Hooper	Mrs. L.S.	11
Hooper	LH	14
Hooper	L.S. Jr	23
Hooper	Catheine	23
Hooper	Thomas	28
Hooper	LS	68
Hooper	Agnes	68
Hooper	LS	71
Hooper	LS	74
Hooper	LS	84
Hooper	LS	85
Hooper	LS	87
Hooper	LS	92
Hooper	Agnes	92
Hooper	LS "Buck"	93
Hooper	Sheaun	128
Houseley	Adam	129
Housely	Daniel	131
Housely	Daniel	133
Hubbard	Johnny	89
Hubbard	Carl	134
Huffman	Alvie	38
Hughes	Murph	47
Hughes		48
Hughes		49
Hughes	C.A.	74
Hunt		49
Hyde	Johnny	80
Hyde	Mike	80
Hyde	Johnny	81
Hydge	Bill	78
Iles	Bobby	65
Iles	Trey	100
Iles	Trey	101
Ingram	Tyson	141
Issac	Tom	121
Ivory	Edwin	140
Jackson	Don	71
Jackson	Don	77
Jackson	Larry	97
Jackson	Mike	100

Jackson	Adam	117
Jackson	Demarrious	151
Jackson	McKenzie	159
Jackson	McKenzie	160
Jackson	McKenzie	163
James		44
Jantz		59
Jeane	Craic	80
Johnson	Norman	47
Johnson	Petey	81
Johnson	Frank	90
Johnson	Donel	92
Johnson	James	101
Johnson	Daniel	104
Johnson	Lester	104
Johnson	Jesse	113
Johnson	Dione	157
Johnson	Dionte	158
Johnston	J. Bennett	25
Joiner	Oscar	32
Joiner	Oscar	102
Joiner	Oscar	103
Joiner	Oscar	104
Joiner	Darryl	140
Jones,	Jimmy	37
Jones,	Roy	43
Jones,		54
Jones,	Tony	101
Jones,	Paul	106
Jones,	Paul	106
Jones,	Clarence	125
Jones,	Kenny	136
Jones,	Kory	154
Kaba	Ibraham	139
Karamales	Dennis	80
Karamales	Dennis	81
Karamatic	Richard	80
Keller		44
Kelly	E.D.	54
Kelly	E.D.	56
Kelly		59
Keltz	Richard	82
Kennedy	John	75
Kenner	Buddy	80
Kern	Jeff	80
Kilgore	Murrell	10
King		54
Kite	Jeff	106

Koen		44
Kulaga	Eugene	78
Kulaga	Eugene	80
Kunkle	Alex	153
LaCaze	Pete	37
LaGrone	Chester	37
Lampo	Sam	92
Lange	Willis	80
Latchison	Titus	125
Latham	Damian	165
Laughlin	Gerald	115
Laughlin	Gerald	117
Laughlin	Gerald	118
Laughlin	Gerald	119
Laurent	Billy	80
Leacock	Jason	138
Lee	Marvin	80
Lee	Marcus	115
Leray	George	60
Lestage	Jimmy	33
Lesure	Lamond	134
Levy	Stan	124
Levy	Steve	129
Lewis	Catherine Agnes	15
Lewis	Nathaniel	15
Lewis	Maurine	15
Lewis	Mary	15
Lewis	E.N.	15
Lewis	Mrs. L.S.	20
Lewis	Agnes	20
Lewis	Leah	27
Lewis	Elbert	28
Lewis	Samuel	28
Lewis	Bill	37
Lewis	Robert	37
Lewis	Robert	38
Lewis	Robert	38
Lewis		45
Lewis	Robert	47
Lewis	Bill	50
Lewis		59
Lewis	Robert	62
Lewis	Billy	62
Lewis	Johnny	67
Lewis	Jimmy	73
Lewis	Johnny	73
Lewis	Jimmy	75
Lewis	Jimmy	78

Lewis	Jimmy	79
Lewis	Jimmy	80
Lewis	Hunter	151
Lewis	Devail	153
Lewis	Dontrell	153
Lewis	Robert	159
Lewis	Robert	160
Lewis	Trevon	160
Liggins	Levander	144
Liggins	Levander	149
Liggins	Levander	150
Lions Club	Bowl	64
Lipscomb	Martin	40
Loftin	Billy	73
Lovely	Andre	151
Lowe	Scott	114
Lowery	Cecil	40
Lyles		44
Lynch	Omar	125
Lyon		59
Lyons		44
Lyons	Clayton	46
Magee	Louis	29
Magee	Kennety	59
Magee	Louis	67
Majeris	Joseph	168
Mangano		59
Mango	Fred	121
Manuel	Mitch	92
Mapu	Johnny	92
Mapu	Raymond	93
Marasalise		59
Mark	Demetrisu	142
Maroney	Mike	80
Marshall	Ricky	73
Martin	John	36
Martin		44
Martin		45
Martin	Howard	46
Martin	Howard	47
Martin	M	48
Martin	K	48
Martin	Stewart	69
Martin	Stuart	75
Martin	Ricky	75
Martin	Randy	80
Martin	Kenyon	139
Martinez	John	76

Mason	Bennie	75
Mason	Rayt	117
Mastrachio	Joe	98
Mattison		44
Mattison		45
Maxwell	Melvin	104
Maxyck	Eric	131
Mayes	Michael	108
Mayes	Roger	138
Mays	Deauntrae	161
Mayzck	Eric	133
McAlpin	Lewis	36
McBroom		44
McCaig	Tom	56
McClain	Ulrich	80
McClendon	Mac	95
McClendon	Theron	97
McClure		44
McClure	Clyde	45
McClure	Cottom	45
McClure	Kyle	46
McClurg	Paul	112
McCoy	Gary	151
McCoy	Cory	157
McCoy	Cory	158
McCoy	Cory	159
McCoy	Cory	160
McCoy	Cory	161
McCoy	Cory	162
McDonald	Edward	70
McInnis	Hubert	40
McIntyre	Bill	72
McNeely	Demond	131
McNeely	Deshun	131
McNeely	Deshun	133
McPherson	Arnold	112
McTear	Tyrell	141
Mctear	Eddie	142
Medina	Thomas	150
Melose		48
Melvin	Angelo	125
Meridith	Eddie	148
Meridith	Eddit	151
Middlebrooks	Andre	125
Mijares	Joseph	167
Miller	Lawrence	80
Miller	Wade	85
Miller	Ryan	137

Mills	Frank	80
Milner	Donald	80
Mitcham	Jeff	112
Mitcham	Jeff	113
Mitchell		40
Mitchell	Curt	101
Mock	Robert	67
Mogridge	Chris	116
Mogridge	Chris	116
Mohl	Butch	80
Montgoery	Ray	67
Montgomery	Charles	92
Moore	TJ	30
Moore	TJ	104
Moore	TJ	105
Moore	TJ	106
Moore	Roosevelt	133
Moore	Tommy	157
Moore	Tommy	159
Moran	Devin	142
Moran	Devin	145
Morein	Jace	150
Morrison		41
Morrison	Wayne	59
Morrison	Wayne	61
Morrison	Sidney	66
Morrison	Ricky	80
Morrow	Ronnie	80
Moses	louis	46
Moses	J	48
Moses		54
Moses	John	75
Mount	Jacob	165
Mount	Jacob	167
Mulkey		59
Mungo	Fred	123
Munyan	Coach	29
Muse	Allen	142
Myers	Josh	134
Nance	Kenneth	138
Nance	Ketih	139
Nanney	A.H.	40
Nartub	Kenyon	139
Nash	Chris	137
Nash	Chris	138
Neace	Scott	110
Nease	Scott	113
Nelson		59

Neubert	Tom	124
Neubert	Tommy	139
Neubert	Tommy	140
Nicholas	Paul	69
Nicholas	Paul	71
Nicholas	Paul	75
Nichols	Ellis	38
Nichols	Jimmy	40
Nickerson	Allen	80
Norris	Warren	64
Nugent	Buckie	73
O'Bryan	Chris	136
Olds		41
Oliver	James	138
O'Neal	David	32
O'Neal		54
O'Neal	Billy	58
O'Neal		59
O'Neal	Tate	141
O'Neal	Tate	142
Ortagus	Billy	134
Ortiz	Victor	84
Ortiz	Vic	85
Osborne	Wood	44
Osborne	Wood	46
Osborne	Wood	47
Osborne	Wood	48
Osbrne	Wood	43
Owen	Creighton	14
Owen	Charles	101
Owen	Charles	102
Owens		41
Palmer	Kenneth	73
Palmer	Lyons	74
Palmer	Dwayne	75
Palmer	Antonio	147
Paris	Coach	29
Paris	Tec	54
Paris	Teddy	55
Paris	Ted	64
Paris	Ted	69
Parker	Wild Bill	47
Parker	V	48
Parker	Joe	74
Parker	Bryce	153
Parker	Bryce	154
Parmley	Brownie	115
Parmley	Brownie	116

Parmley	Eric	147
Parmley	Eric	155
Parmley	Brady	163
Parmley	Brady	165
Parmley	Brady	167
Parmley	Brady	168
Patterson	Howard	37
Paye	A.E.	36
Payton	Demetrius	113
Peavey	Louis	67
Peavy	Tom	102
Penrod		54
Perkins		54
Pernici		41
Perry		41
Perry	Allen	145
Perry	Allen	146
Peters	Ray	127
Peters	Derrick	128
Petersen	Butch	70
Petersen	Ray	125
Peterson	Stuart	141
Peterson	Samuel	142
Peterson	Samuel	144
Peterson	Samuel	145
Peterson	Samuel	146
Pierce	Craig	110
Pierce	Craig	110
Pinchback	Bobby	47
Pinchback	R	48
Pinchbak		49
Pinkley	Steve	80
Piranio	Sam	59
Piranio	Sam	61
Pollard		54
Polmboeuf	Walter	36
Polmboeuf	Blewett	36
Porter	Raymond	113
Porter	James	139
Poteet	Jared	136
Powell	Lawrence	123
Powell	Lawrence	125
Pressell	Bill	80
Pursley	Zac	161
Pursley	Zac	162
Pye	Perry	40
Pynes	Jimmy	47
Pynes	Robert	61

Pynes	Robert	104
Quayhagen	Josh	139
Ramano	Dana	101
Rathburn	Richard	80
Rayburn	Sam	12
Reder	D'Angelo	153
Reder	D'Angelo	155
Reder	D'Angelo	156
Reder	D'Angelo	157
Reders	D'Angelo	154
Reyes	Xavier	163
Reynolds	Heggie	117
Reynolds	Heggie	121
Rhane	Larry	76
Rhodes	Eric	106
Rhodes	Eric	108
Richardson	Remone	125
Richmond	Stephen	142
Richmond	Stephen	147
Roberts	Tommy	80
Roberts	Tommy	82
Roberts	Herbert	116
Robertson	Elos	44
Robertson	Chris	106
Robichaux	Julius	94
Robinson		44
Robinson	H	44
Robinson		45
Robinson	Homer	46
Robinson	Robert	125
Robinson	Ronnie	131
Roe	Frank	57
Roebuck	Carol	36
Rolon	Roger	124
Rolon	Kap	153
Rone	Greg	125
Rone	Greg	127
Roosevent	Franklin	9
Ross	Charles	80
Rowzee	Fred	40
Rowzee	Fred	40
Rowzee		41
Rush	Tony	113
Russell		44
Russell		59
Russell	Jerry	70
Russell	H. Lynn	90
Russell	H. Lynn	93

Salim	Billy	71
Salim	Billy	75
Salim	Billy	78
Sandahl	Al	89
Sandahl	Al	92
Sanders	Bill	37
Sanders	Andy	102
Sanders	Andy	103
Sanders	Andy	104
Sartin	Dougla	46
Sawyer	Darius	165
Sawyer	Darius	166
Sawyer	Darius	168
Schaller	Joe	123
Schlag	John	142
Schmidt		59
Schoonover	Chris	163
Schwartz	Richard	67
Schwartz	Richard	71
Schwartz	Richard	75
Scobee	Hanson	47
Scobee	R	48
Scobee	H	48
Scott	Doug	119
Scott	Sam	134
Scott	Sam	135
Scott	Quentiza	139
Self	James	92
Sepeda		44
Sepeda		45
Sepeda	John	46
Sepeda		57
Septeda		46
Sexton		59
Shapkoff	Jimbo	106
Sharpless	Marvin	37
Shaw	Ed	37
Sherrill	Albert	92
Shirley	Dank	37
Shirley	James	53
Shirley	James	54
Shirley	Paul	79
Shirley	Paul	80
Shirley	Paul	82
Shockley	Mike	71
Sigler		41
Simmons	Ray	38
Simmons	Jimmy	52

Simmons	Larry	58
Simmons	Larry	59
Simmons	Larry	59
Simmons	Larry	100
Simmons	David	114
Simons	Larry	100
Skinner	Jimmy	78
Slaydon	Boddy	64
Slaydon	Bobby	64
Sliman	PJ	14
Sliman	Pete	46
Sliman	Paul	85
Smart	R	44
Smart	M	44
Smart	Ducky	44
Smart		45
Smart	Darrell	46
Smart	Malcom	46
Smart	Dawin	57
Smart	Charles	59
Smart	Harles	136
Smith	Shirley	67
Smith	George	67
Smith	John	80
Smith	Kevin	114
Smith	Kevin	116
Smith	Danny	119
Smith	Tyrone	120
Smith	Danny	121
Smith	Danny	123
Smith	Danny	125
Smith	Danny	127
Smith	Danny	128
Smith	Danny	129
Smith	Stan	131
Smith	Dustin	131
Smith	Keith	131
Smith	Andy	131
Smith	Andy	131
Smith	Danny	133
Smith	Andy	133
Smith	Keith	133
Smith	Danny	134
Smith	Danny	135
Smith	Kole	151
Smith	Marshall	151
Smith	Kole	153
Spann	Steve	78

Spann	Steve	80
Spann	Steve	82
Spence	Chris	98
Spikes	Thurman	106
Squyres	Zach	150
Squyres	Zach	151
St. Clergy	Jessie	153
Stafford	John	40
Stallworth	Travante	141
Stallworth	Travante	142
Stallworth	Travante	143
Stallworth	Travante	145
Stallwroth	Travante	144
Stanley		44
Stanley	J	48
Steele	Jeff	110
Stenson	Delano	151
Stephens	Bobby	98
Sterling	G	48
Stevens		41
Stevens	Williams	97
Stevenson	Kenric	117
Stevenson	Kenric	119
Stevenson	Kenric	120
Steward	Markese	131
Steward	Tevon	142
Stewart		59
Storer	John	121
Storer	John	123
Storer	John	128
Storer	John	129
Storer	John	131
Storer	Johnny	131
Storer	John	133
Storms	Bill	80
Stracner	Hubert	38
Swearingen		41
Sweet	Ralph	37
Swilley	Clarence	79
Swilley	Clarence	80
Swilley	Clarence	82
Sylvest	Bennie	106
Symons	Ro	100
Taylor	Derrick	138
Taylor	Derrick	139
Taylor	Djuan	141
Taylor	Shadrick	142
Taylor	DeJuan	142

Taylor	Landon	159
Taylor	Landon	160
Tellis	Donnie	137
Tellis	Donnie	138
Tellis	Donnie	139
Temple	Rusty	54
Temple	Ryan	131
Terry	Pete	38
Terry	John	64
Tester	Raymond	82
Teston	Bob	75
Teston	Raymond	80
Teston	Robert	80
Teston	Ray	81
Thomas	Greg	108
Thomas	Greg	110
Thomas	Greg	111
Thomas	Greg	112
Thomas	Altheus	115
Thomas	Brandon	140
Thomas	Charles	114
Thurman	Marcus	128
Thurman	Diontay	144
Thurman	Diontay	145
Thurman	Clinton	152
Thurman	Jalyn	165
Thurman	Jalyn	167
Thurmann	Clinton	151
Tolbert	Moses	155
Tolbert	Moses	156
Tolbert	Moses	157
Tolbert	Moses	158
Tolbert	Amone	158
Toney	Michael	138
Tousba	Noble	47
Trahan	Roy	67
Trahan	Roy	75
Trahan	Brain	148
Travis	Charles	80
Treme	Gary	75
Tucker	Kemmp	46
Tucker	Jim	100
Turick	Danny	92
Turner	Bill	40
Turner		54
Turrick	Danny	93
Vargas	Chris	163
Vaughn	Gary	59

Vaughn		59
Vaughn	Adrian	59
Vaughn	Garey	59
Ventrella	Vinny	153
Ventrella	Vinny	154
Venturella	Darrell	116
Venturella	Vinny	151
Victor	Justin	143
Victor	Drew	153
Victor	Drew	155
Victor	Drew	156
Vidler		44
Vinson	Casey	140
Wahers	F.A.	47
Walker	George	46
Walters	James	104
Ward	Brown	80
Warren	John	37
Warren	Harry	37
Watson		44
Wayne	John	13
Webb	Donald	13
Weinning	Albert	125
Weinning	John	133
Weissman	Morton	20
Welborn		41
Welborn		59
Welborn	Robert	59
Welborn	John	73
Welch	J.C.	59
Welch	Rodger	80
Welden		54
Welldon	Rudolph	47
Wells		44
Werner	Dale	55
Westerchil	Brady	160
Westerchil	Theron	161
Westerchil	Theron	162
Westmoreland	John	112
Whatley	Stan	113
Wheel34	Cadet	160
Wheeler	Caden	156
Wheeler	Caden	157
Wheeler	Cadet	158
Wheeler	Caden	159
Whiddon	Billy	67
Whiddon	Buddy	88
White	George	37

White	George	38
White	Lois	38
White		54
White		59
Whitfield	Jason	134
Wiegand	Donald	80
Wiggins	Lloyd	38
Wilbanks	Gene	81
Wilcox	Tim	115
Wildblood	Lloyd	89
Wilhelmy	Mark	80
Williams	Cyril	47
Williams	C	48
Williams		59
Williams	Carl	80
Williams	Stacy	100
Williams	Chris	108
Williams	Joe	114
Williams	Mike	121
Williams	Arliss	136
Williams	Derek	137
Williams	Marquis	140
Williams	Danny	141
Williams	Terrance	144
Williams	Terrance	145
Williamson	Arliss	136
Willians	Danny	142
Willis		48
Willis	Clinton	142
Willis	Clinton	145
Wilson	Chalmicah	34
Wilson	Jimmie	157
Wilson	Jimmie	158
Winberry	Percy	37
Winfield	Daniel	148
Winfree	RL	14
Winfree		41
Winton	Walt	80
Wood	Allen	46
Wood	Billy	87
Woods	Marion	127
Woods	Marlon	127
Woods	Adam	148
Woods	Adam	151
Word		44
Word	J	48
Word	W	48
Worthen	Vance	141

Worthen	Vance	142
Wosley	G	48
Wright	Deonte	158
Wyatt	Daniel	80
Wyatt	Daniel	82
Zaunbrecher	Copeland	155
1910	LHS Team	36
1911	DHS Team	37
1920	DHSTeam	37
1922	DHS Team	37
1929	LHS Team	38
1938	LHS Team	45
1940	LHS Team	46
1941	LHS Team	47
1945	DHS Team	51
1946	LHS Team	52
1963	LHS Seniors	71
1967	DHS Seniors	84
1969	DHS Team	88
1975	DHS Team	96
1982	DHS Seniors	107
1993	DHS Team	124

www.ingramcontent.com/pod-product-compliance
Lightning Source LLC
Chambersburg PA
CBHW081216230426
43666CB00015B/2747